A Kodansha Trade Paperback Original

Vampire Dormitory 1 copyright © 2019 Ema Toyama
English translation copyright © 2021 Ema Toyama

Published in the United States by
Kodansha USA Publishing, LLC, New York.

Publication rights for this English edition arranged through
Kodansha Ltd., Tokyo.

ISBN 978-1-64651-329-1

Printed in the United States of America.

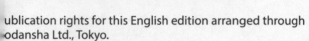

987654321

Translation: Devon Corwin
Lettering: Noelle Yamagami
Editing: Sarah Tilson, Ryan Holmberg
KS Services LLC/SKY JAPAN, Inc.
Kodansha USA Publishing edition cover design by My Truong

Publisher: Kiichiro Sugawara

Director of Publishing Services: Ben Applegate
Associate Director of Operations: Stephen Pakula
Publishing Services Managing Editors: Madison Salters, Alanna Ruse
Production Managers: Emi Lotto, Angela Zurlo

KODANSHA.US

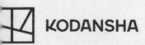

Vampire Dormitory

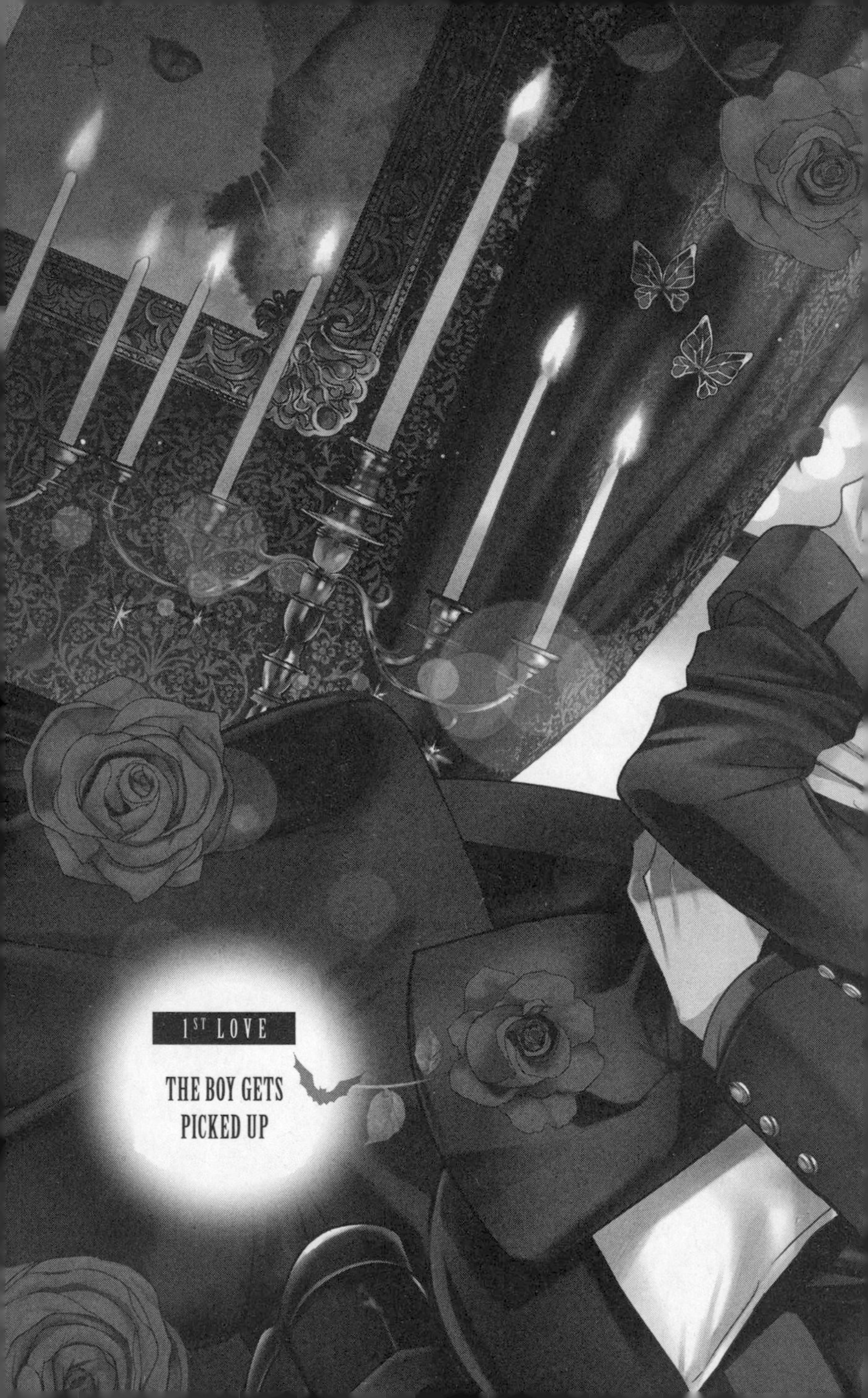
1ST LOVE
THE BOY GETS PICKED UP

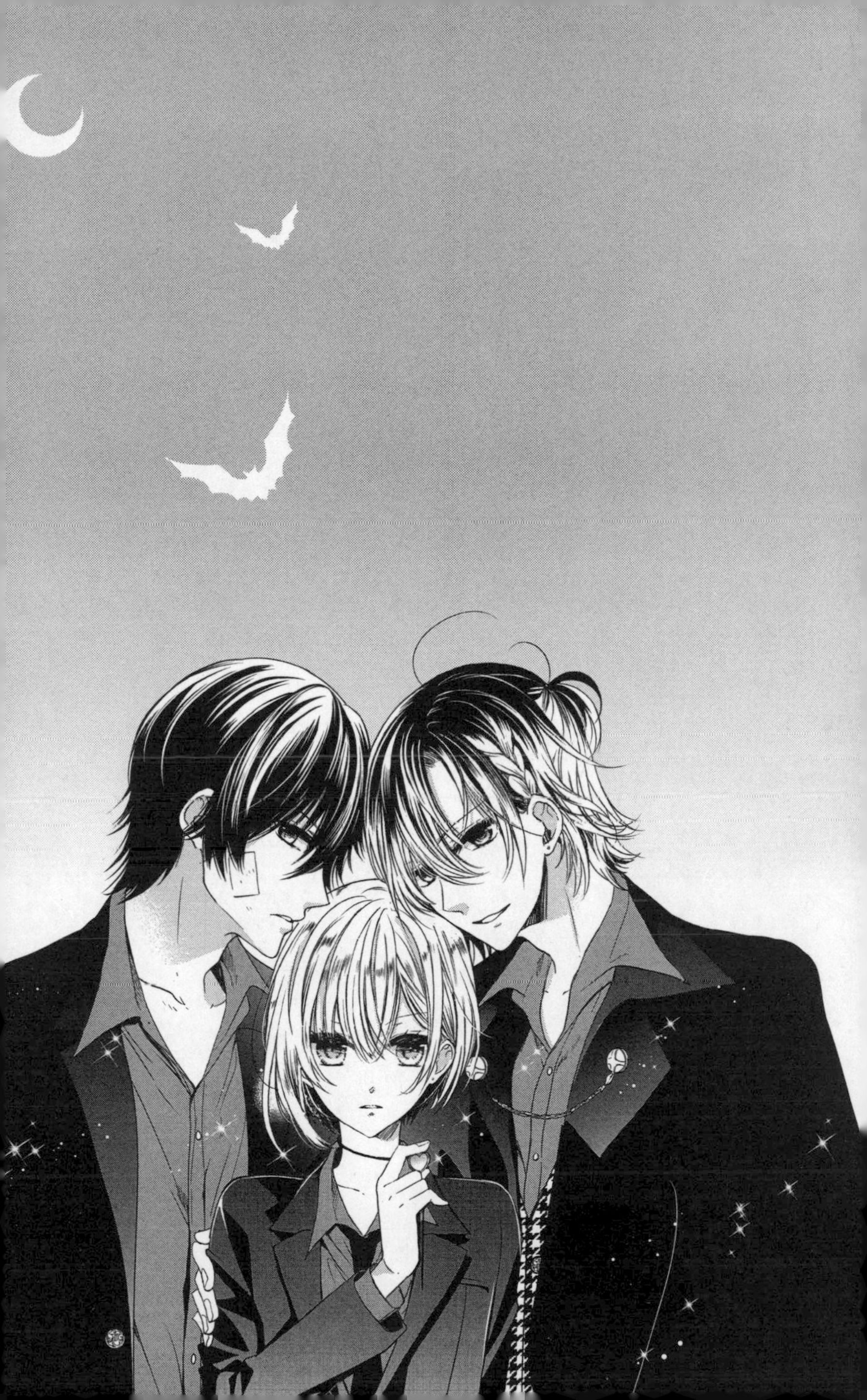

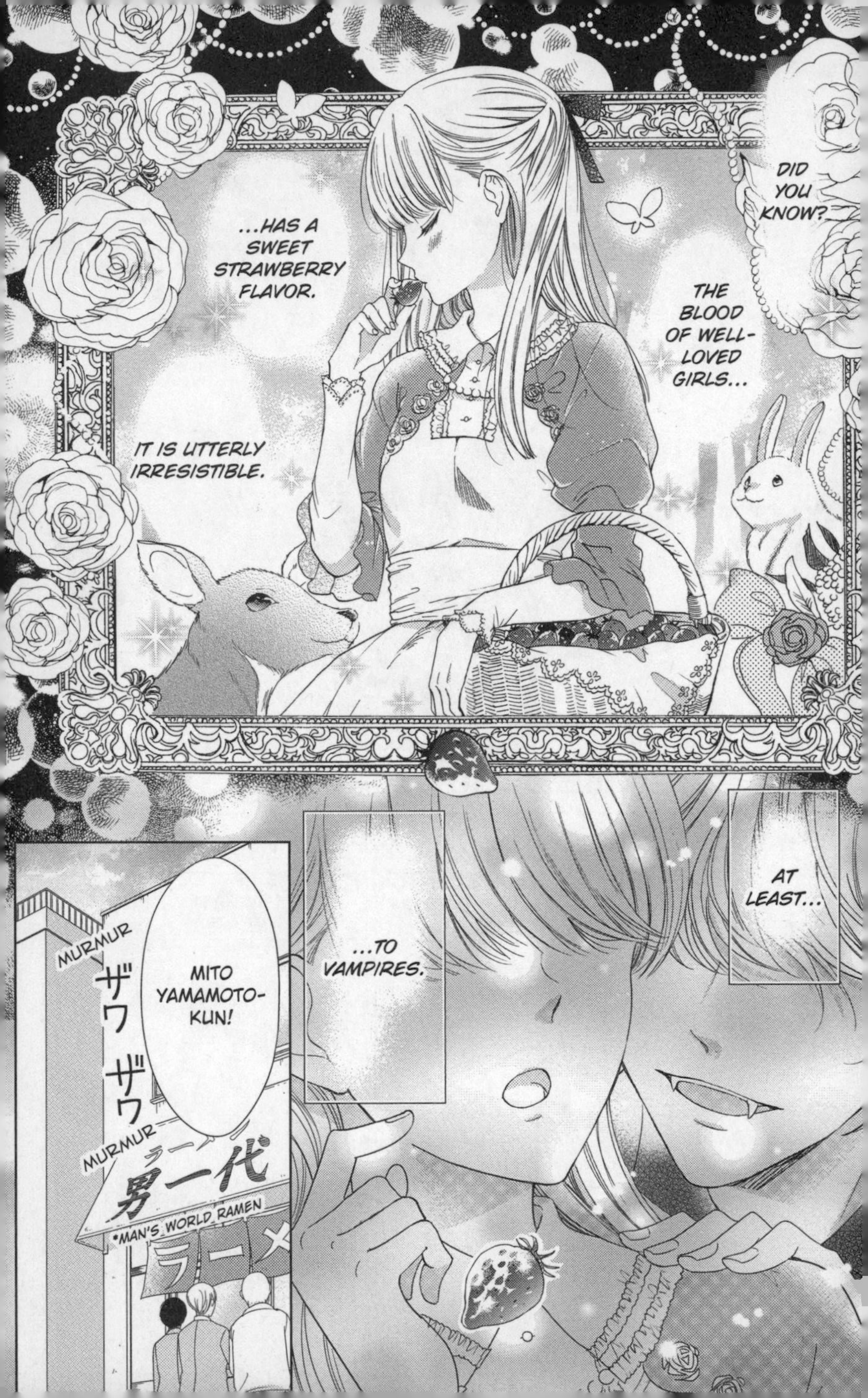
DID YOU KNOW?
THE BLOOD OF WELL-LOVED GIRLS...
...HAS A SWEET STRAWBERRY FLAVOR.
IT IS UTTERLY IRRESISTIBLE.
AT LEAST...
...TO VAMPIRES.
MITO YAMAMOTO-KUN!
ザワ MURMUR
ザワ MURMUR
男一代
ラーメン
*MAN'S WORLD RAMEN

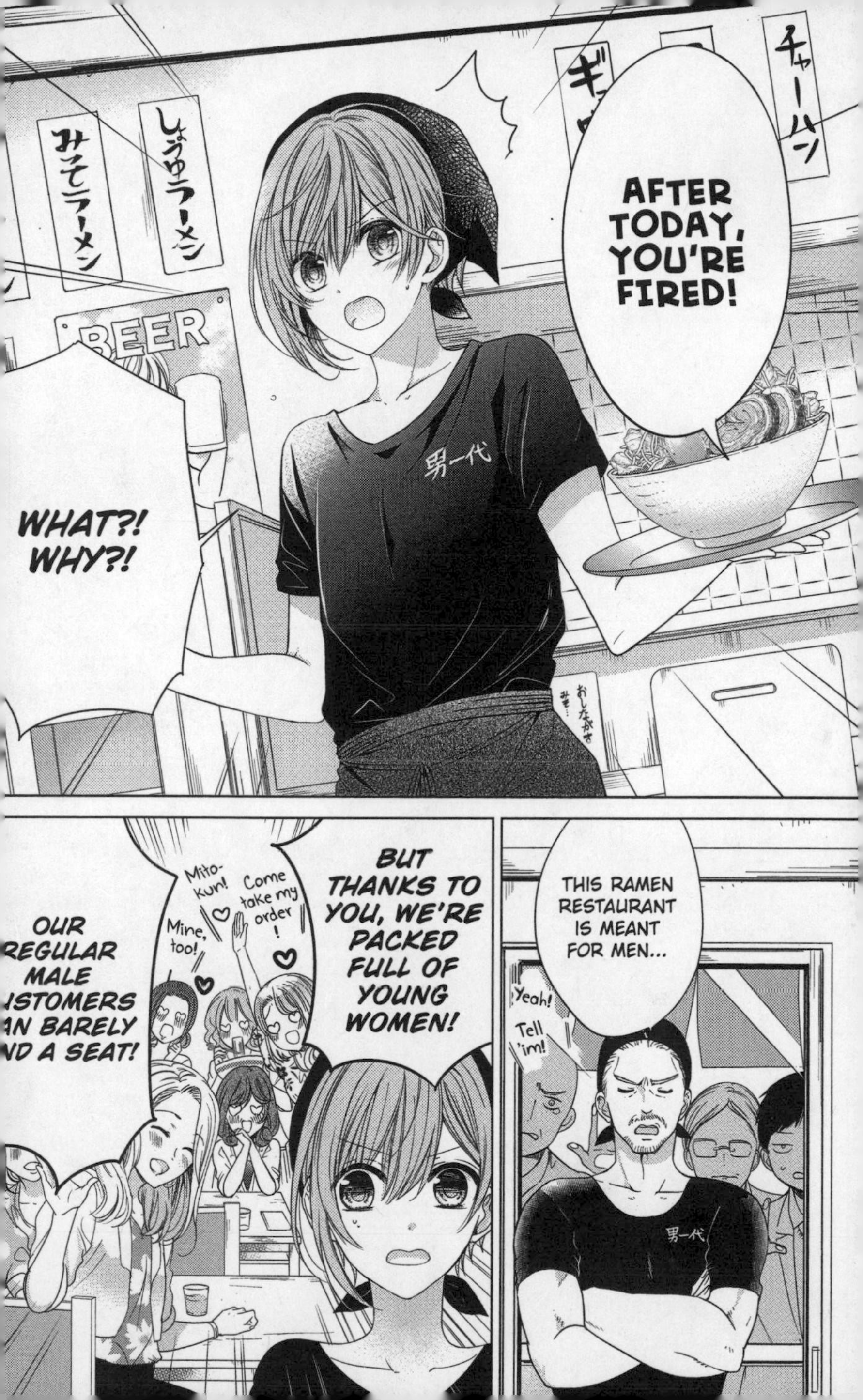
チャーハン
しょうゆラーメン
みそラーメン
BEER
AFTER TODAY, YOU'RE FIRED!
男一代
WHAT?! WHY?!
THIS RAMEN RESTAURANT IS MEANT FOR MEN...
Yeah!
Tell 'im!
男一代
BUT THANKS TO YOU, WE'RE PACKED FULL OF YOUNG WOMEN!
Mito-kun!
Come take my order!
Mine, too!
OUR REGULAR MALE ISTOMERS AN BARELY ND A SEAT!

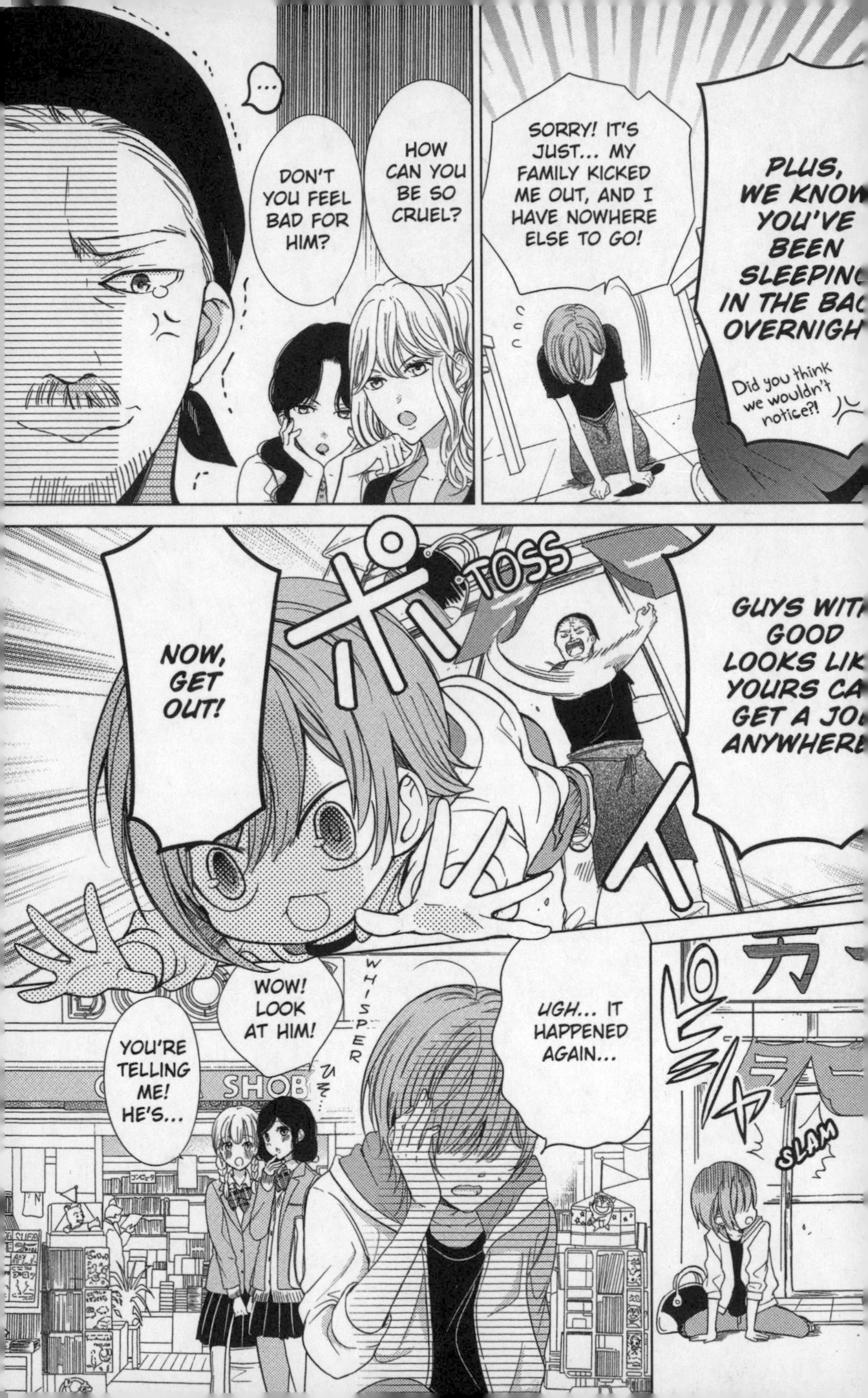
PLUS, WE KNOW YOU'VE BEEN SLEEPIN IN THE BAC OVERNIGH
Did you think we wouldn't notice?!
SORRY! IT'S JUST... MY FAMILY KICKED ME OUT, AND I HAVE NOWHERE ELSE TO GO!
HOW CAN YOU BE SO CRUEL?
DON'T YOU FEEL BAD FOR HIM?
...
GUYS WIT GOOD LOOKS LIK YOURS CA GET A JO ANYWHERE
TOSS
ポイッ
NOW, GET OUT!
SLAM
ピシャ
UGH... IT HAPPENED AGAIN...
WOW! LOOK AT HIM!
WHISPER
YOU'RE TELLING ME! HE'S...
SHOB

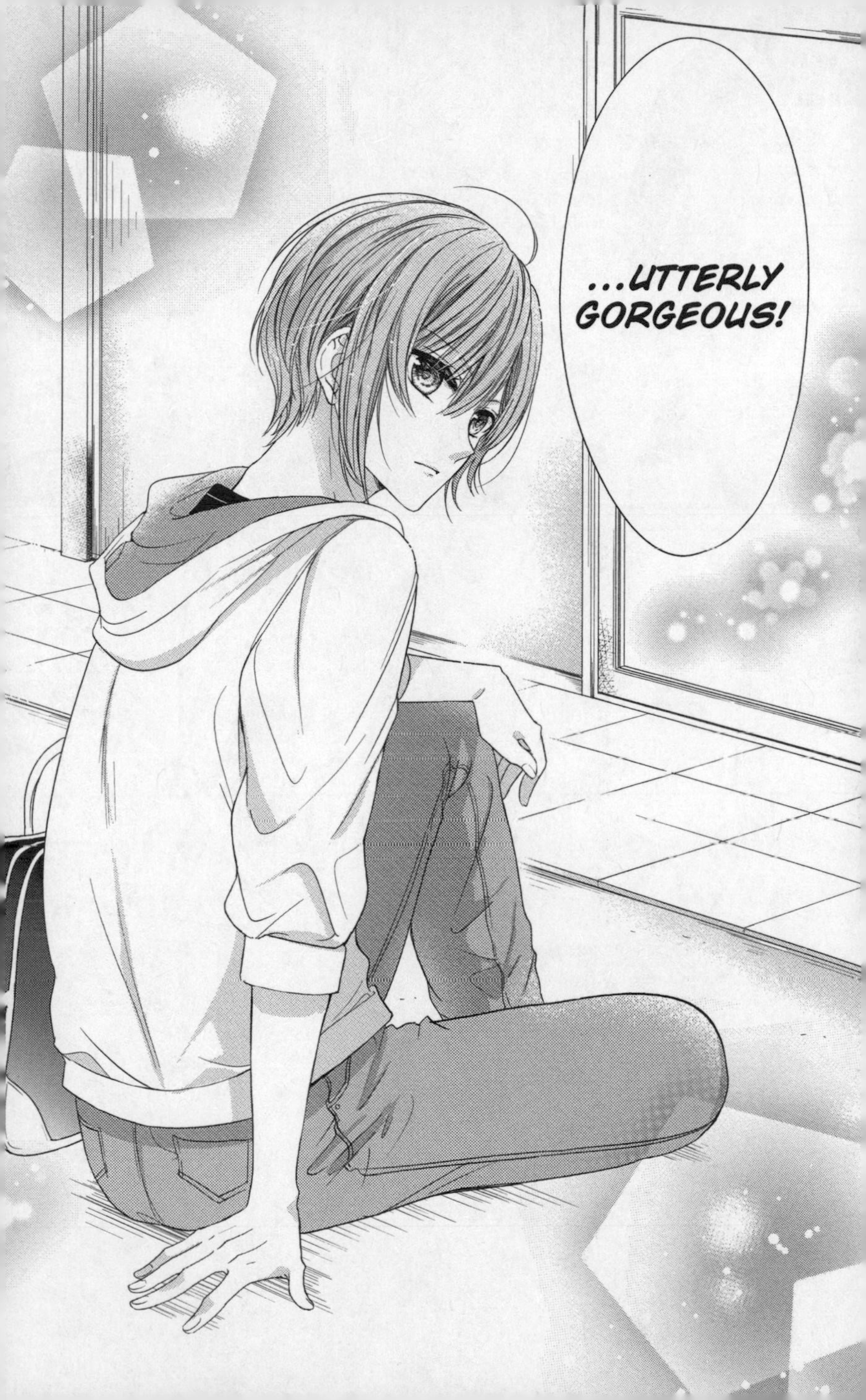
...UTTERLY GORGEOUS!

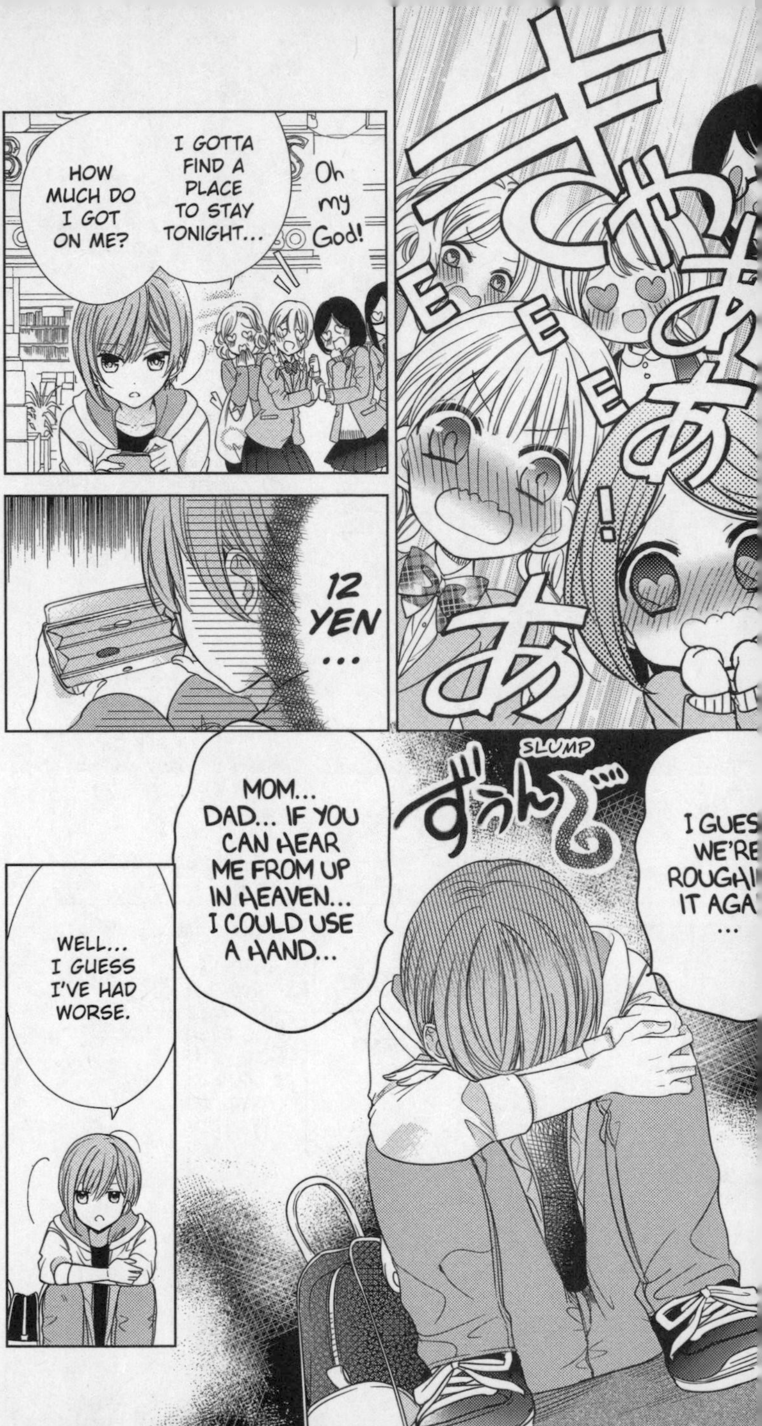
きゃあああ
E
E
E
!
I GOTTA FIND A PLACE TO STAY TONIGHT...
HOW MUCH DO I GOT ON ME?
Oh my God!
12 YEN ...
SLUMP
ずぅん
I GUES WE'RE ROUGHI IT AGA ...
MOM... DAD... IF YOU CAN HEAR ME FROM UP IN HEAVEN... I COULD USE A HAND...
WELL... I GUESS I'VE HAD WORSE.

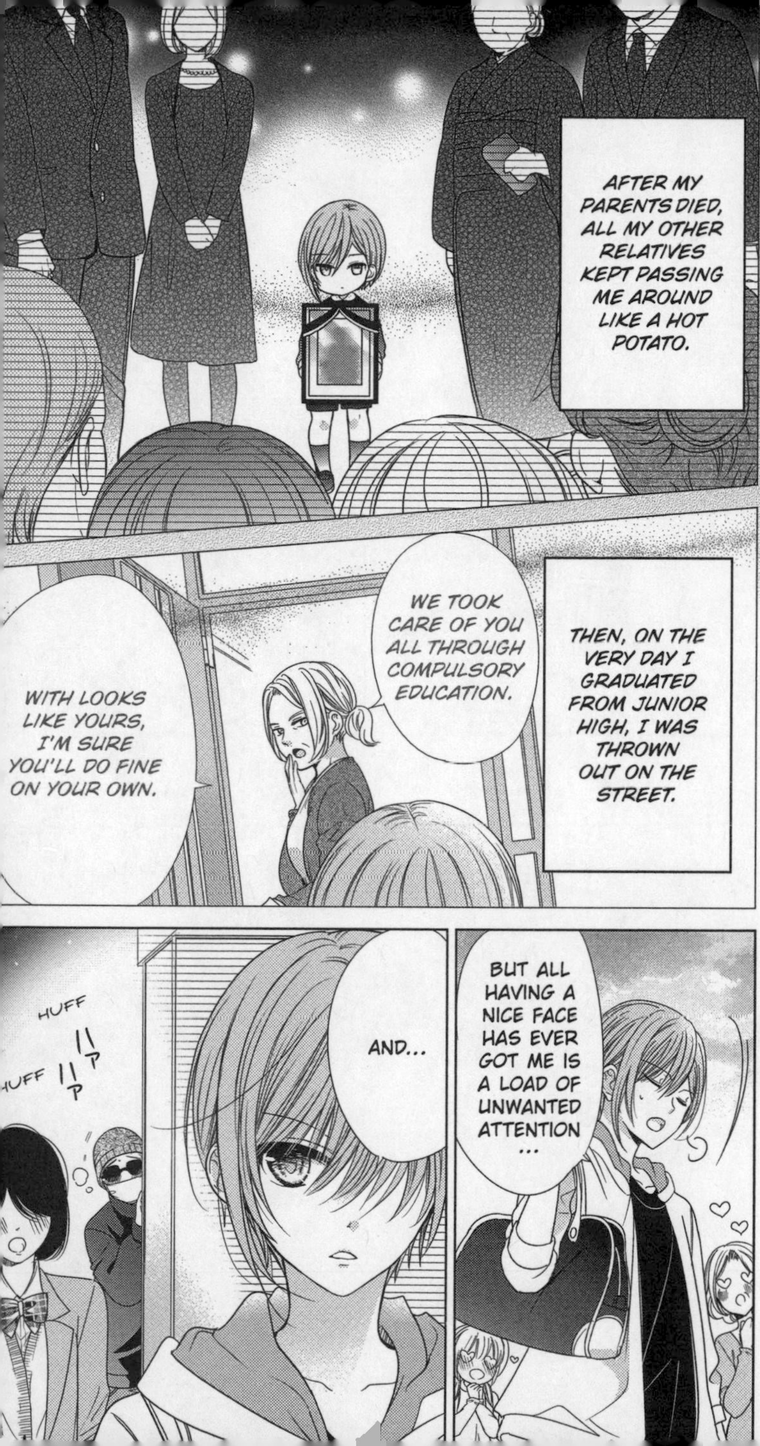
AFTER MY PARENTS DIED, ALL MY OTHER RELATIVES KEPT PASSING ME AROUND LIKE A HOT POTATO.
THEN, ON THE VERY DAY I GRADUATED FROM JUNIOR HIGH, I WAS THROWN OUT ON THE STREET.
WE TOOK CARE OF YOU ALL THROUGH COMPULSORY EDUCATION.
WITH LOOKS LIKE YOURS, I'M SURE YOU'LL DO FINE ON YOUR OWN.
BUT ALL HAVING A NICE FACE HAS EVER GOT ME IS A LOAD OF UNWANTED ATTENTION ...
AND...
HUFF
HUFF

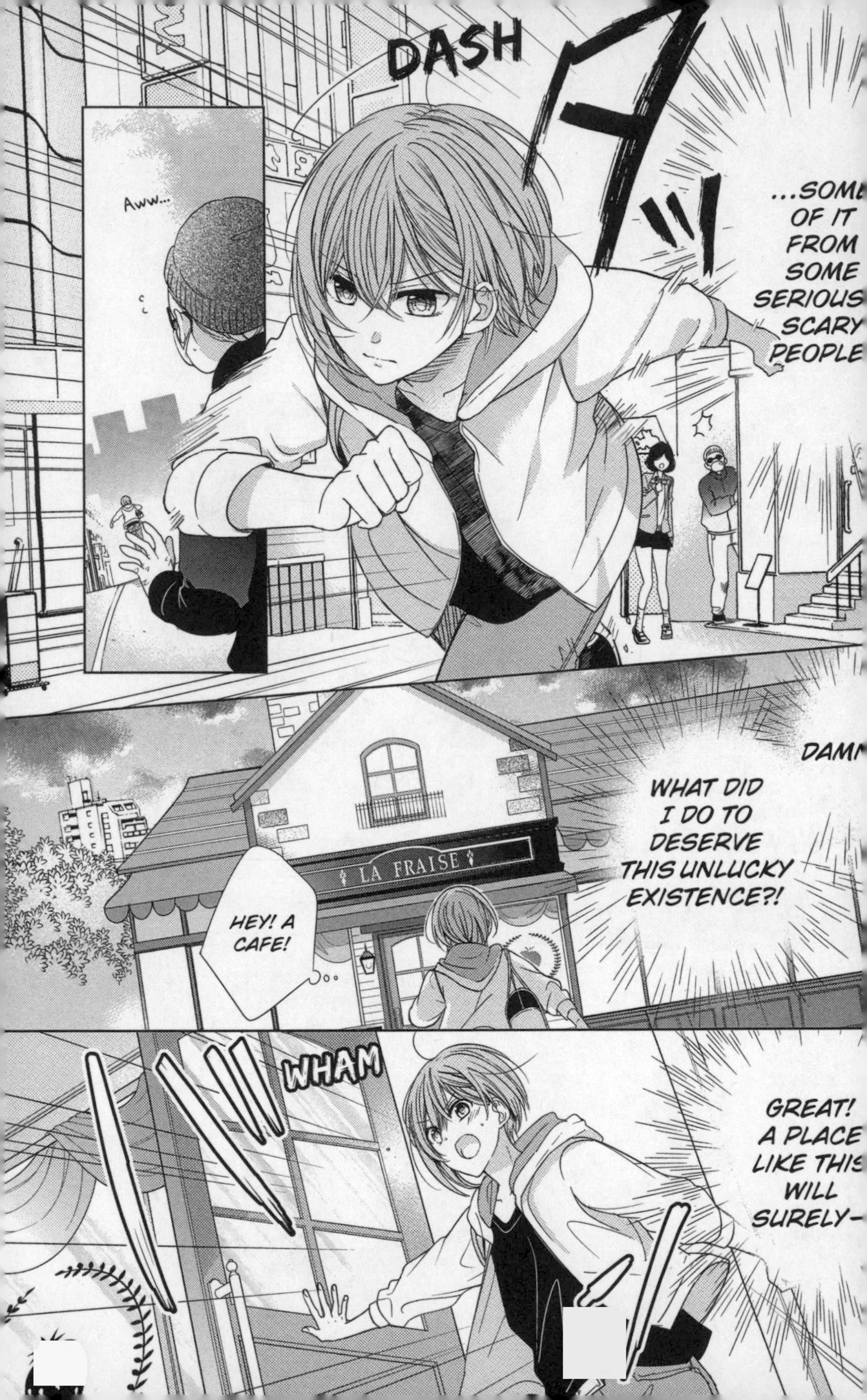
DASH
...SOM OF IT FROM SOME SERIOUS SCARY PEOPLE
Aww...
DAM
WHAT DID I DO TO DESERVE THIS UNLUCKY EXISTENCE?!
LA FRAISE
HEY! A CAFE!
GREAT! A PLACE LIKE THIS WILL SURELY—
WHAM

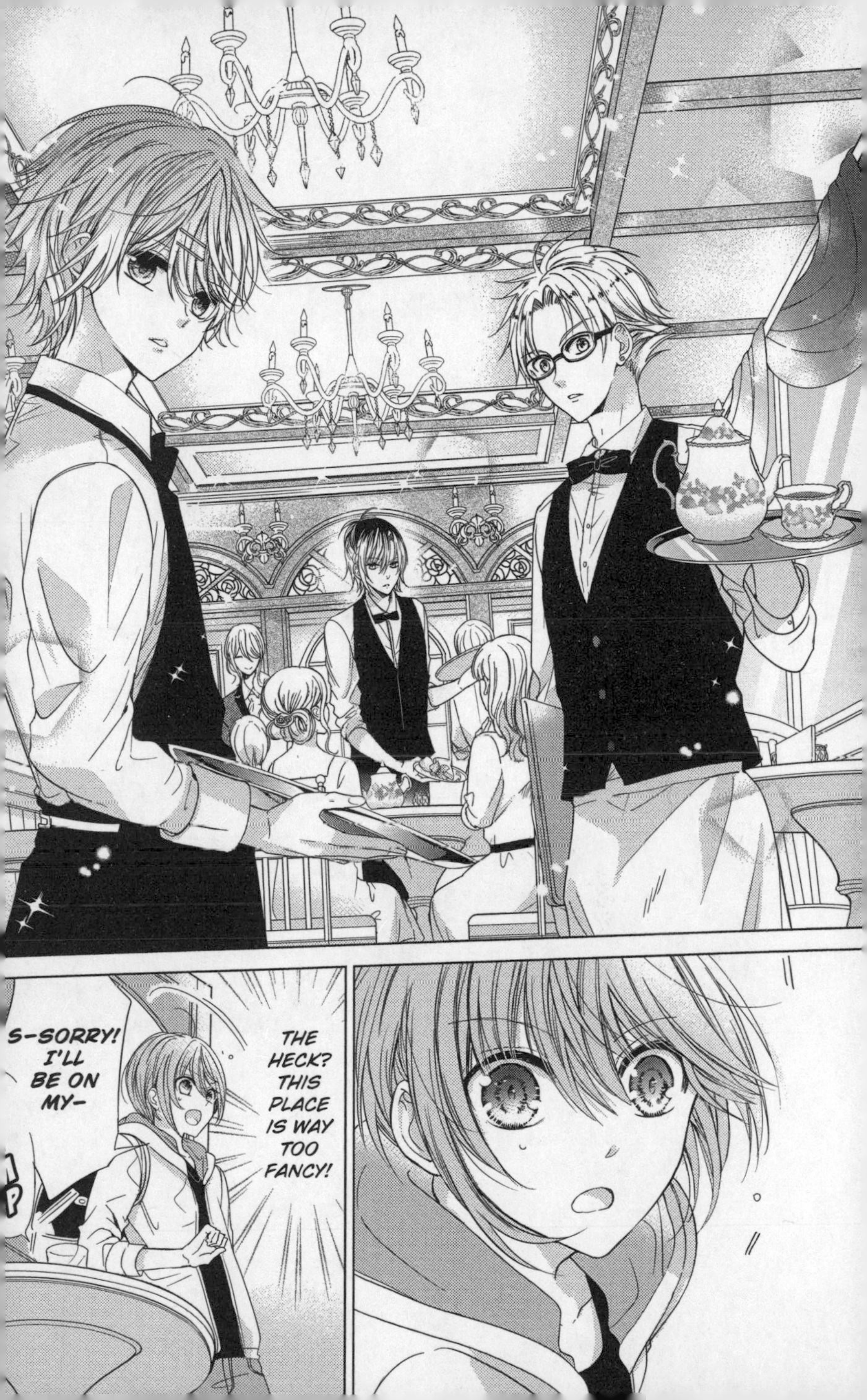
THE HECK? THIS PLACE IS WAY TOO FANCY!
S-SORRY! I'LL BE ON MY-

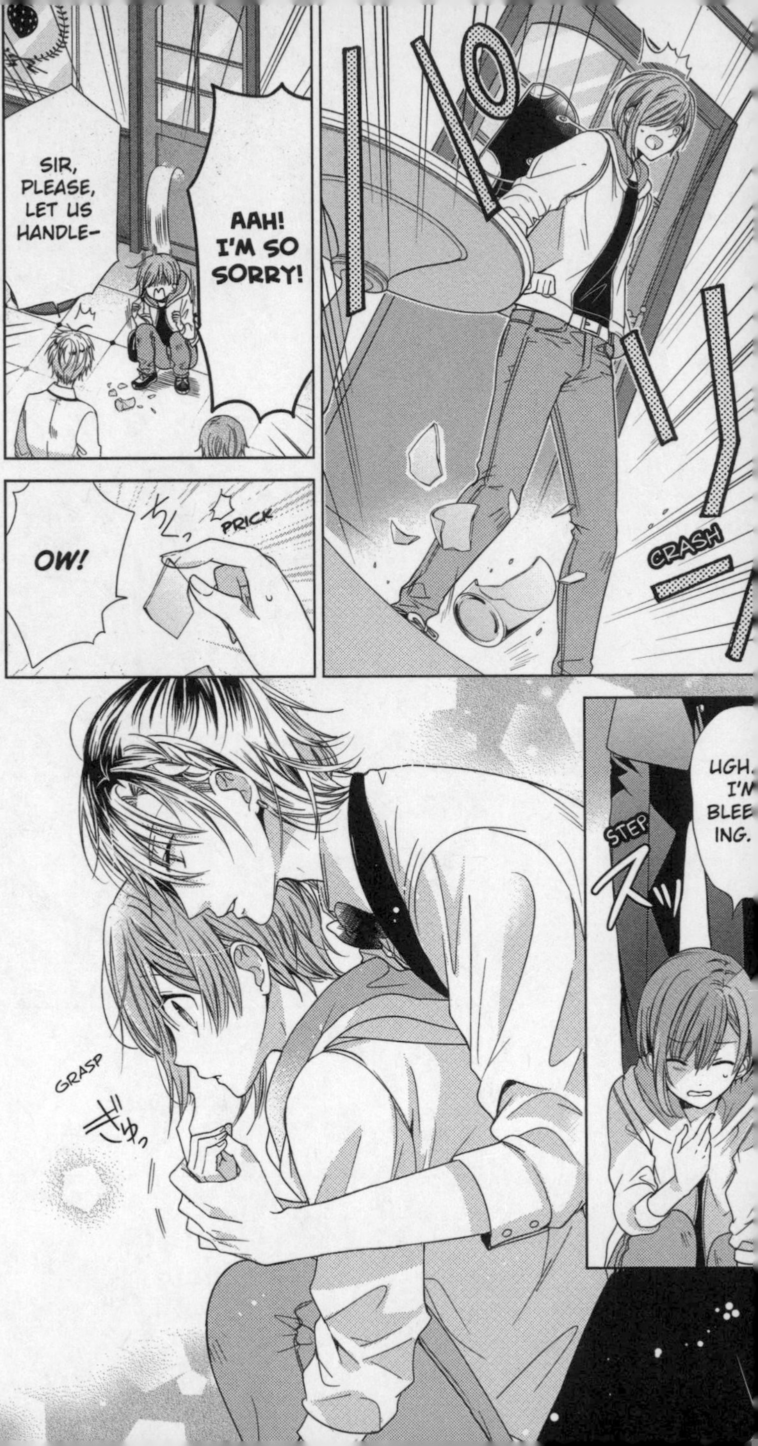
CRASH
AAH! I'M SO SORRY!
SIR, PLEASE, LET US HANDLE-
ちくっ
PRICK
OW!
UGH. I'M BLEE ING.
スッ
STEP
ぎゅっ
GRASP

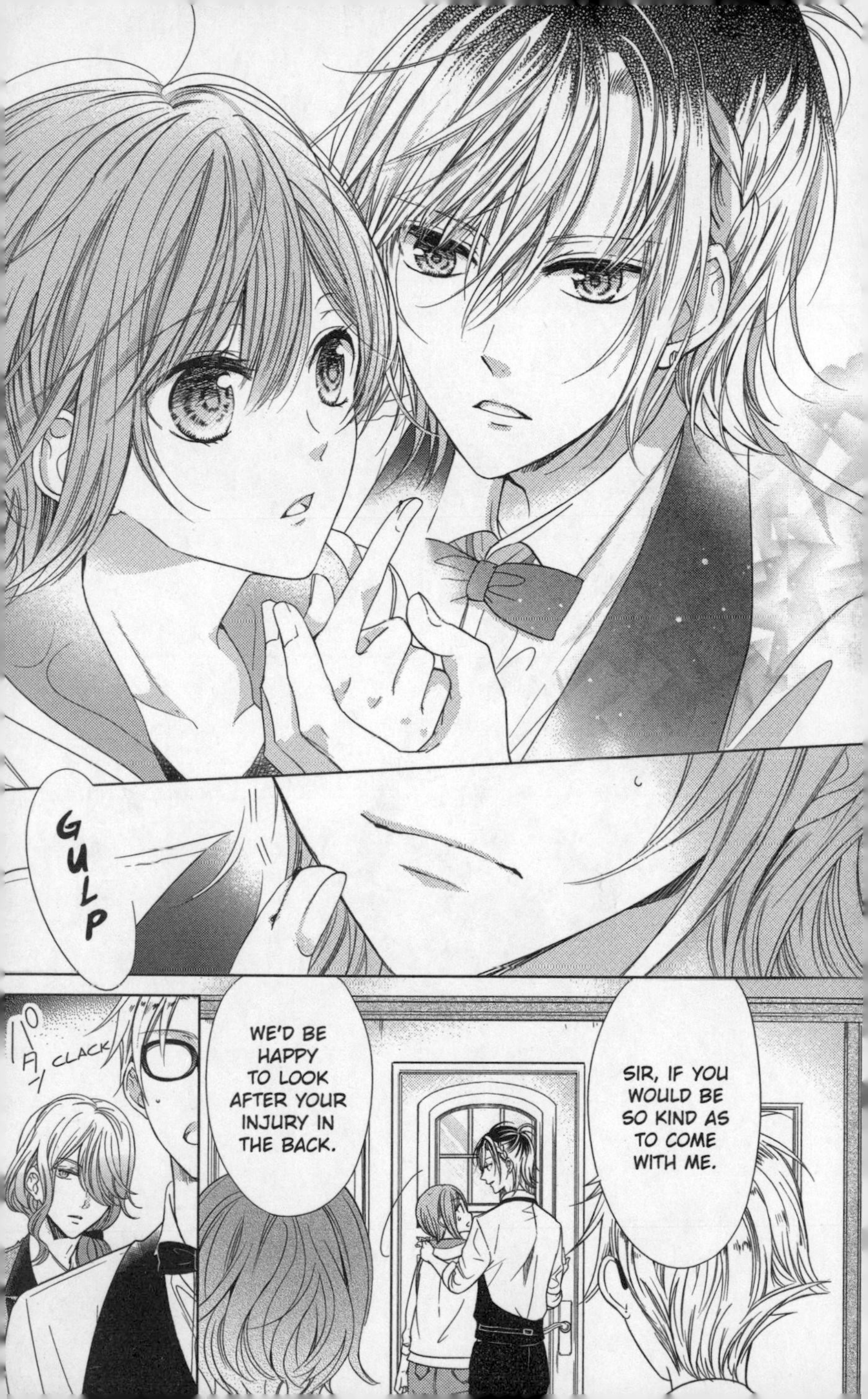
GULP
SIR, IF YOU WOULD BE SO KIND AS TO COME WITH ME.
WE'D BE HAPPY TO LOOK AFTER YOUR INJURY IN THE BACK.
CLACK

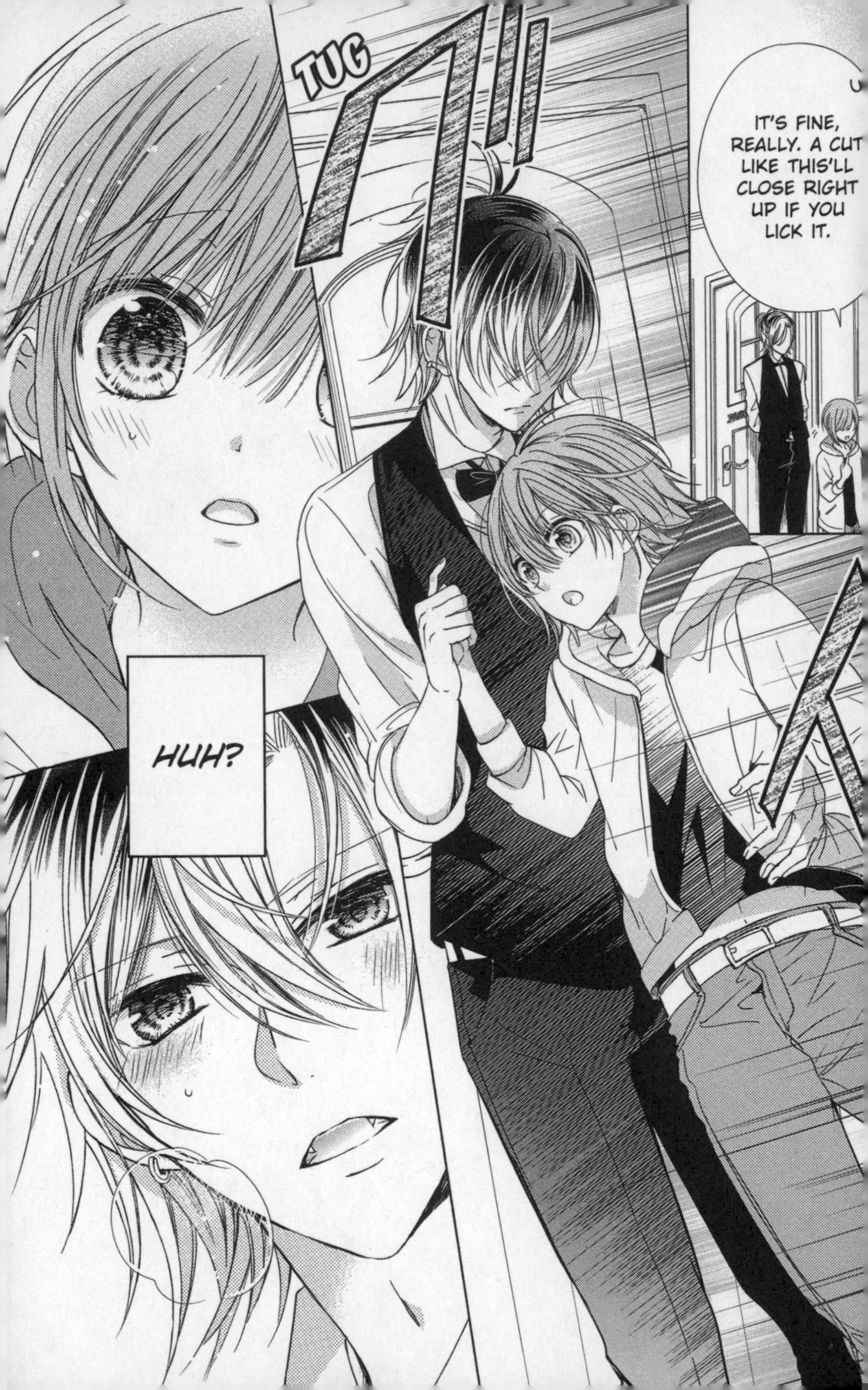
IT'S FINE, REALLY. A CUT LIKE THIS'LL CLOSE RIGHT UP IF YOU LICK IT.
TUG
HUH?

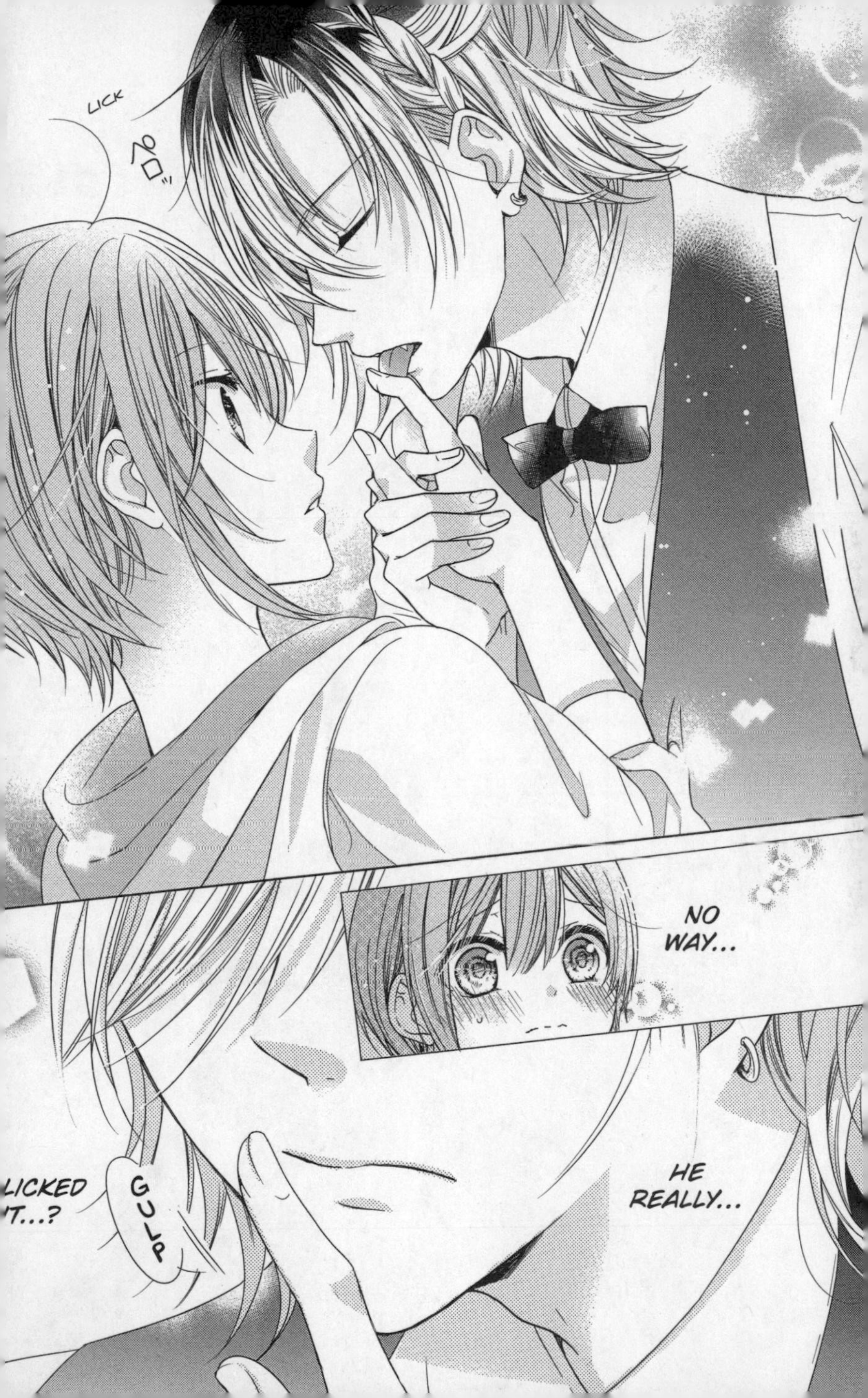
LICK
ペロッ
NO WAY...
HE REALLY...
LICKED IT...?
GULP

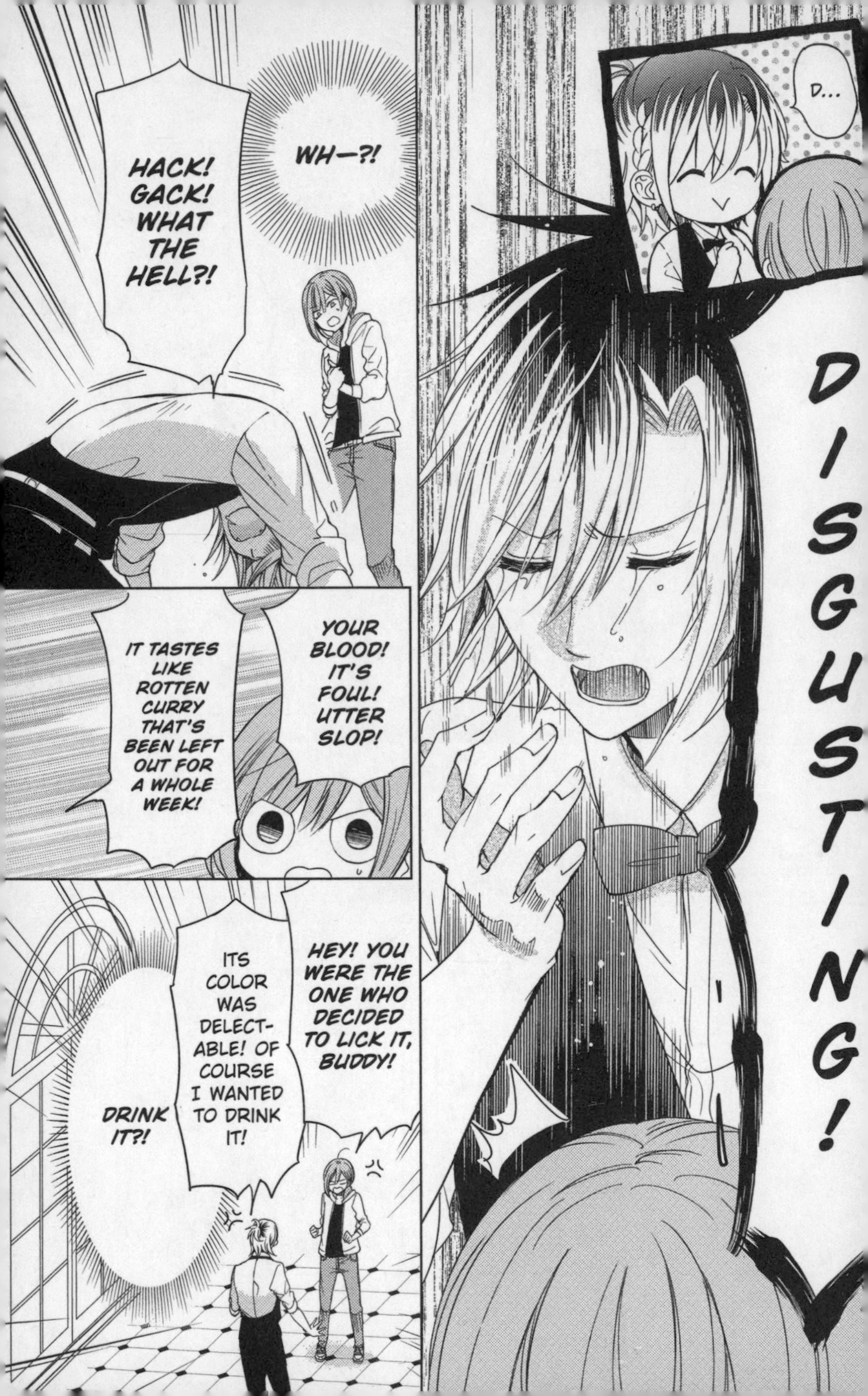
D...
DISGUSTING!
WH—?!
HACK! GACK! WHAT THE HELL?!
YOUR BLOOD! IT'S FOUL! UTTER SLOP!
IT TASTES LIKE ROTTEN CURRY THAT'S BEEN LEFT OUT FOR A WHOLE WEEK!
HEY! YOU WERE THE ONE WHO DECIDED TO LICK IT, BUDDY!
ITS COLOR WAS DELECT-ABLE! OF COURSE I WANTED TO DRINK IT!
DRINK IT?!

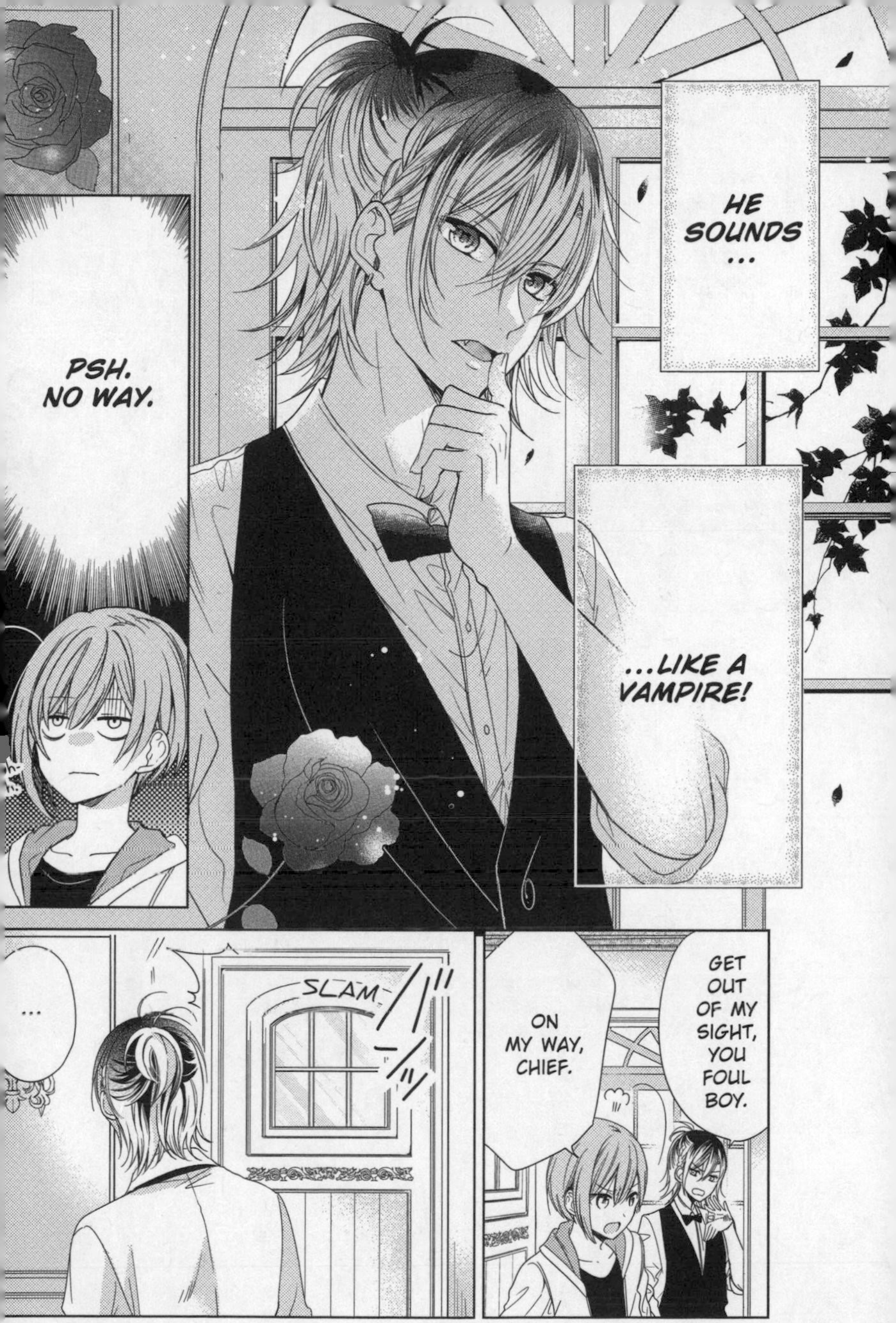
HE SOUNDS...
...LIKE A VAMPIRE!
PSH. NO WAY.
GET OUT OF MY SIGHT, YOU FOUL BOY.
ON MY WAY, CHIEF.
SLAM
...

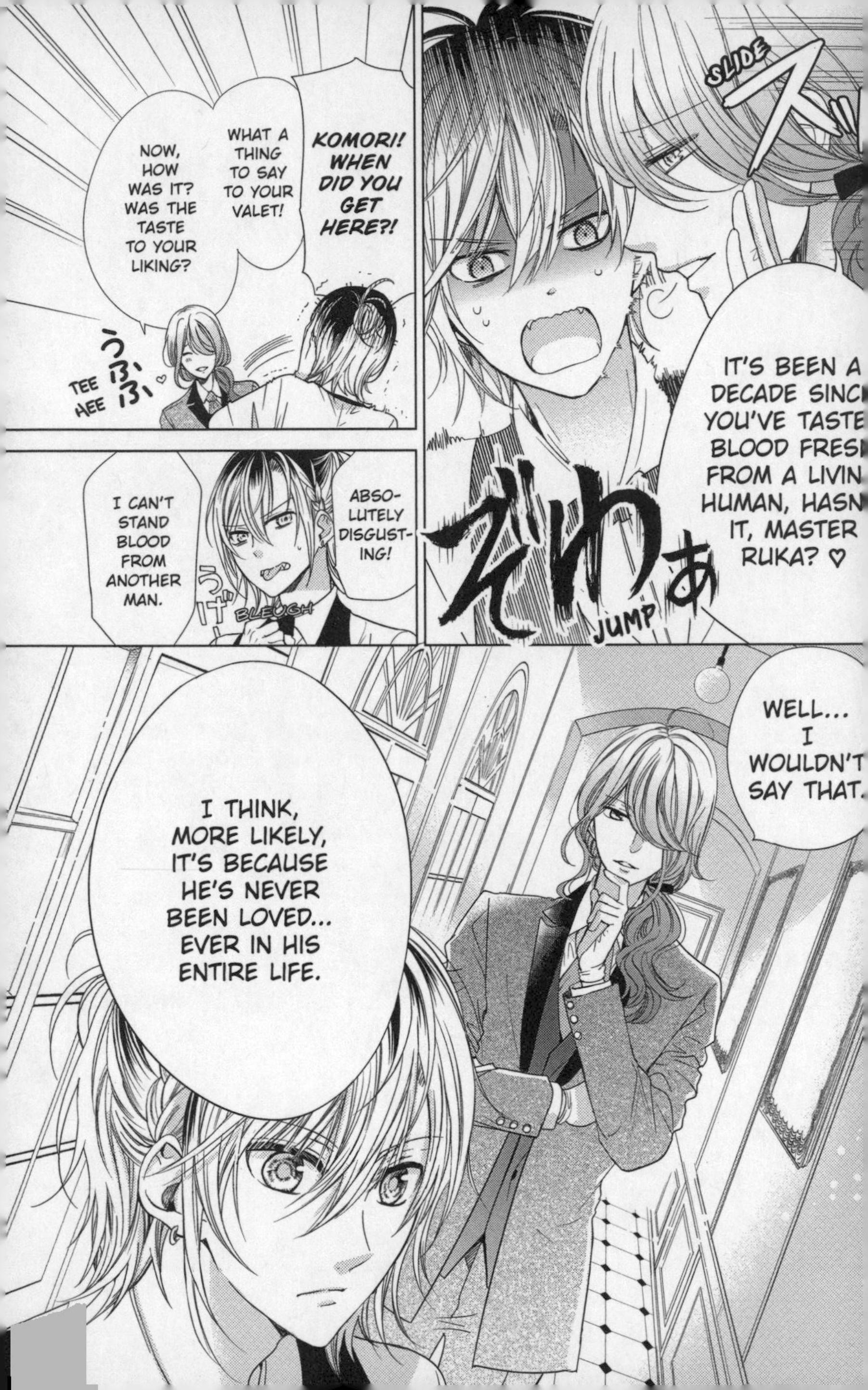
SLIDE
IT'S BEEN A DECADE SINC YOU'VE TASTE BLOOD FRES FROM A LIVIN HUMAN, HASN IT, MASTER RUKA? ♡
ぞわあ
JUMP
KOMORI! WHEN DID YOU GET HERE?!
WHAT A THING TO SAY TO YOUR VALET!
NOW, HOW WAS IT? WAS THE TASTE TO YOUR LIKING?
うふふ
TEE HEE
ABSOLUTELY DISGUSTING!
I CAN'T STAND BLOOD FROM ANOTHER MAN.
うげ
BLEUGH
WELL... I WOULDN'T SAY THAT.
I THINK, MORE LIKELY, IT'S BECAUSE HE'S NEVER BEEN LOVED... EVER IN HIS ENTIRE LIFE.

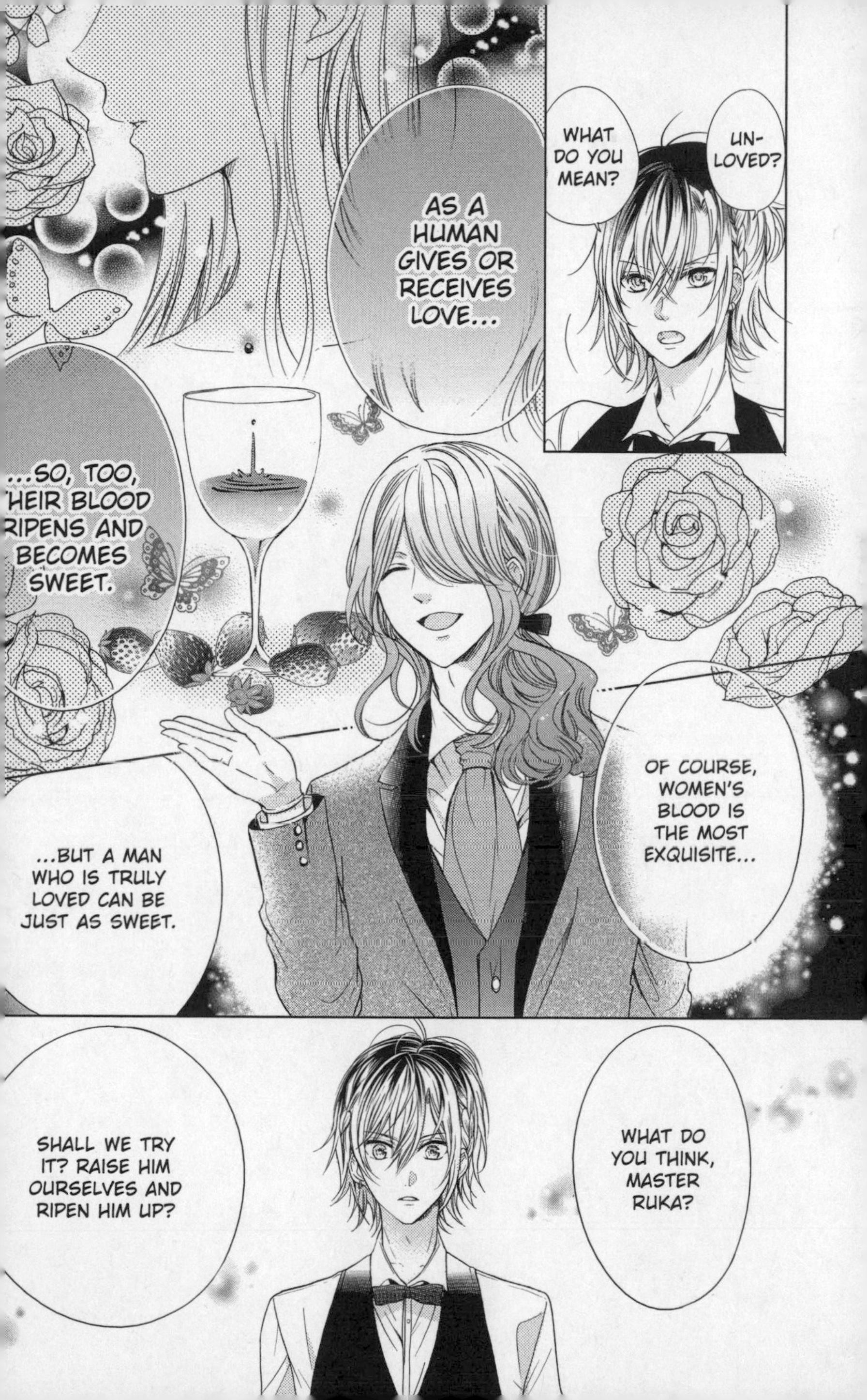
UN-LOVED?
WHAT DO YOU MEAN?
AS A HUMAN GIVES OR RECEIVES LOVE...
...SO, TOO, THEIR BLOOD RIPENS AND BECOMES SWEET.
OF COURSE, WOMEN'S BLOOD IS THE MOST EXQUISITE...
...BUT A MAN WHO IS TRULY LOVED CAN BE JUST AS SWEET.
WHAT DO YOU THINK, MASTER RUKA?
SHALL WE TRY IT? RAISE HIM OURSELVES AND RIPEN HIM UP?

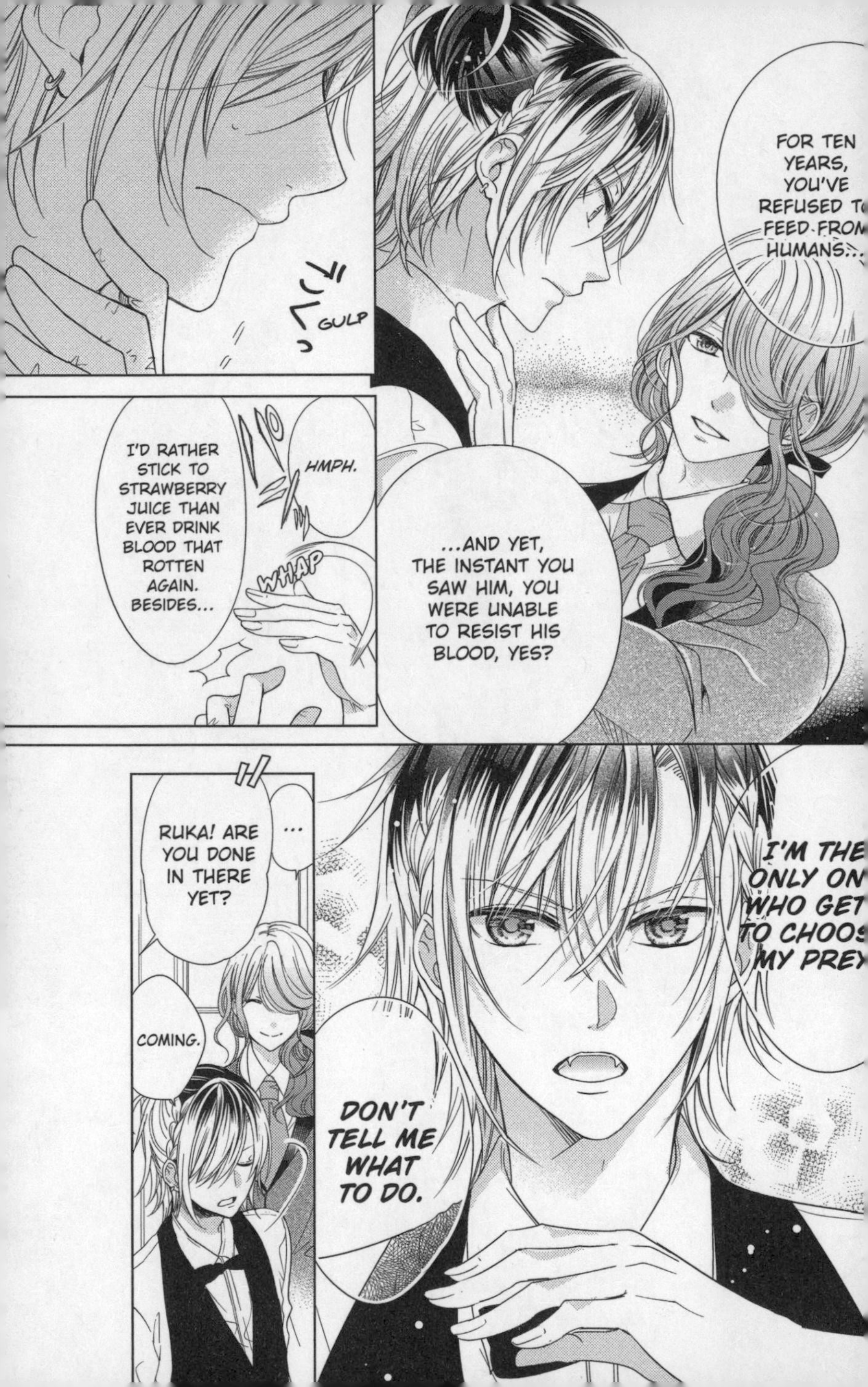
FOR TEN YEARS, YOU'VE REFUSED T FEED FROM HUMANS...
GULP
...AND YET, THE INSTANT YOU SAW HIM, YOU WERE UNABLE TO RESIST HIS BLOOD, YES?
HMPH.
I'D RATHER STICK TO STRAWBERRY JUICE THAN EVER DRINK BLOOD THAT ROTTEN AGAIN. BESIDES...
WHAP
I'M THE ONLY ON WHO GET TO CHOOS MY PRE
DON'T TELL ME WHAT TO DO.
...
RUKA! ARE YOU DONE IN THERE YET?
COMING.

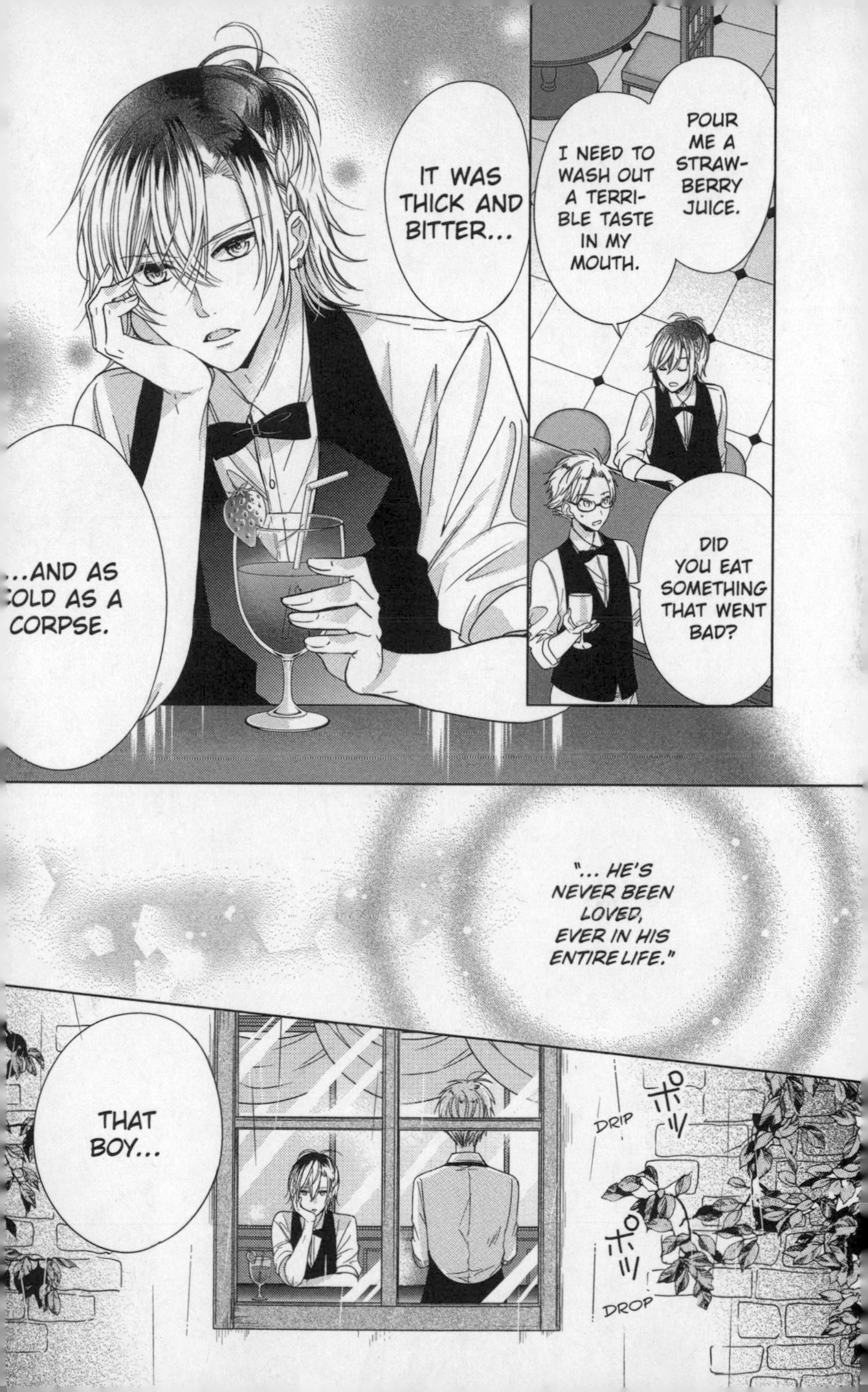
POUR ME A STRAWBERRY JUICE.
I NEED TO WASH OUT A TERRIBLE TASTE IN MY MOUTH.
DID YOU EAT SOMETHING THAT WENT BAD?
IT WAS THICK AND BITTER...
...AND AS COLD AS A CORPSE.
"... HE'S NEVER BEEN LOVED, EVER IN HIS ENTIRE LIFE."
ポツ
DRIP
ポツ
DROP
THAT BOY...

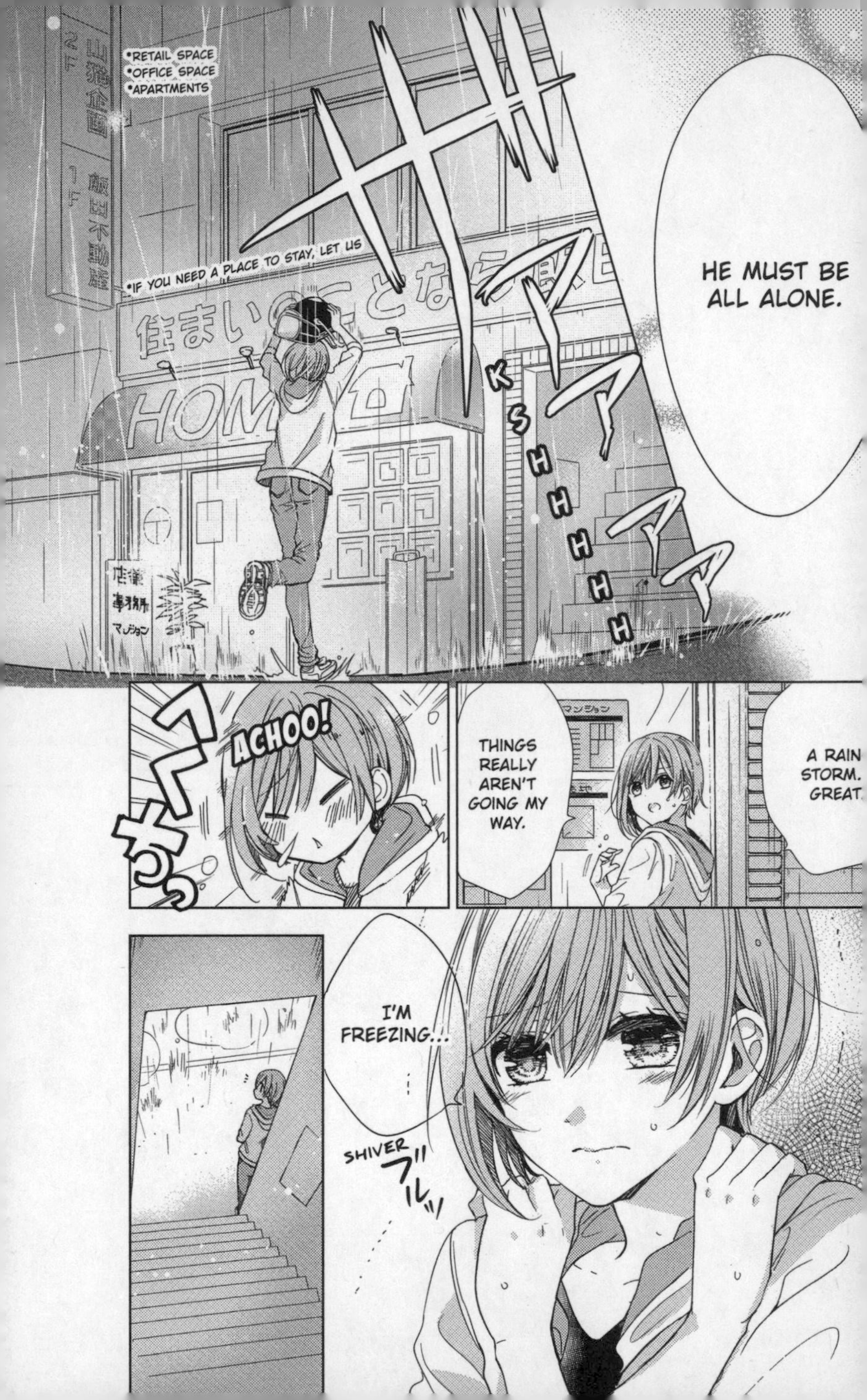
•RETAIL SPACE
•OFFICE SPACE
•APARTMENTS
•IF YOU NEED A PLACE TO STAY, LET US
HOM
HE MUST BE ALL ALONE.
KSHHHHH
A RAIN STORM. GREAT.
THINGS REALLY AREN'T GOING MY WAY.
ACHOO!
I'M FREEZING...
SHIVER

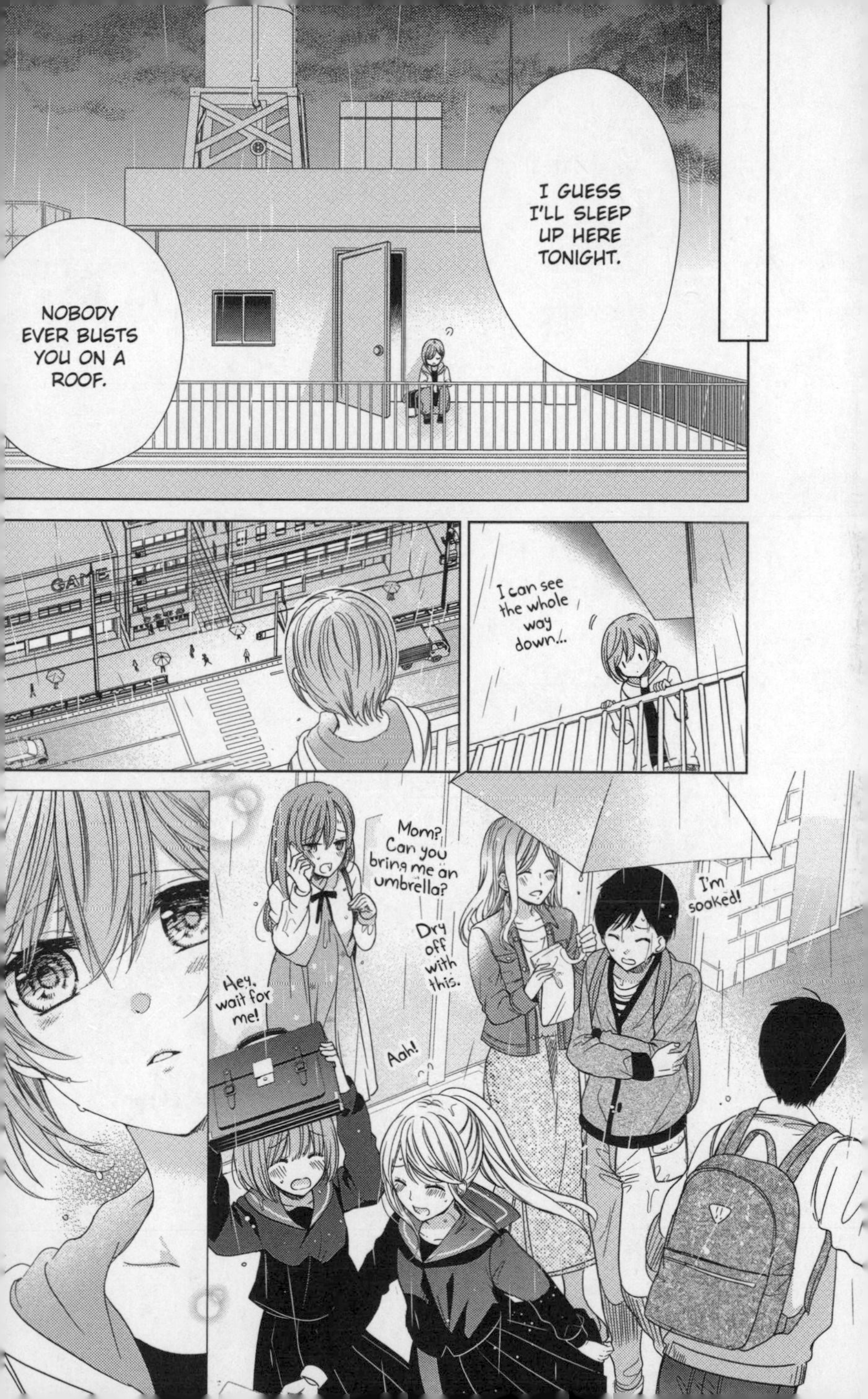
I GUESS I'LL SLEEP UP HERE TONIGHT.
NOBODY EVER BUSTS YOU ON A ROOF.
I can see the whole way down...
I'm sooked!
Dry off with this.
Mom? Can you bring me an umbrella?
Aah!
Hey, wait for me!

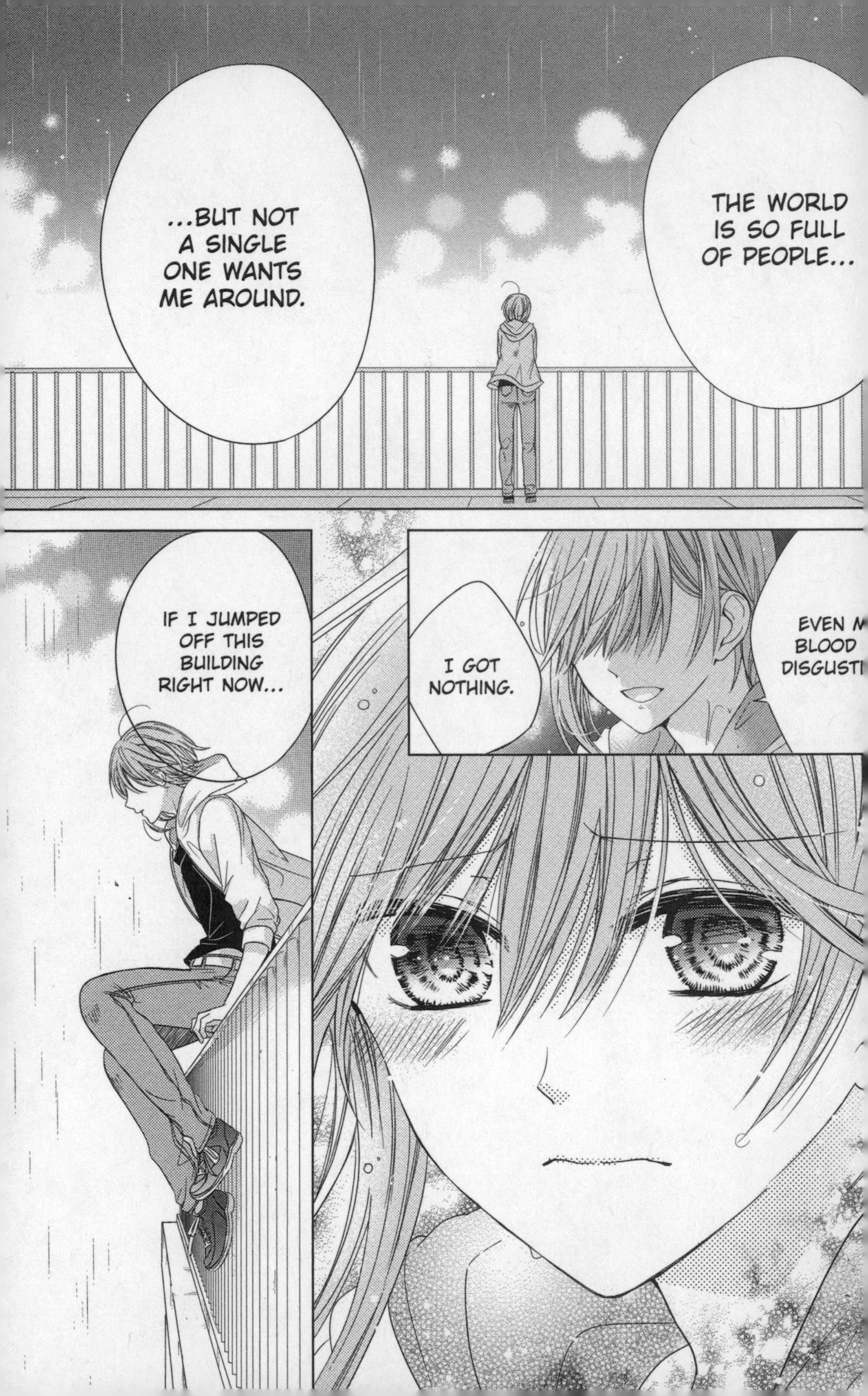
THE WORLD IS SO FULL OF PEOPLE...
...BUT NOT A SINGLE ONE WANTS ME AROUND.
EVEN M BLOOD DISGUSTI
I GOT NOTHING.
IF I JUMPED OFF THIS BUILDING RIGHT NOW...

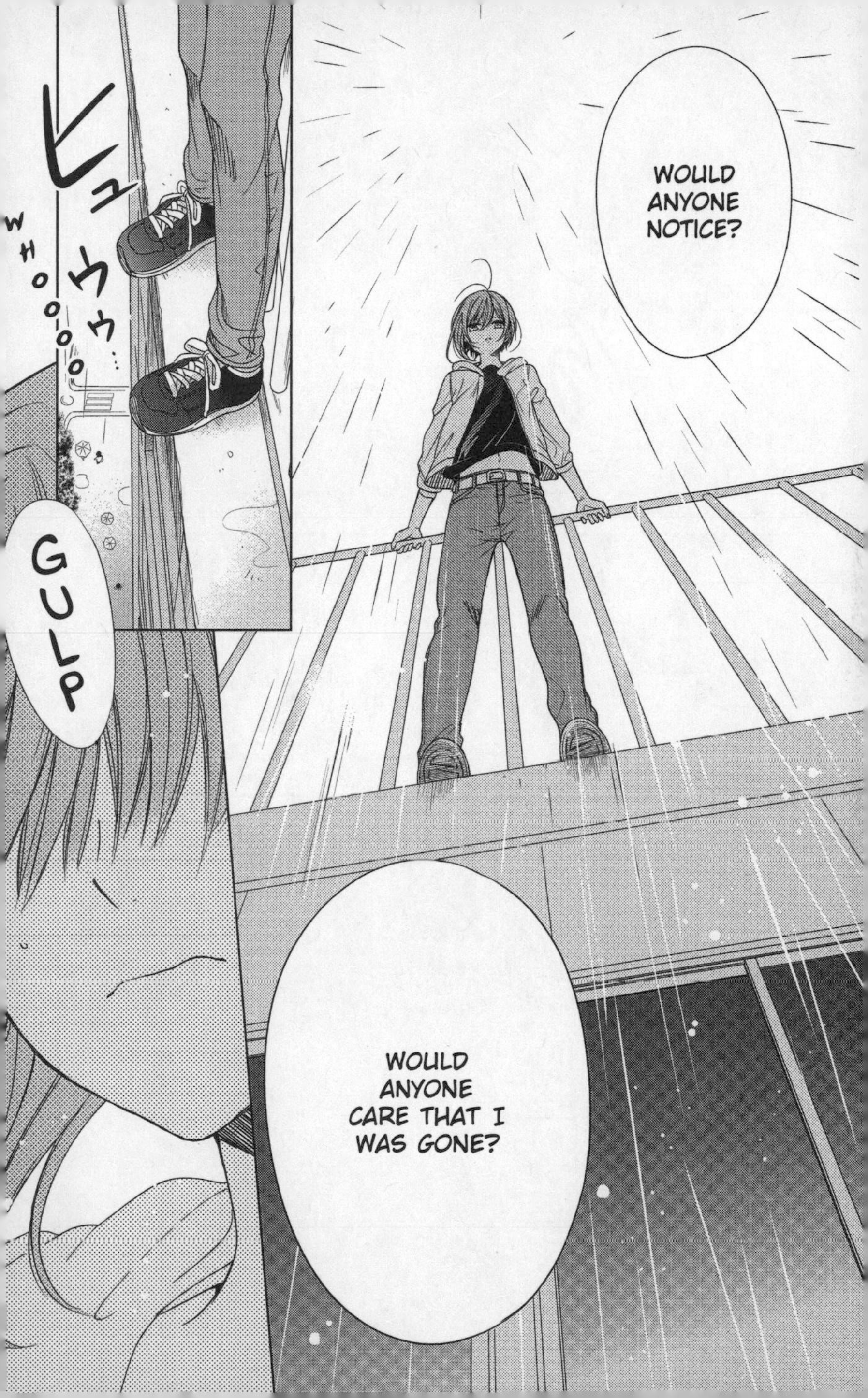
WOULD ANYONE NOTICE?
WOULD ANYONE CARE THAT I WAS GONE?
ヒュウウ…
WHOOOO
GULP

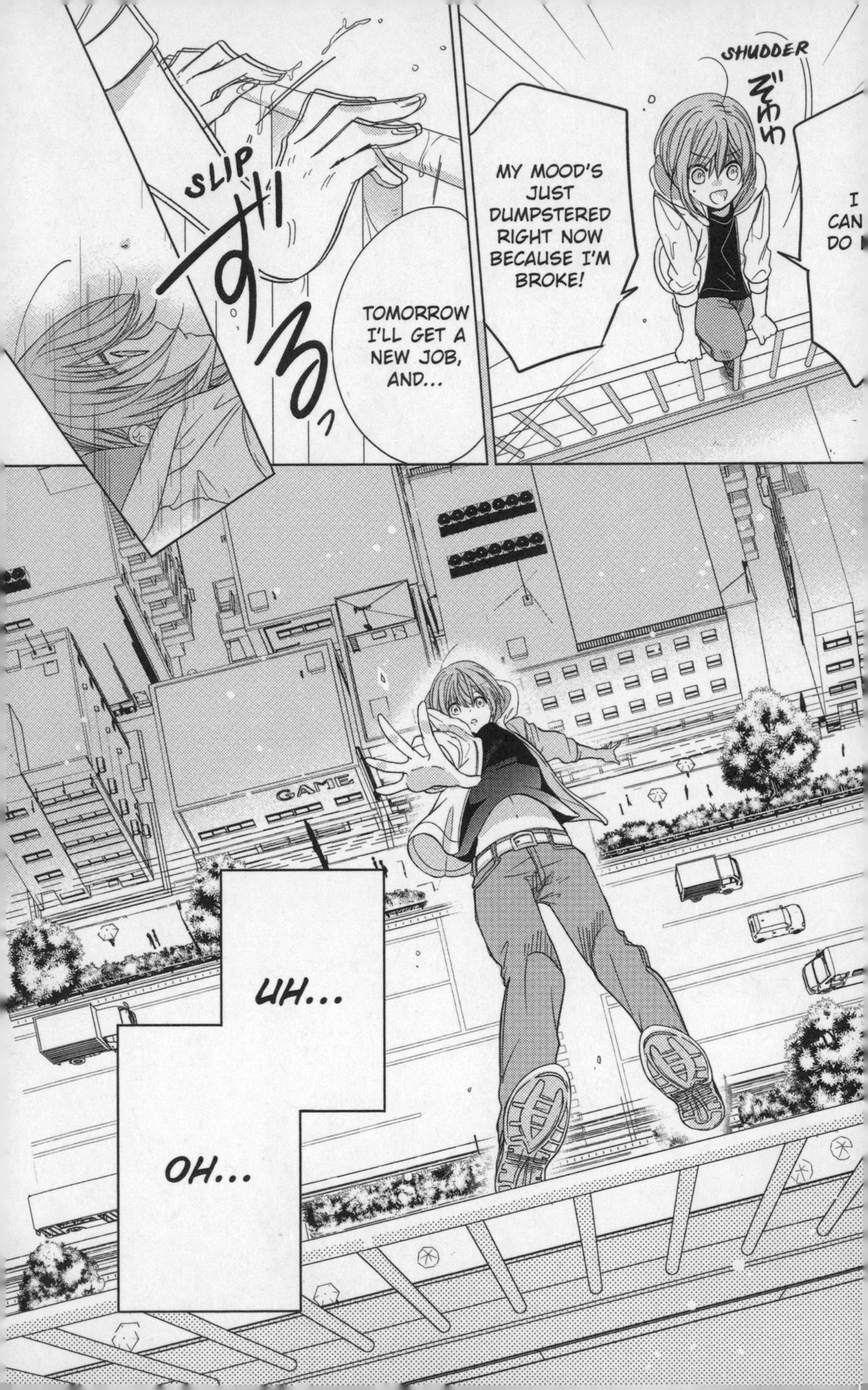
SHUDDER
ぞわわ
I CAN DO
MY MOOD'S JUST DUMPSTERED RIGHT NOW BECAUSE I'M BROKE!
TOMORROW I'LL GET A NEW JOB, AND...
SLIP
ずる
UH...
OH...

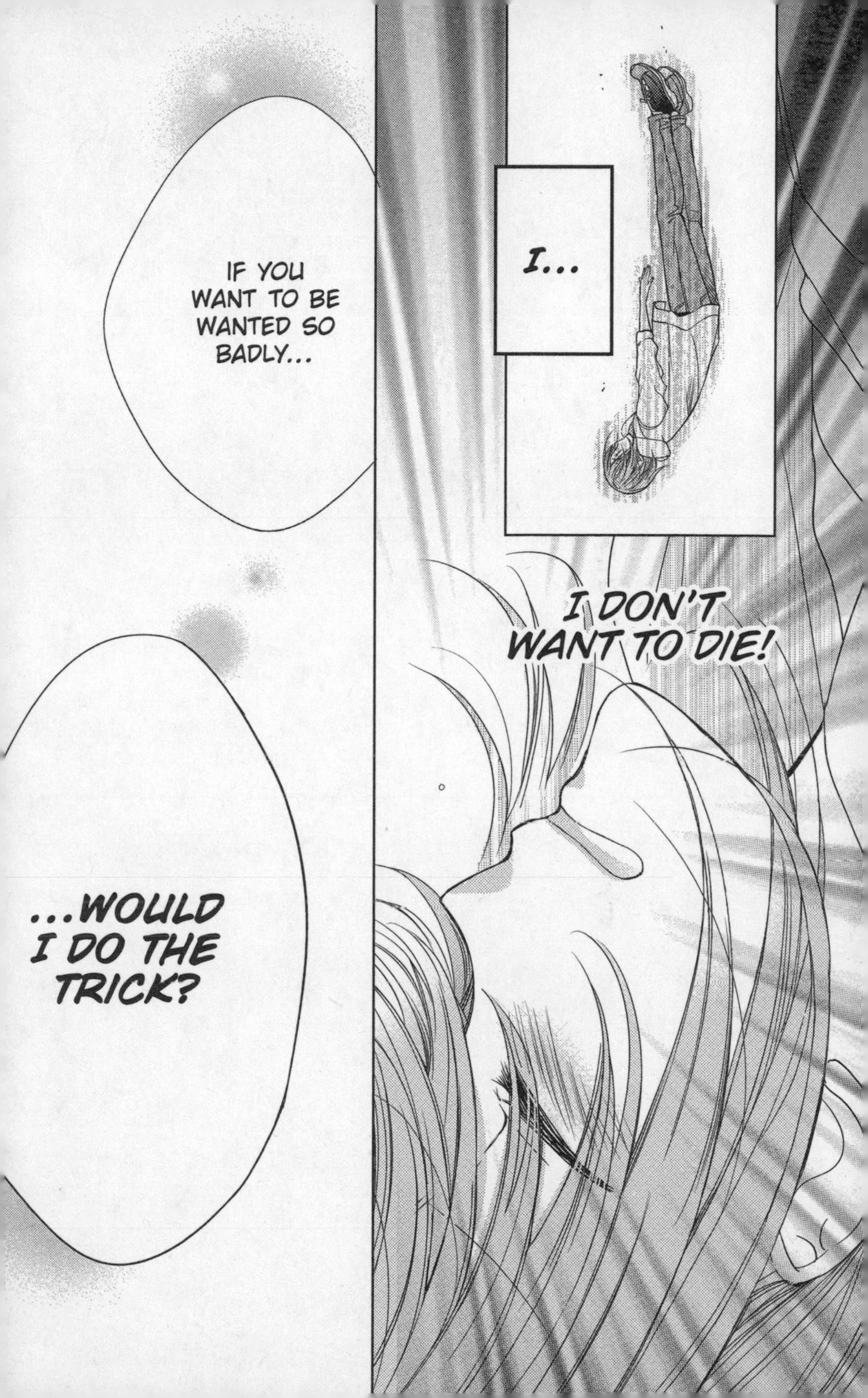
I...
I DON'T WANT TO DIE!
IF YOU WANT TO BE WANTED SO BADLY...
...WOULD I DO THE TRICK?

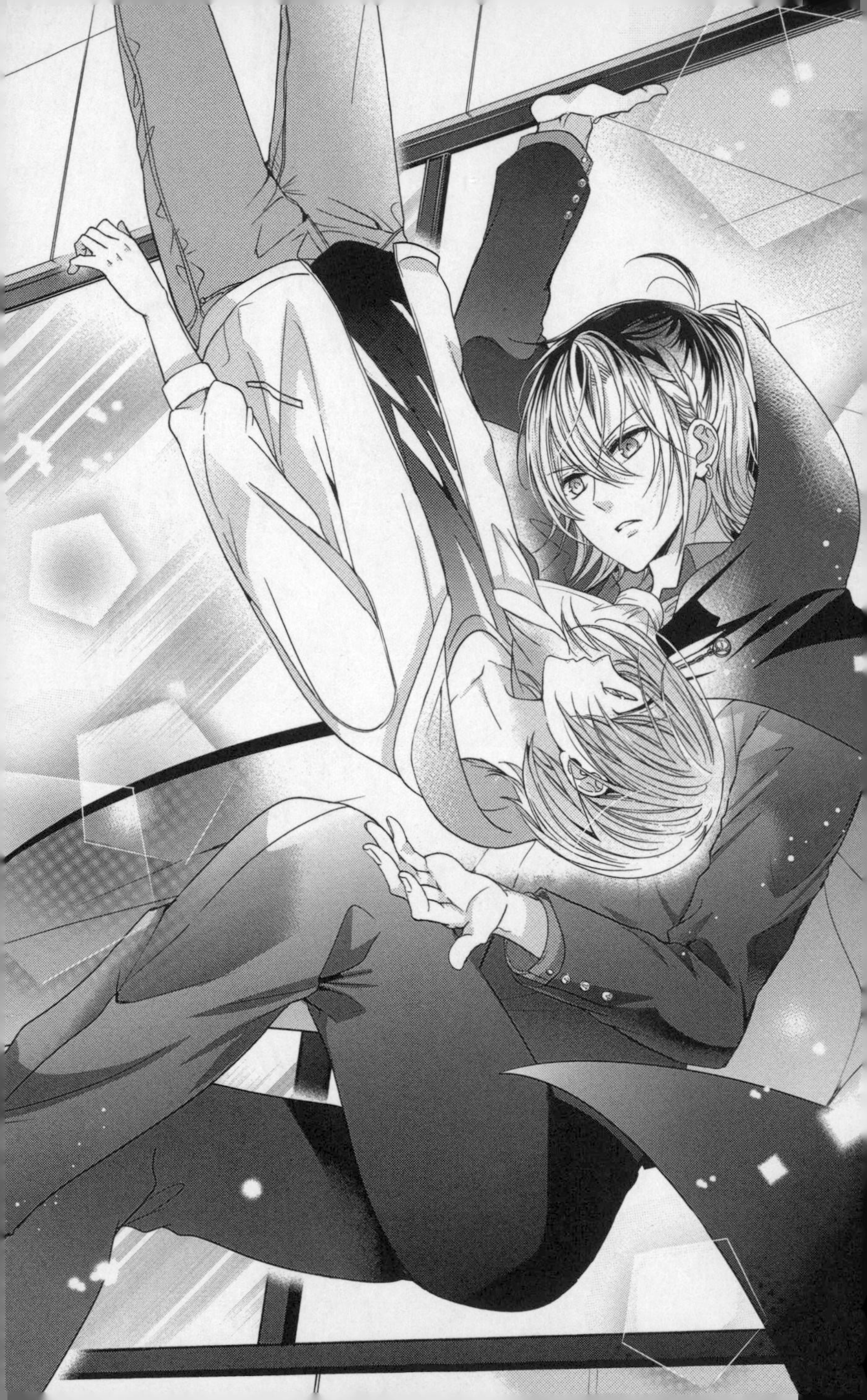

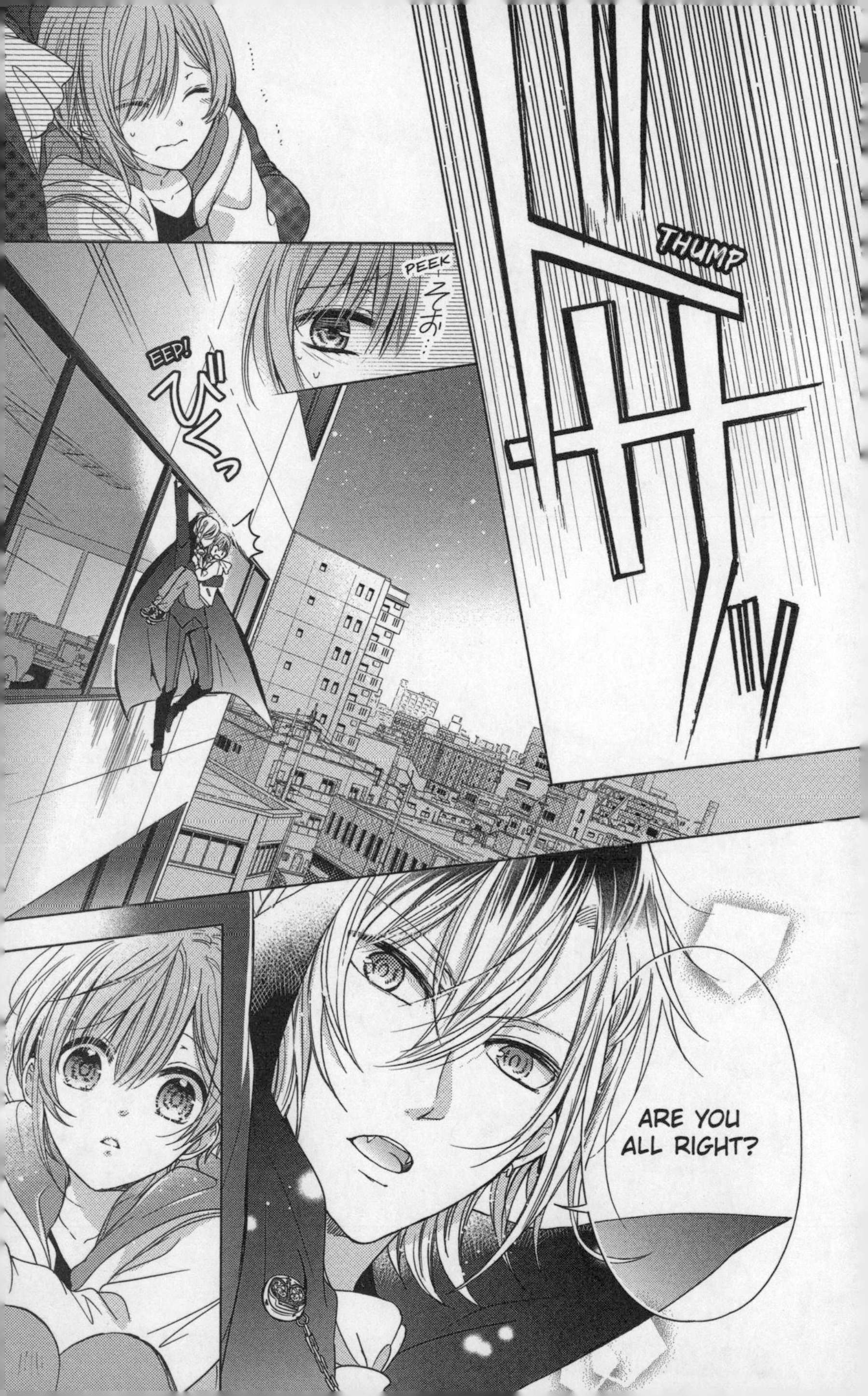
THUMP
PEEK
そぉ…
EEP!
びくっ
ARE YOU ALL RIGHT?

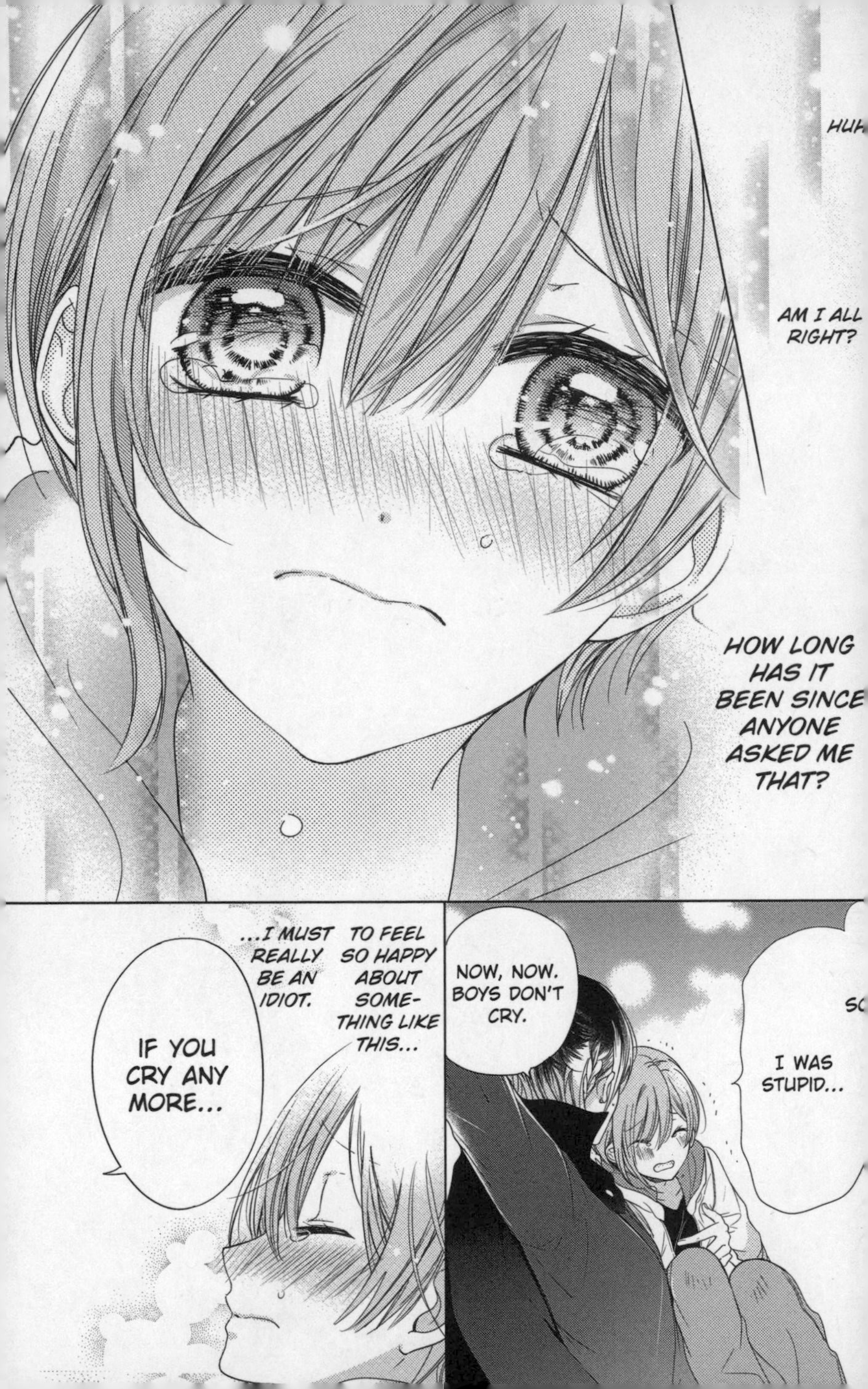
HUH
AM I ALL RIGHT?
HOW LONG HAS IT BEEN SINCE ANYONE ASKED ME THAT?
I WAS STUPID...
NOW, NOW. BOYS DON'T CRY.
TO FEEL SO HAPPY ABOUT SOME-THING LIKE THIS...
...I MUST REALLY BE AN IDIOT.
IF YOU CRY ANY MORE...

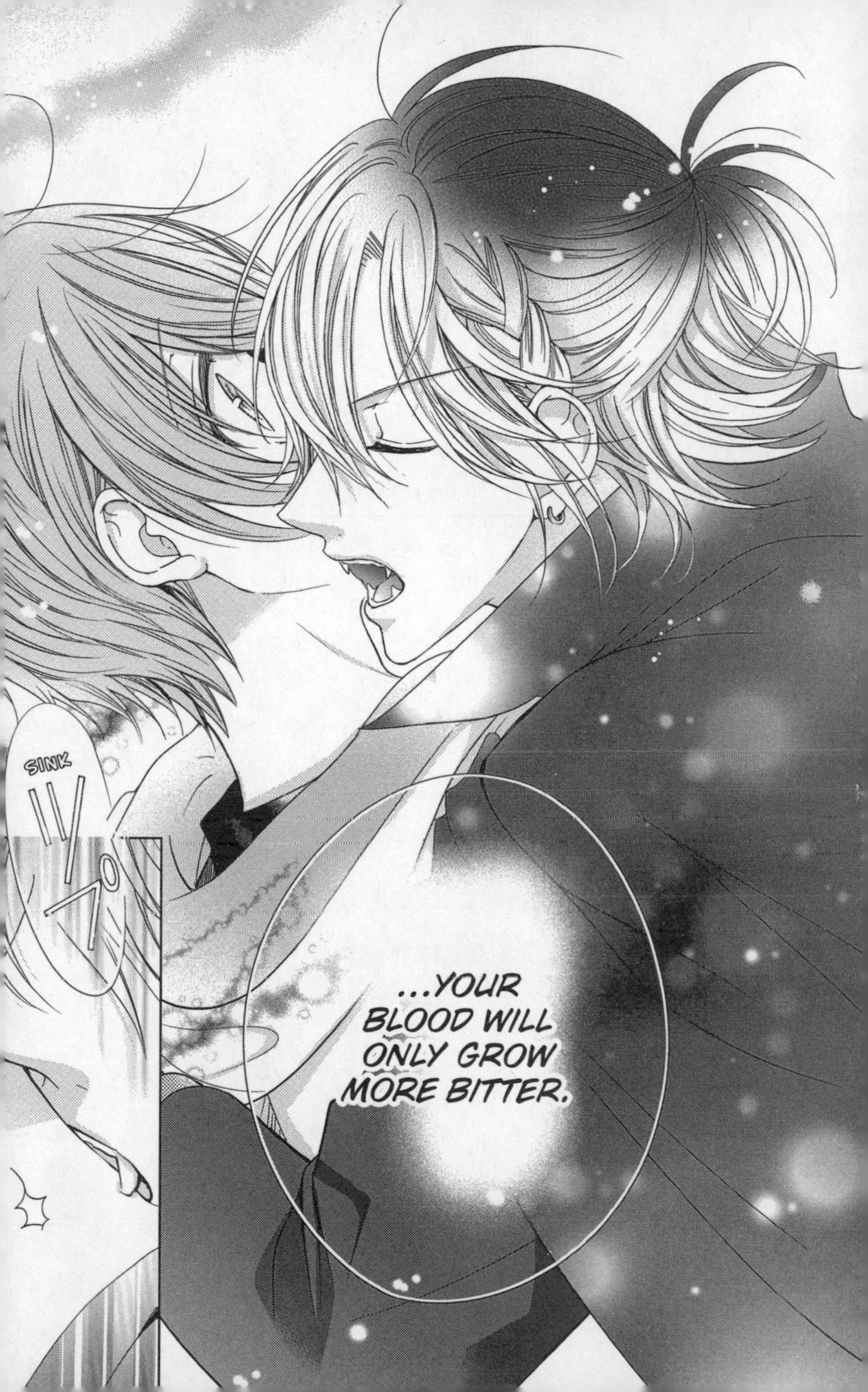
SINK
...YOUR BLOOD WILL ONLY GROW MORE BITTER.

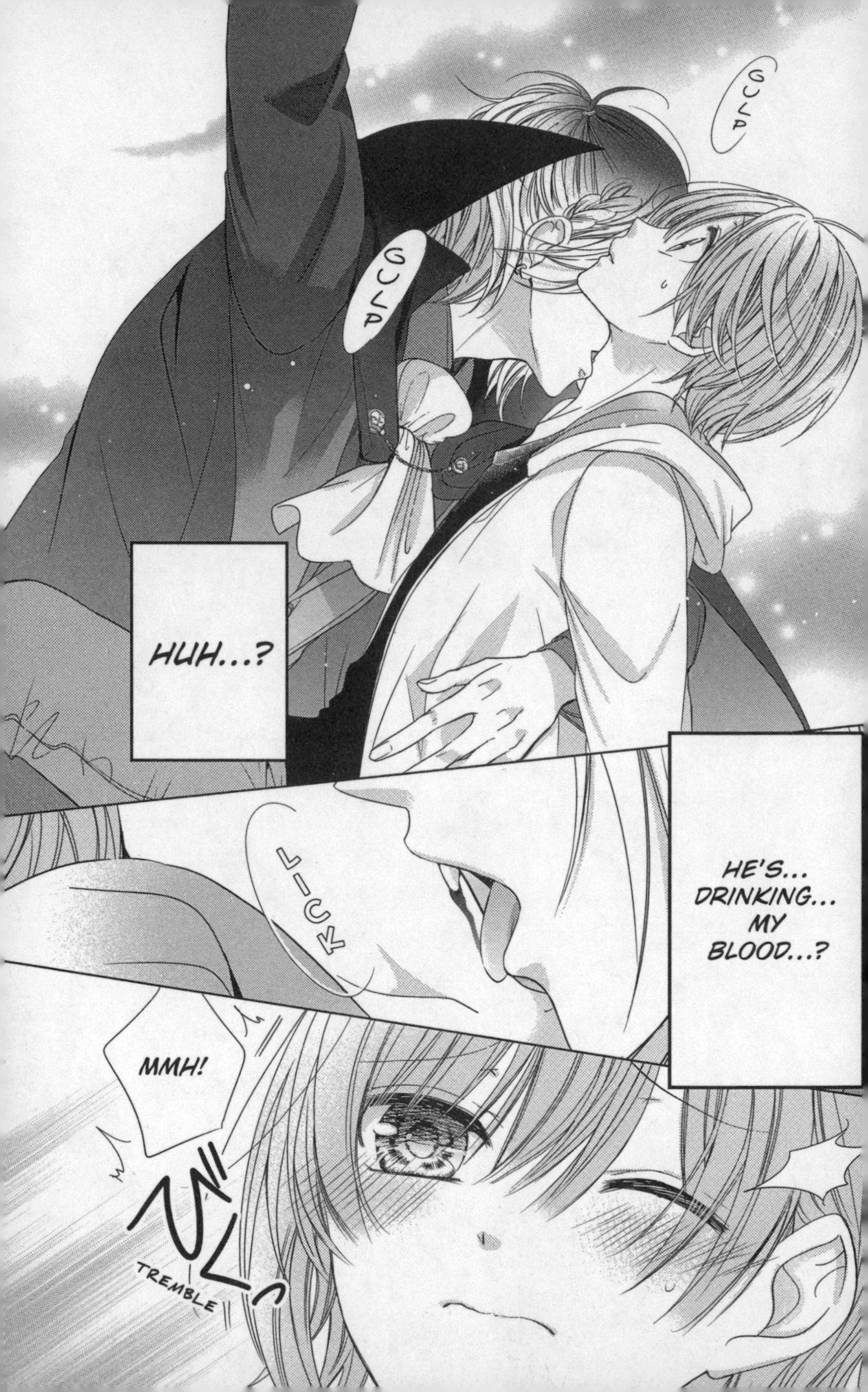
GULP
GULP
HUH...?
HE'S... DRINKING... MY BLOOD...?
LICK
MMH!
TREMBLE

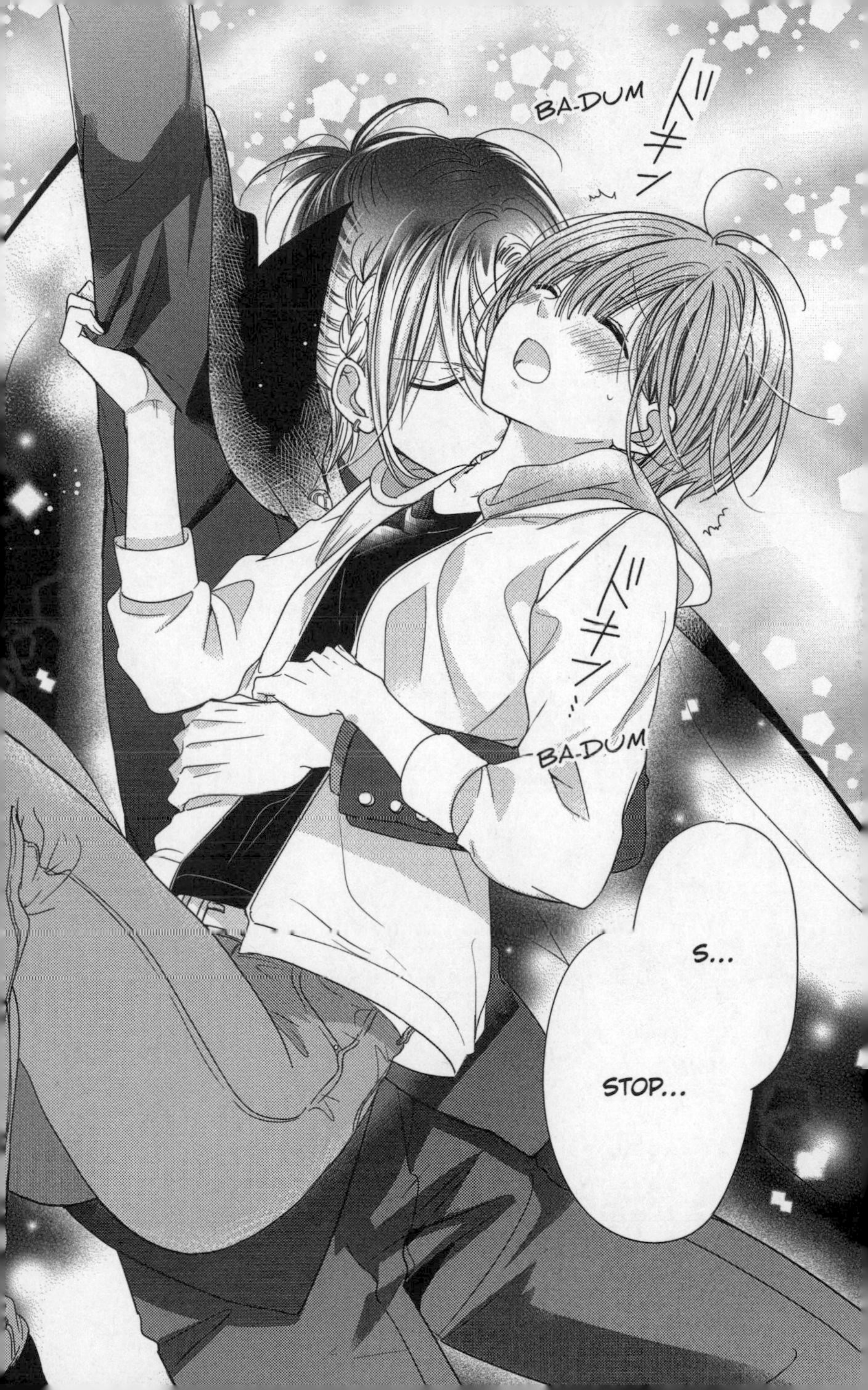
BA-DUM
ドキン
ドキン!!
BA-DUM
S...
STOP...

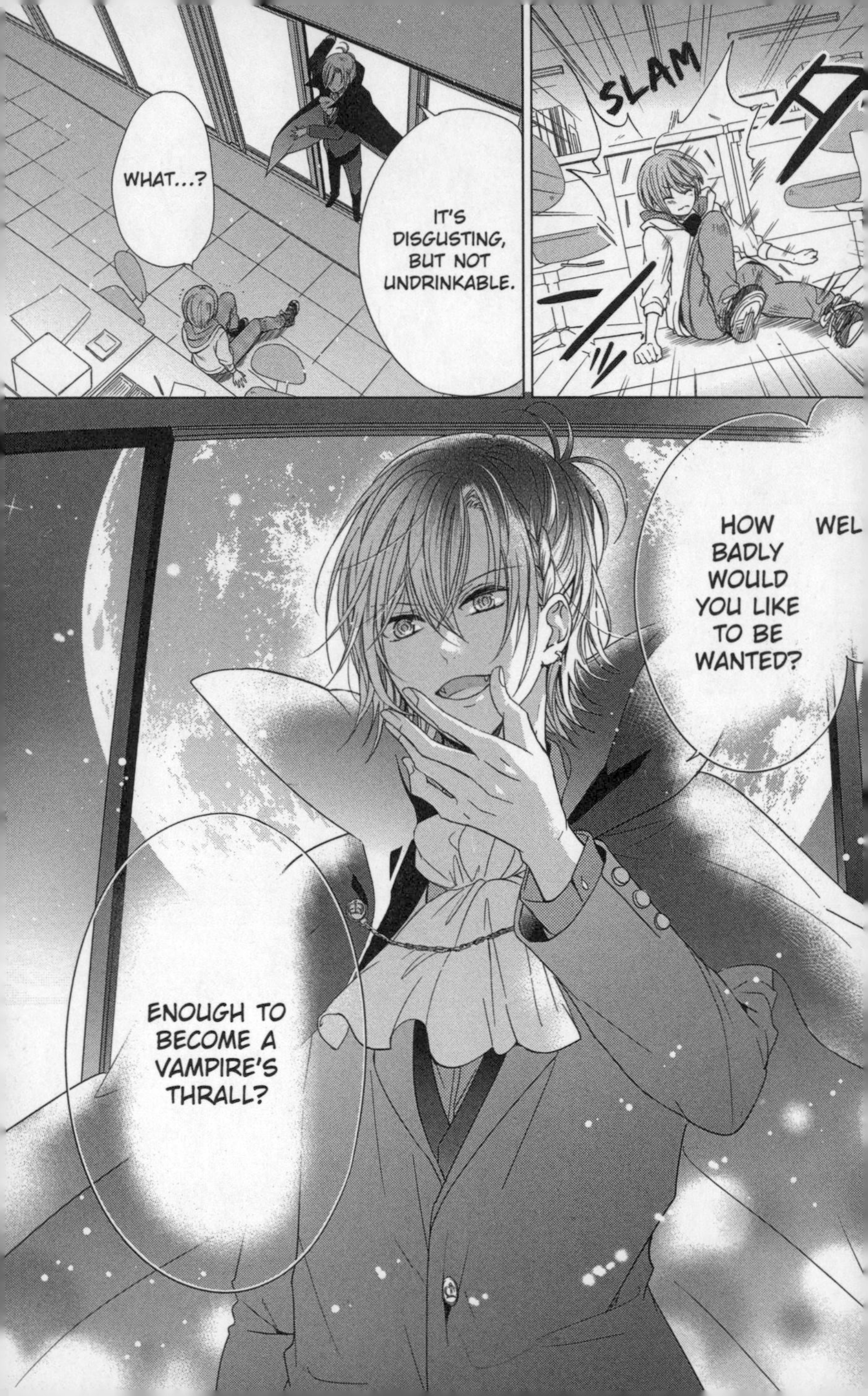
SLAM
IT'S DISGUSTING, BUT NOT UNDRINKABLE.
WHAT...?
WEL
HOW BADLY WOULD YOU LIKE TO BE WANTED?
ENOUGH TO BECOME A VAMPIRE'S THRALL?

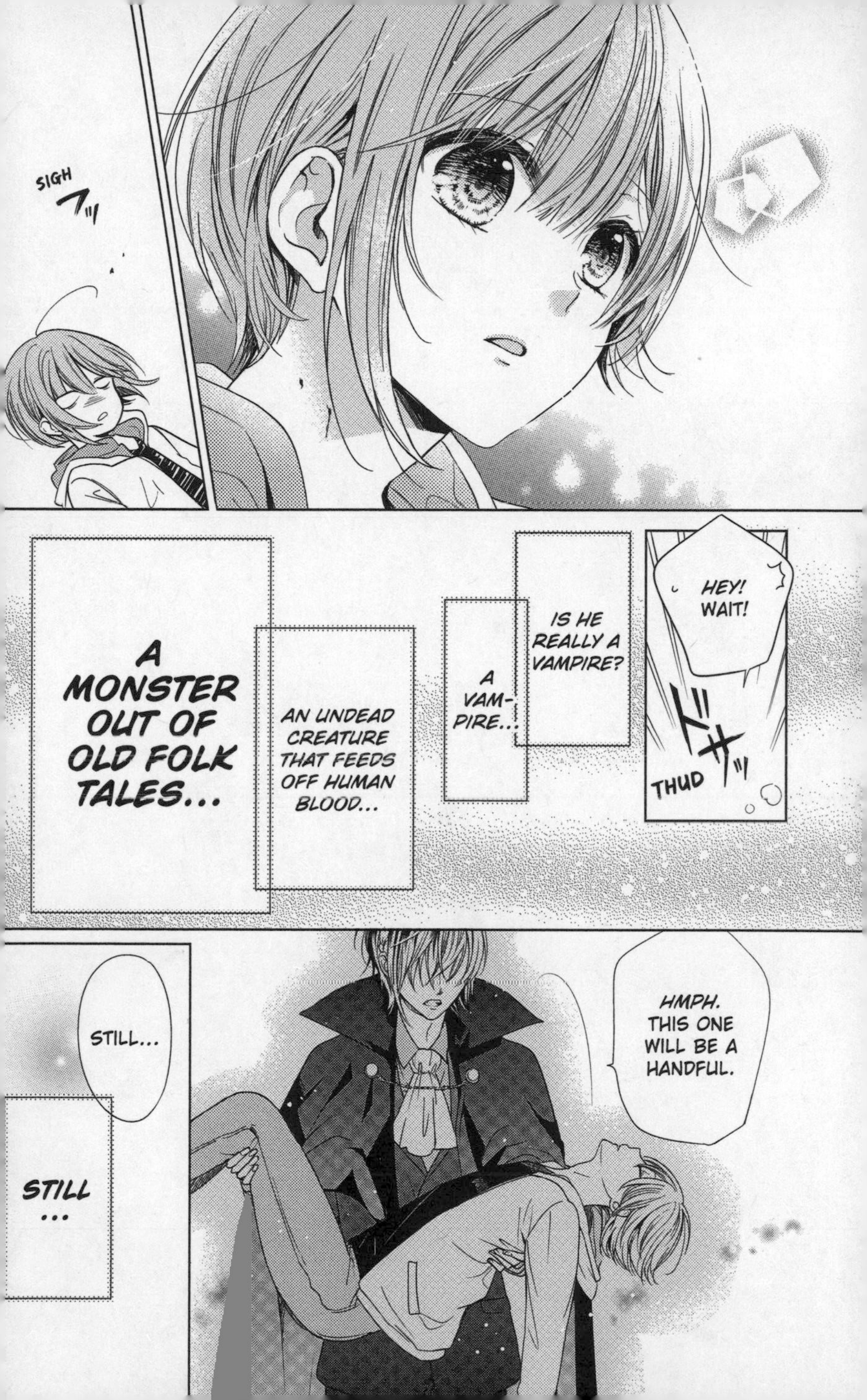
SIGH
HEY! WAIT!
THUD
IS HE REALLY A VAMPIRE?
A VAM-PIRE...
AN UNDEAD CREATURE THAT FEEDS OFF HUMAN BLOOD...
A MONSTER OUT OF OLD FOLK TALES...
HMPH. THIS ONE WILL BE A HANDFUL.
STILL...
STILL...

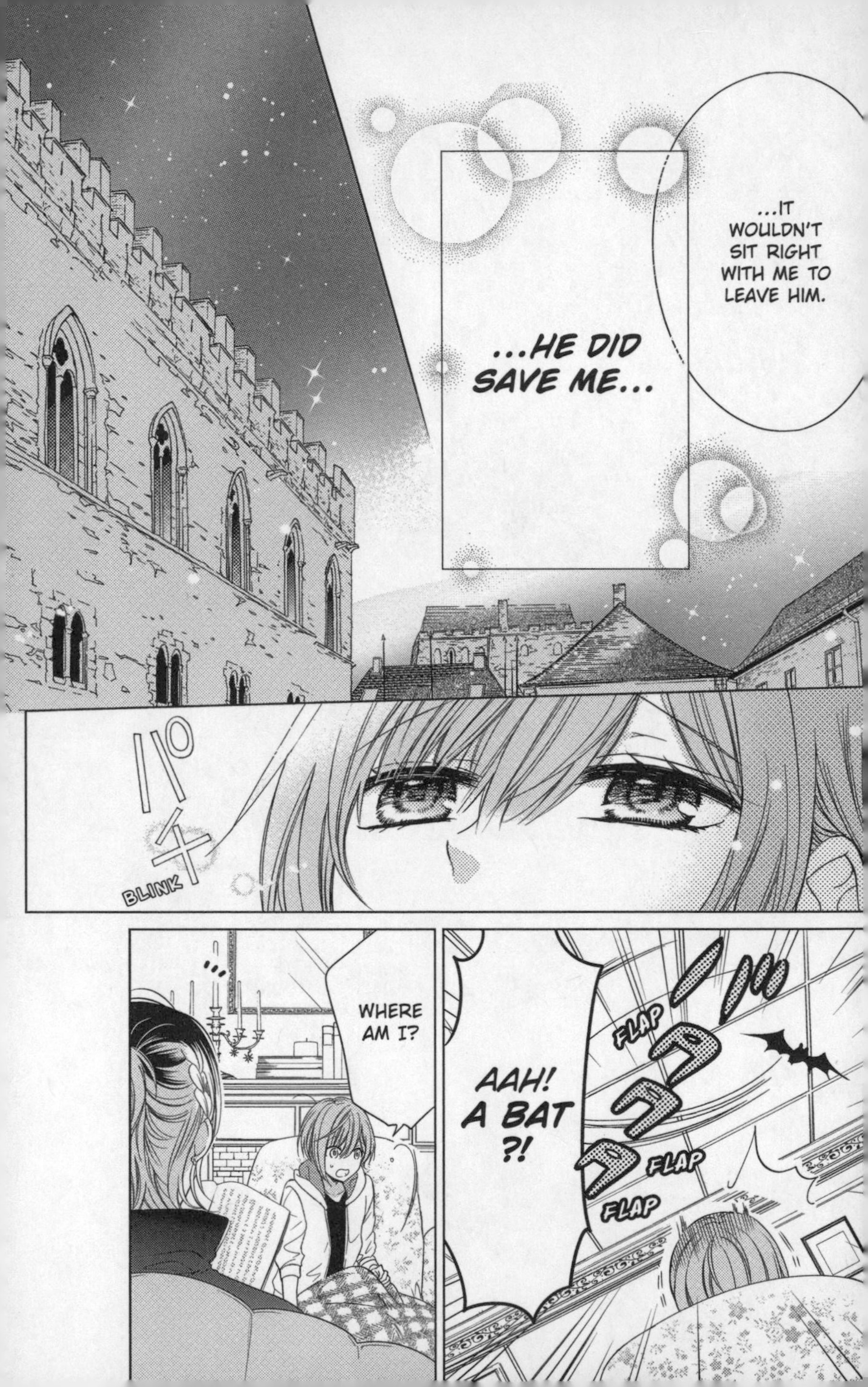
...IT WOULDN'T SIT RIGHT WITH ME TO LEAVE HIM.
...HE DID SAVE ME...
パチ
BLINK
AAH! A BAT ?!
FLAP
FLAP
FLAP
...
WHERE AM I?

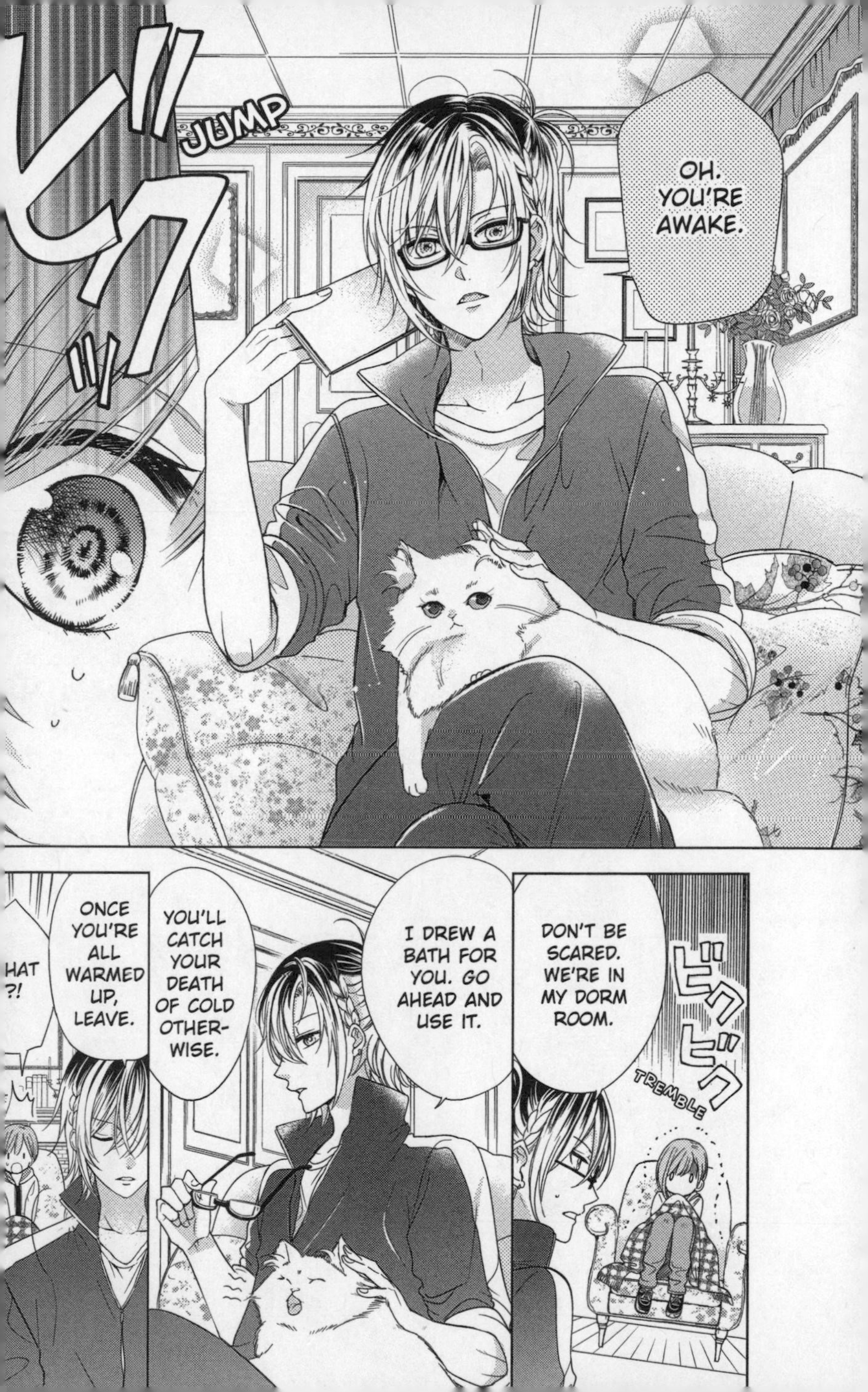
OH. YOU'RE AWAKE.
ビクッ
JUMP
ビクビク
TREMBLE
DON'T BE SCARED. WE'RE IN MY DORM ROOM.
I DREW A BATH FOR YOU. GO AHEAD AND USE IT.
YOU'LL CATCH YOUR DEATH OF COLD OTHER-WISE.
ONCE YOU'RE ALL WARMED UP, LEAVE.
HAT ?!

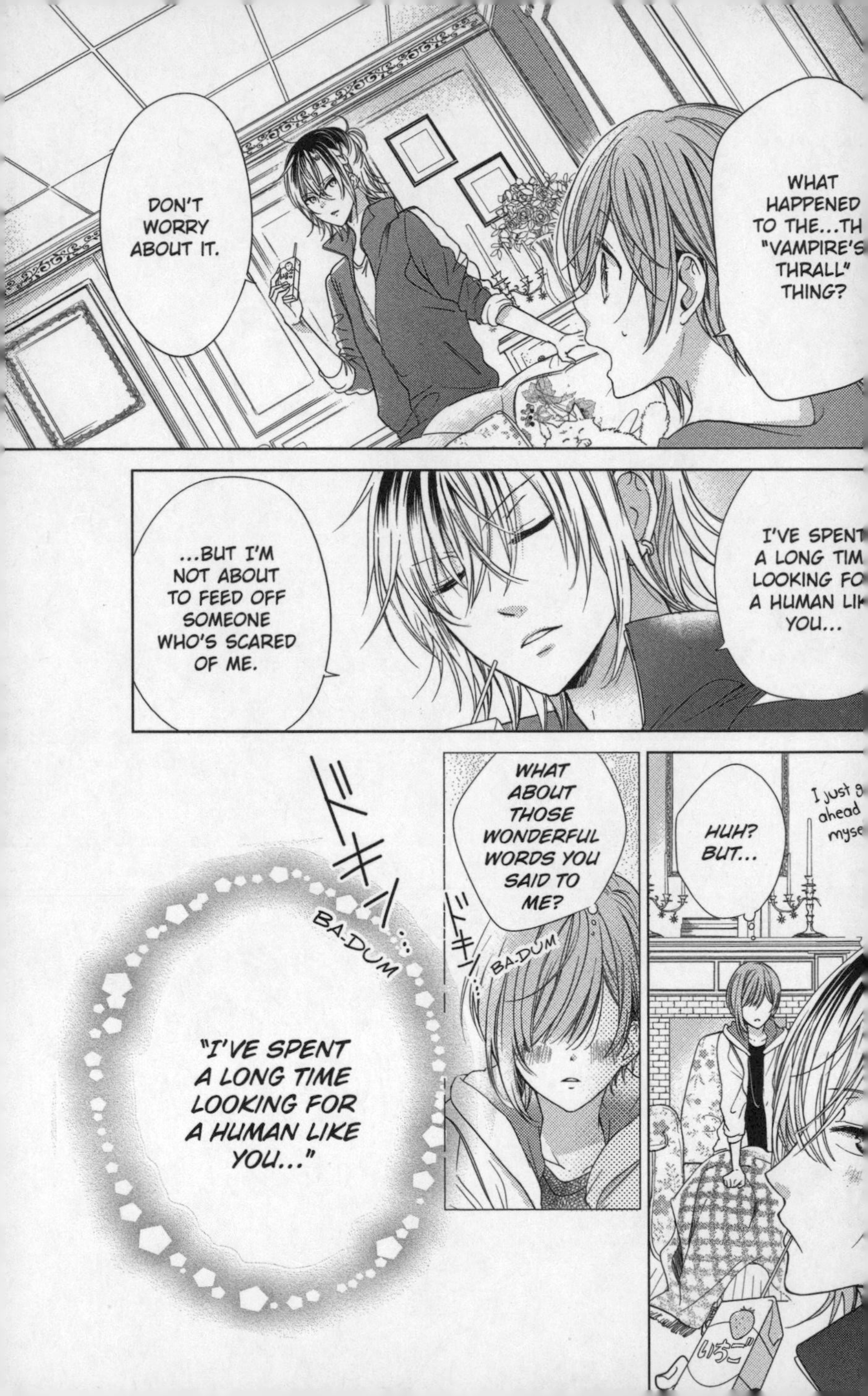
WHAT HAPPENED TO THE...TH "VAMPIRE'S THRALL" THING?
DON'T WORRY ABOUT IT.
I'VE SPENT A LONG TIME LOOKING FO A HUMAN LIK YOU...
...BUT I'M NOT ABOUT TO FEED OFF SOMEONE WHO'S SCARED OF ME.
I just g ahead myse
HUH? BUT...
WHAT ABOUT THOSE WONDERFUL WORDS YOU SAID TO ME?
BA-DUM
BA-DUM
"I'VE SPENT A LONG TIME LOOKING FOR A HUMAN LIKE YOU..."

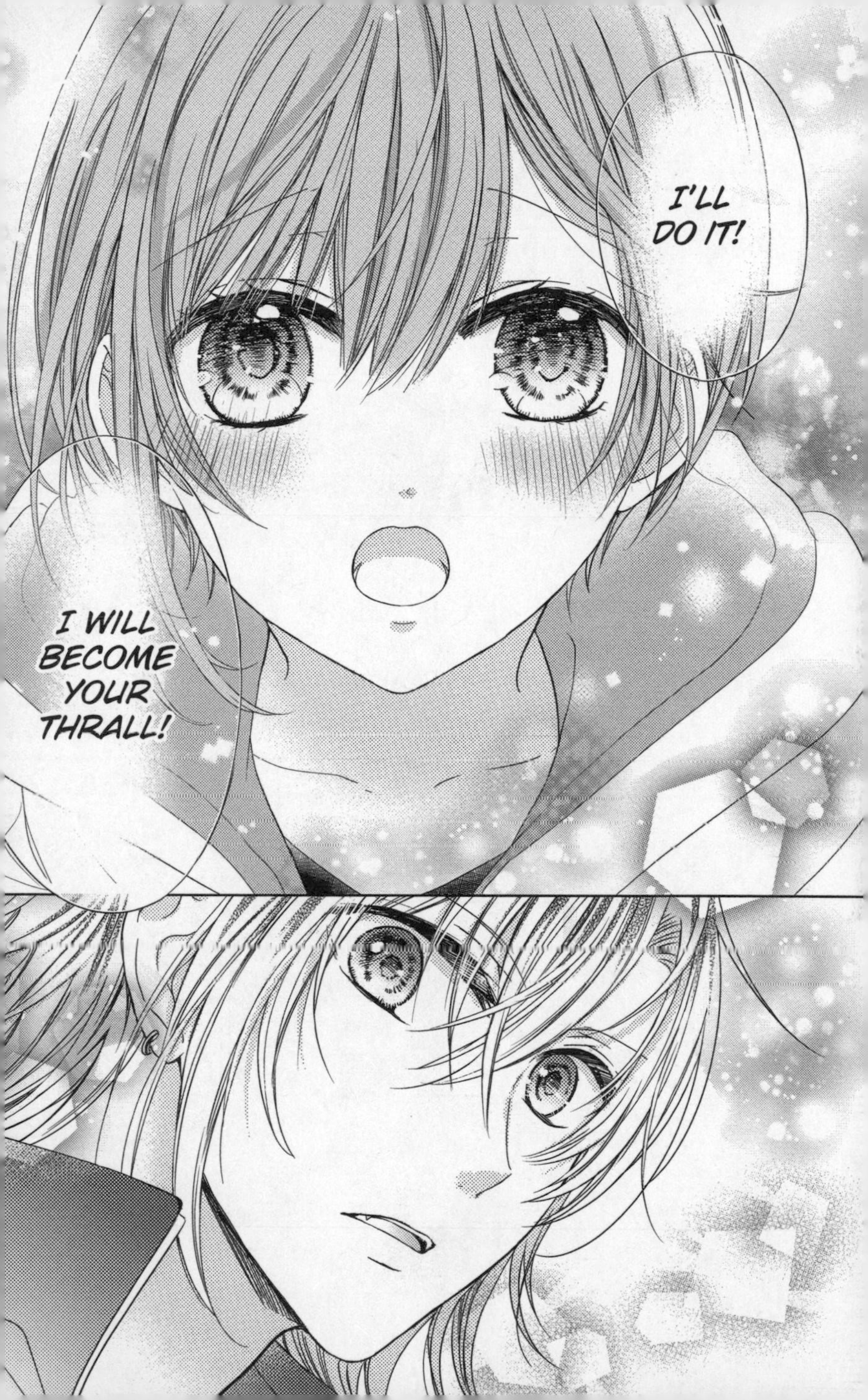
I'LL DO IT!
I WILL BECOME YOUR THRALL!

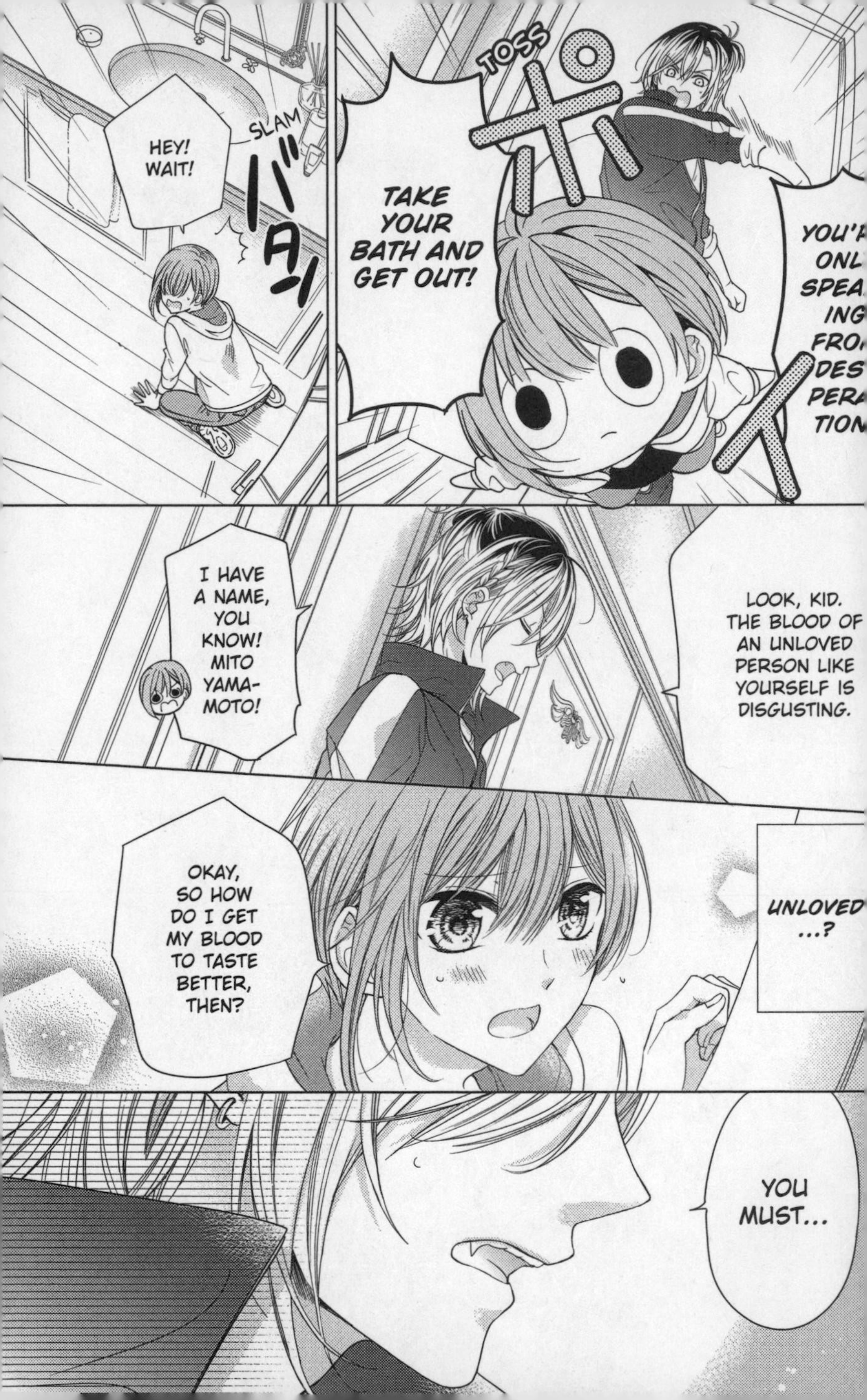
TOSS
YOU'R ONL SPEA ING FRO DES PERA TION
TAKE YOUR BATH AND GET OUT!
SLAM
HEY! WAIT!
LOOK, KID. THE BLOOD OF AN UNLOVED PERSON LIKE YOURSELF IS DISGUSTING.
I HAVE A NAME, YOU KNOW! MITO YAMA-MOTO!
UNLOVED ...?
OKAY, SO HOW DO I GET MY BLOOD TO TASTE BETTER, THEN?
YOU MUST...

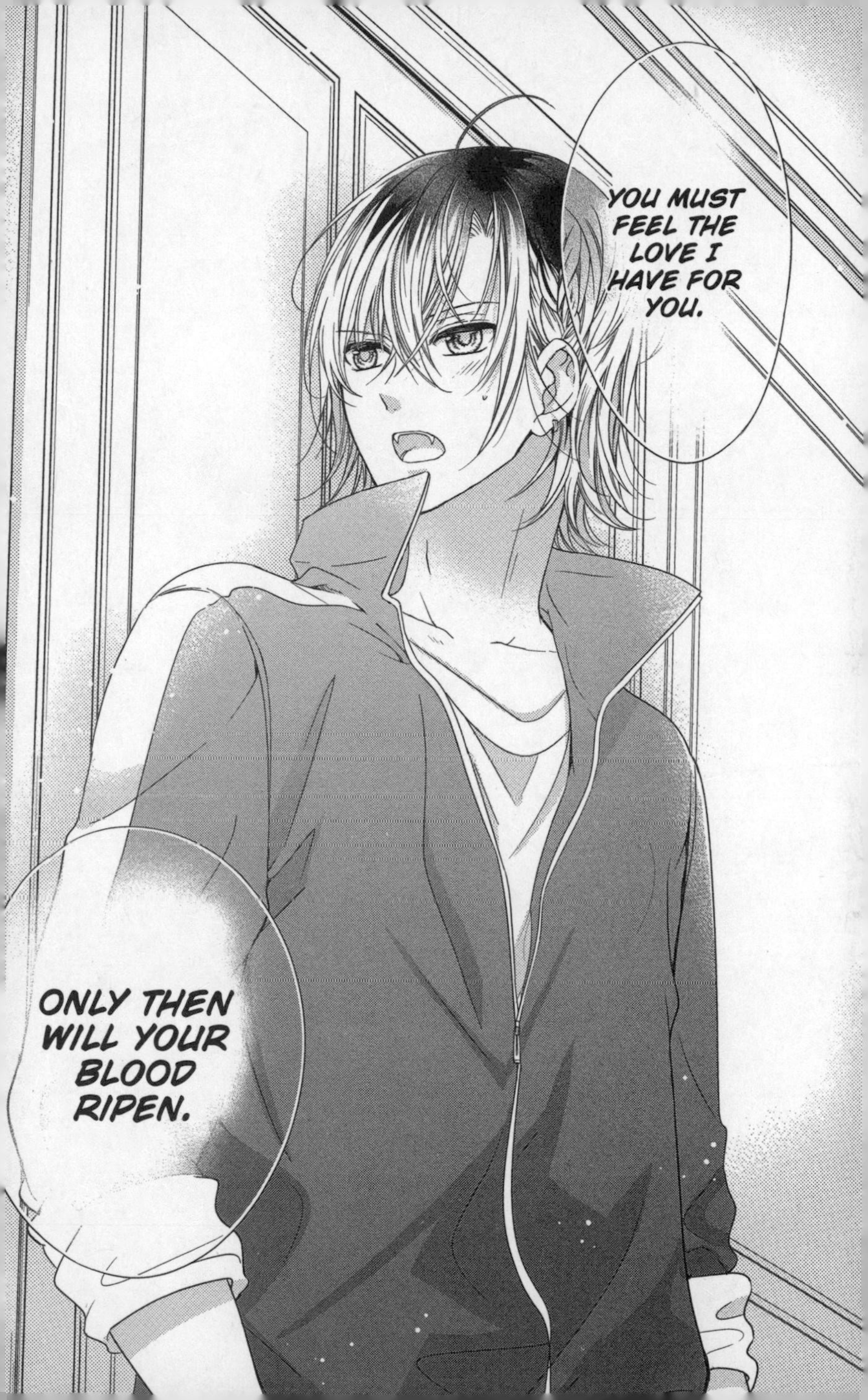
YOU MUST FEEL THE LOVE I HAVE FOR YOU.
ONLY THEN WILL YOUR BLOOD RIPEN.

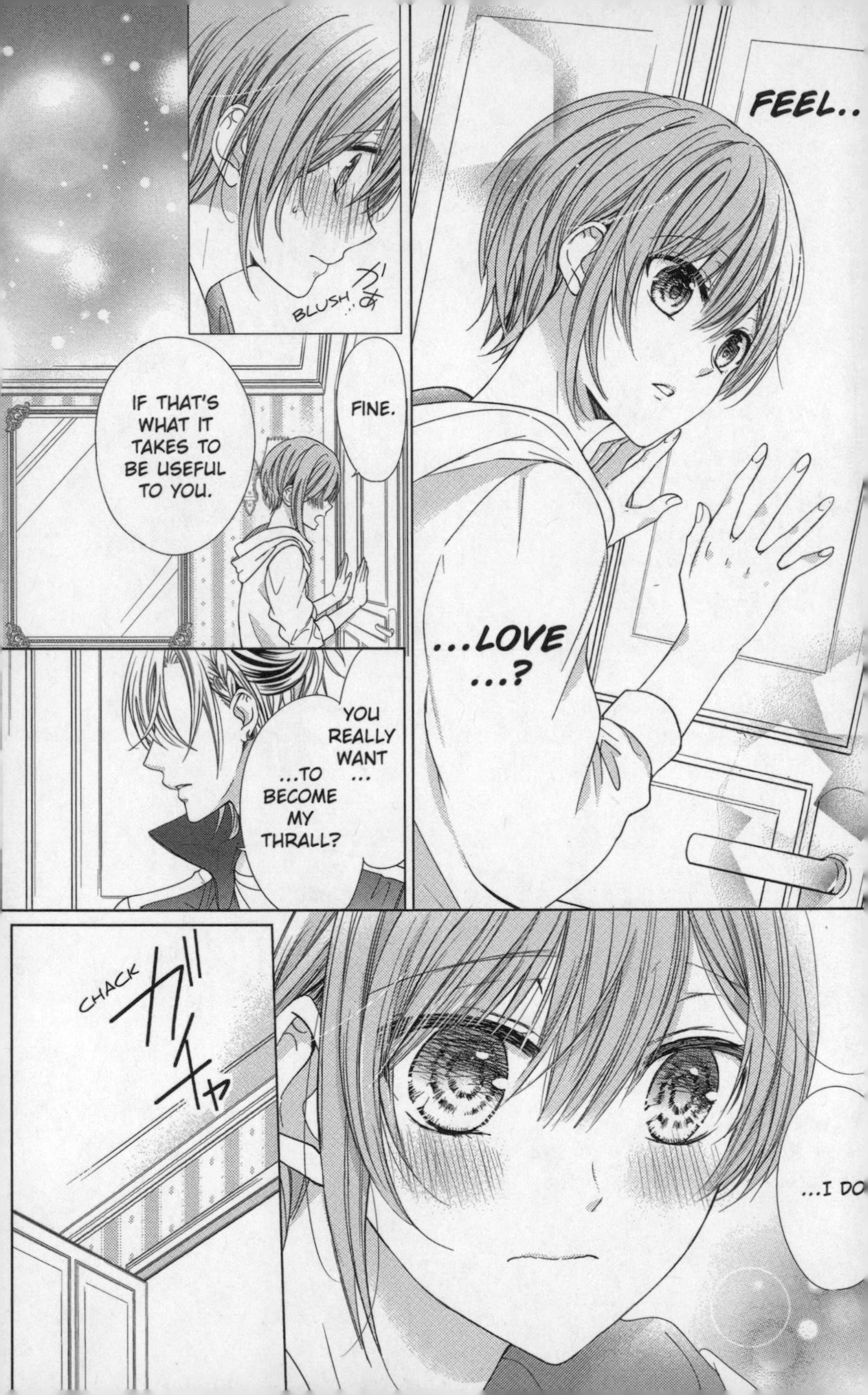
FEEL...
...LOVE ...?
BLUSH
FINE.
IF THAT'S WHAT IT TAKES TO BE USEFUL TO YOU.
YOU REALLY WANT... ...TO BECOME MY THRALL?
...I DO
CHACK
ガチャ

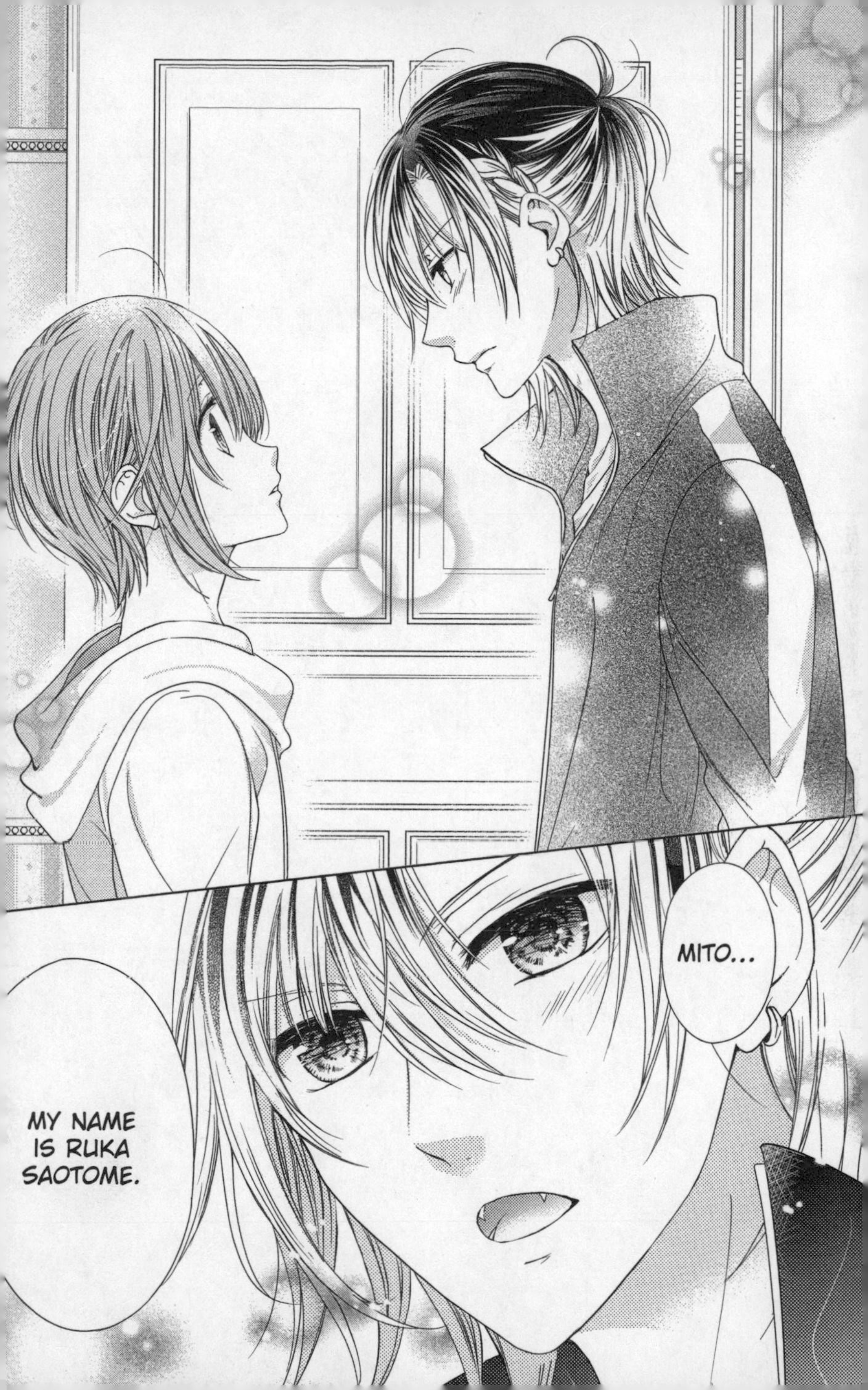
MITO...
MY NAME IS RUKA SAOTOME.

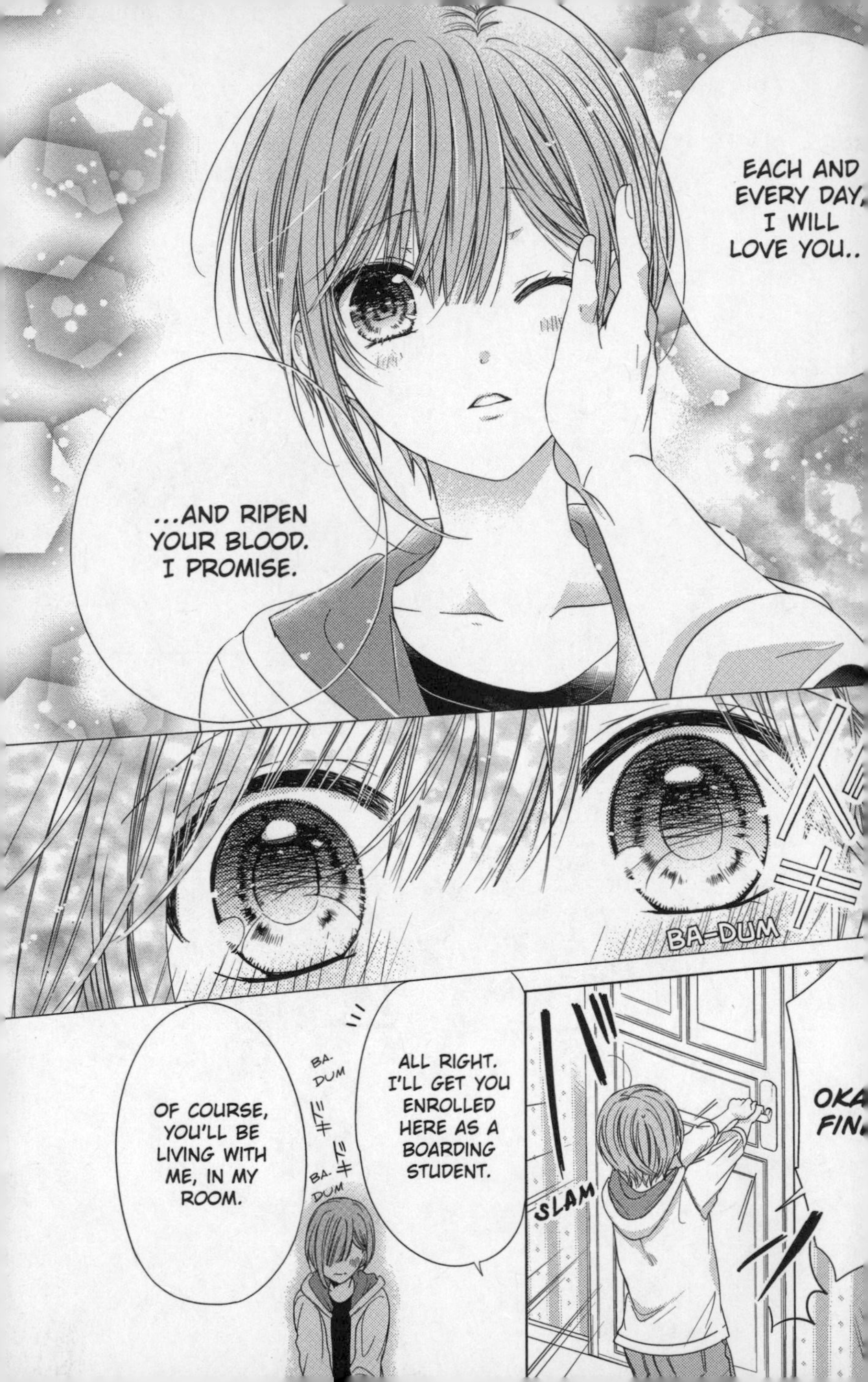
EACH AND EVERY DAY, I WILL LOVE YOU...
...AND RIPEN YOUR BLOOD. I PROMISE.
BA-DUM
OKA FIN.
SLAM
ALL RIGHT. I'LL GET YOU ENROLLED HERE AS A BOARDING STUDENT.
BA-DUM
BA-DUM
OF COURSE, YOU'LL BE LIVING WITH ME, IN MY ROOM.

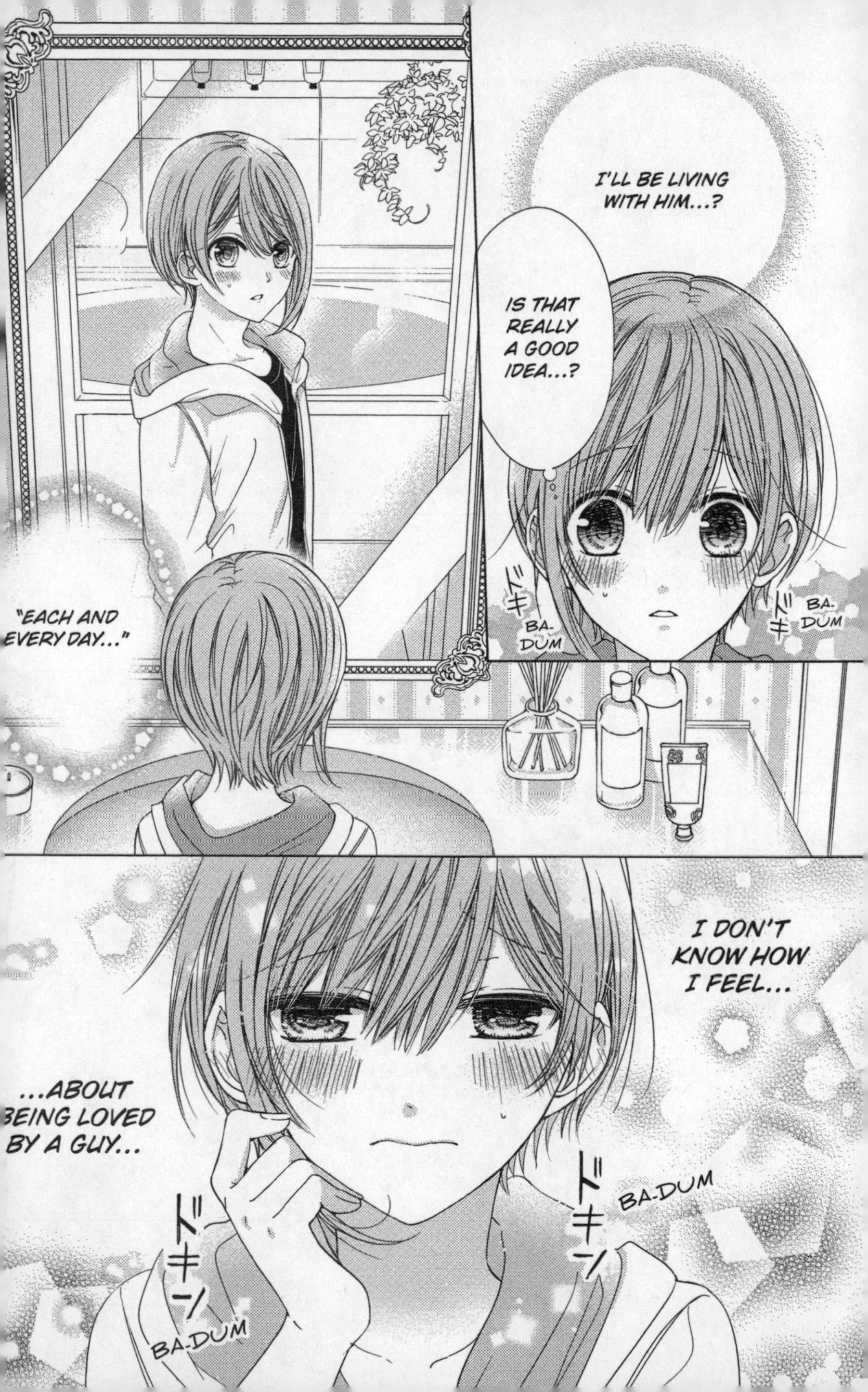
I'LL BE LIVING WITH HIM...?
IS THAT REALLY A GOOD IDEA...?
ドキ
BA-DUM
ドキ
BA-DUM
"EACH AND EVERY DAY..."
I DON'T KNOW HOW I FEEL...
...ABOUT BEING LOVED BY A GUY...
ドキーン
BA-DUM
ドキーン
BA-DUM

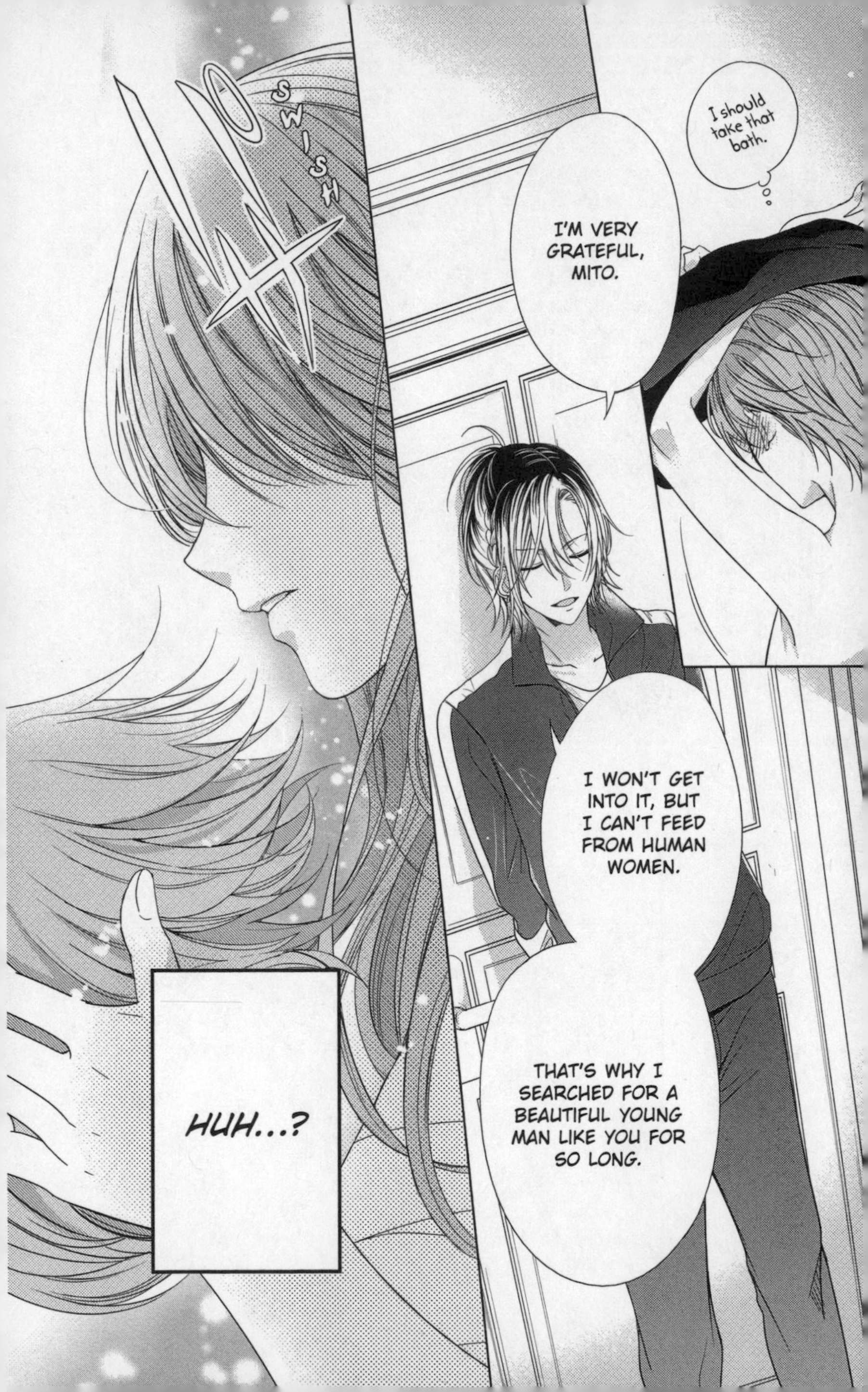
I should take that bath.
I'M VERY GRATEFUL, MITO.
I WON'T GET INTO IT, BUT I CAN'T FEED FROM HUMAN WOMEN.
THAT'S WHY I SEARCHED FOR A BEAUTIFUL YOUNG MAN LIKE YOU FOR SO LONG.
SWISH
HUH...?

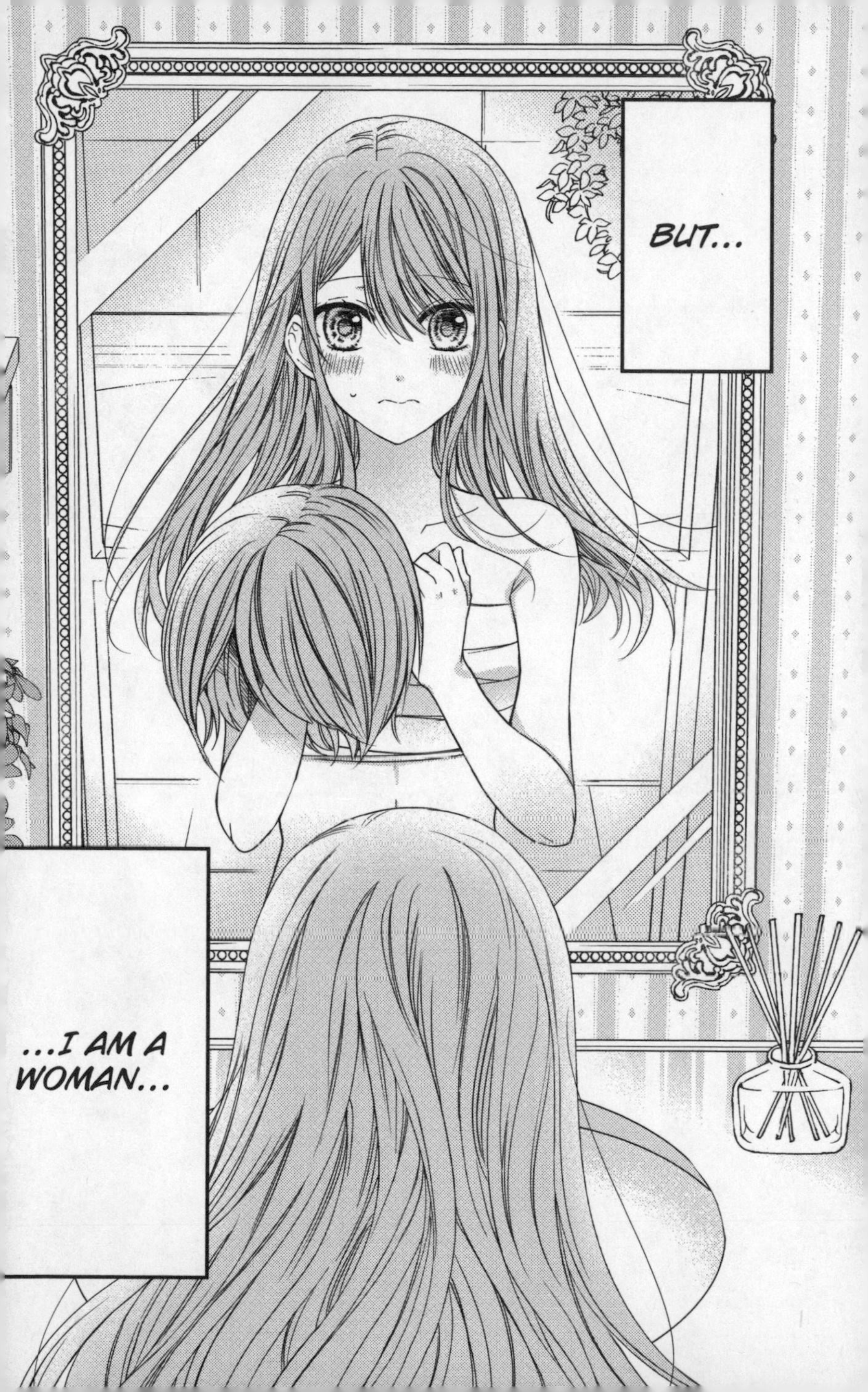
BUT...
...I AM A WOMAN...

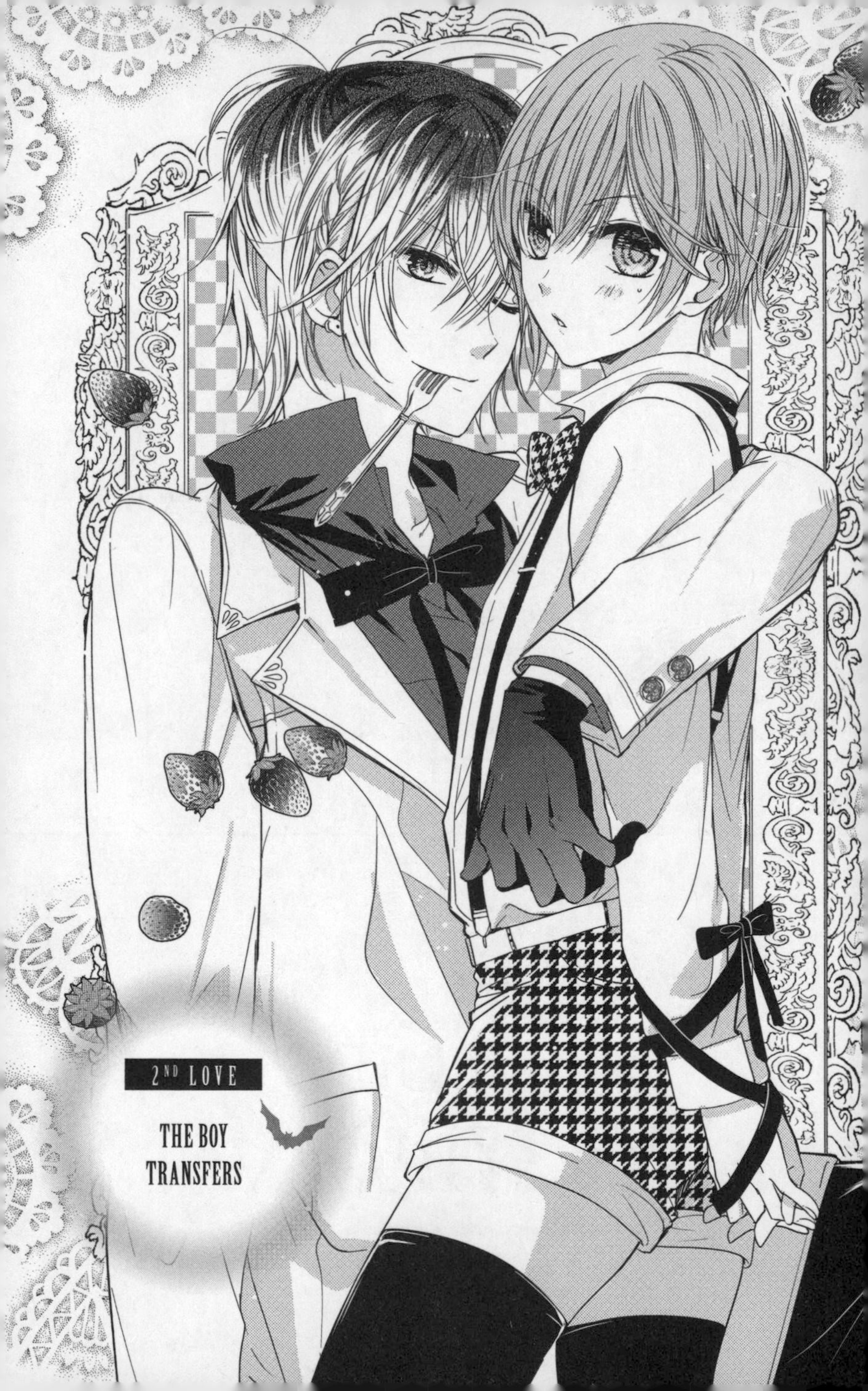
2ND LOVE
THE BOY TRANSFERS

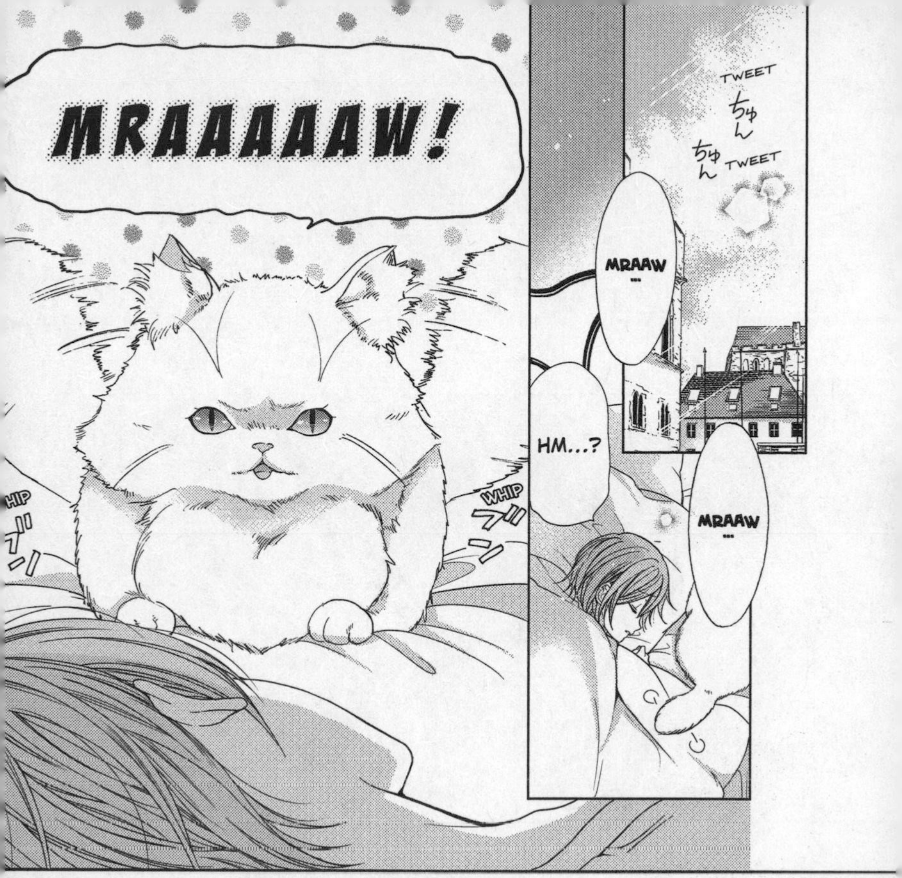
TWEET
ちゅん
ちゅん
TWEET
MRAAW...
HM...?
MRAAW...
MRAAAAAW!
WHIP
ブン
HIP
ブン

Vampire Dormitory

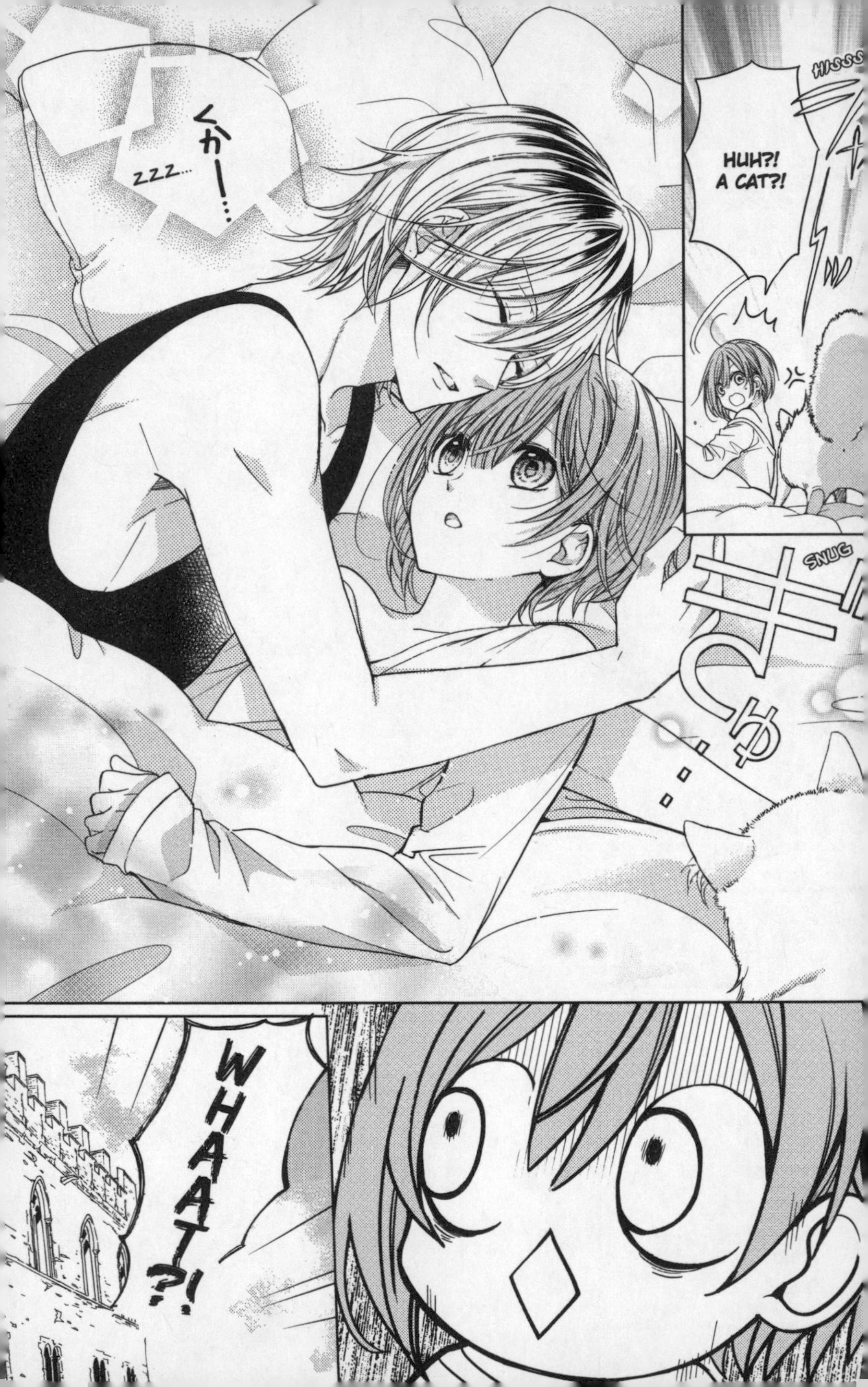
HISSS
HUH?! A CAT?!
くかー…
ZZZ…
SNUG
ぎゅ…
WHAAAT?!

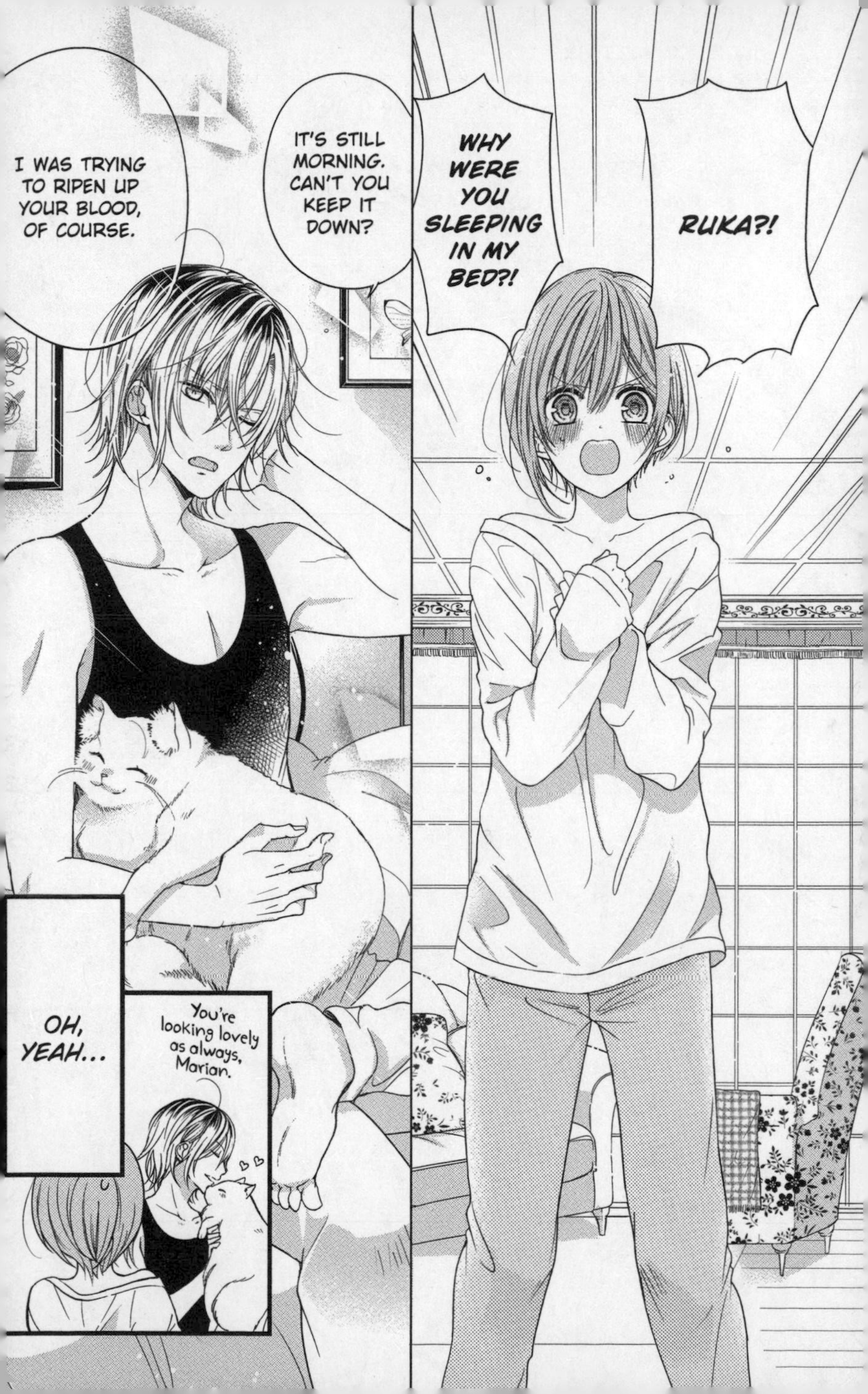
RUKA?!
WHY WERE YOU SLEEPING IN MY BED?!
IT'S STILL MORNING. CAN'T YOU KEEP IT DOWN?
I WAS TRYING TO RIPEN UP YOUR BLOOD, OF COURSE.
You're looking lovely as always, Marian.
OH, YEAH...

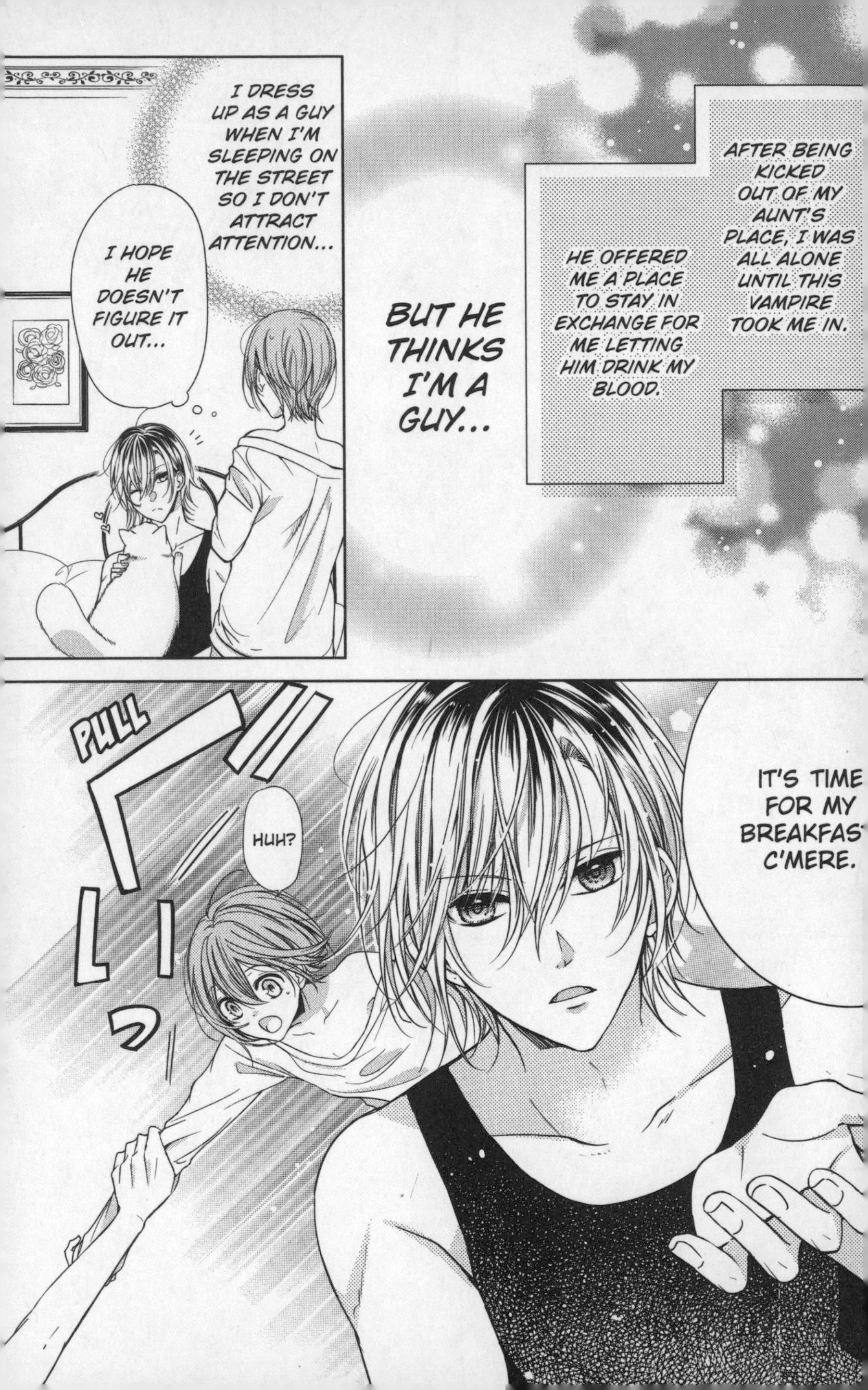
AFTER BEING KICKED OUT OF MY AUNT'S PLACE, I WAS ALL ALONE UNTIL THIS VAMPIRE TOOK ME IN.
HE OFFERED ME A PLACE TO STAY IN EXCHANGE FOR ME LETTING HIM DRINK MY BLOOD.
BUT HE THINKS I'M A GUY...
I DRESS UP AS A GUY WHEN I'M SLEEPING ON THE STREET SO I DON'T ATTRACT ATTENTION...
I HOPE HE DOESN'T FIGURE IT OUT...
IT'S TIME FOR MY BREAKFAS
C'MERE.
PULL
HUH?

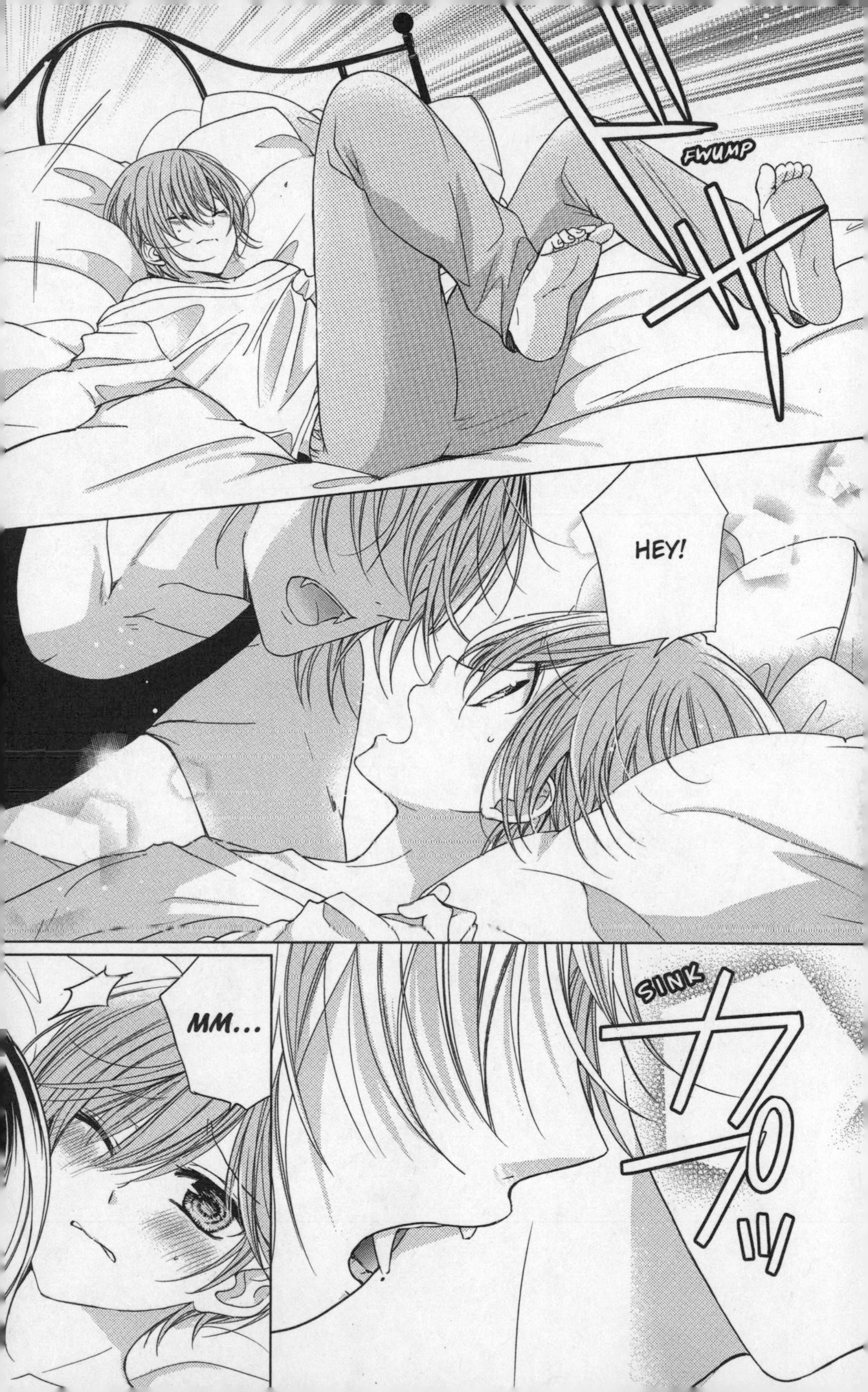
FWUMP
HEY!
SINK
MM...

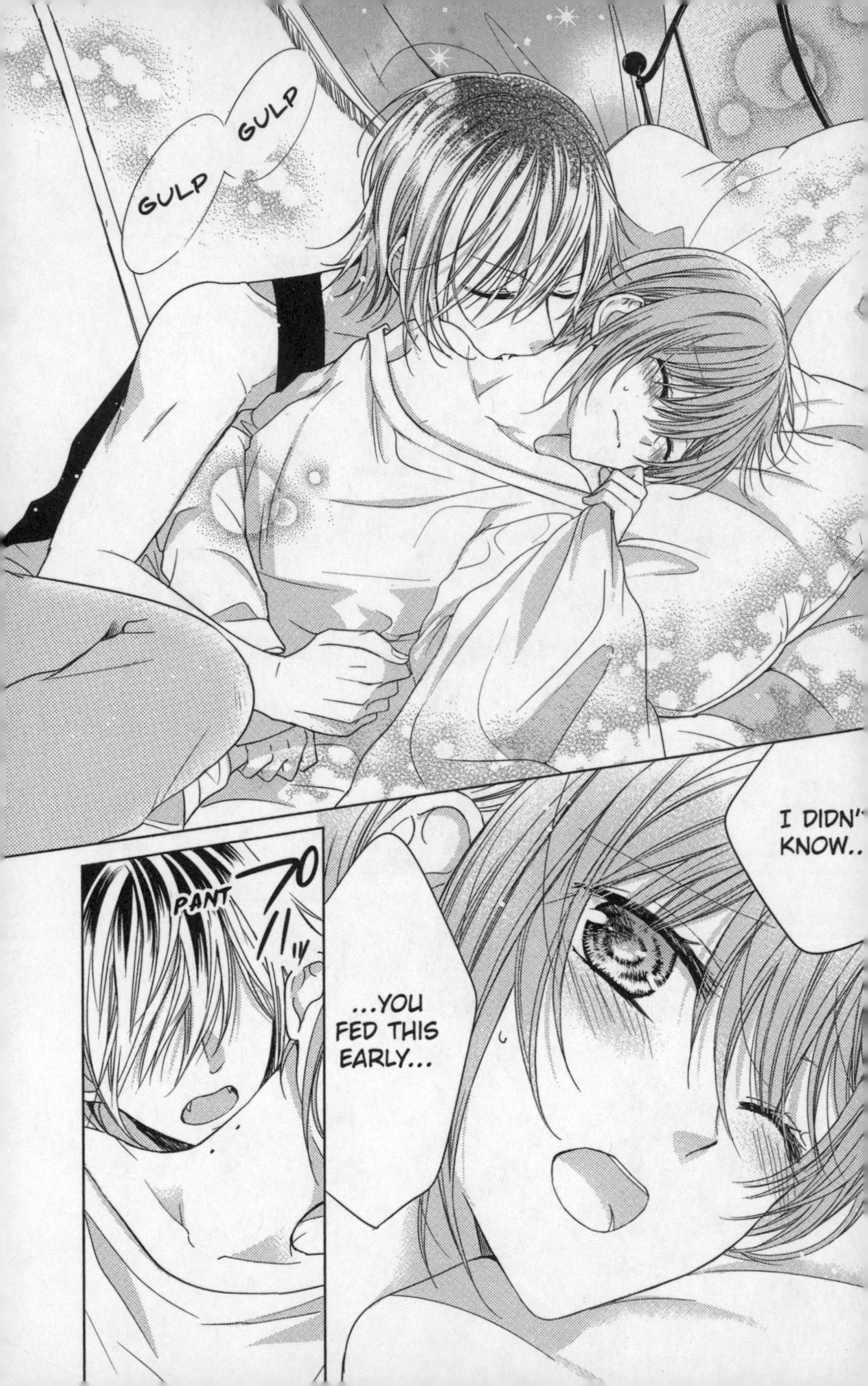
GULP
GULP
GULP
I DIDN'
KNOW..
...YOU FED THIS EARLY...
PANT

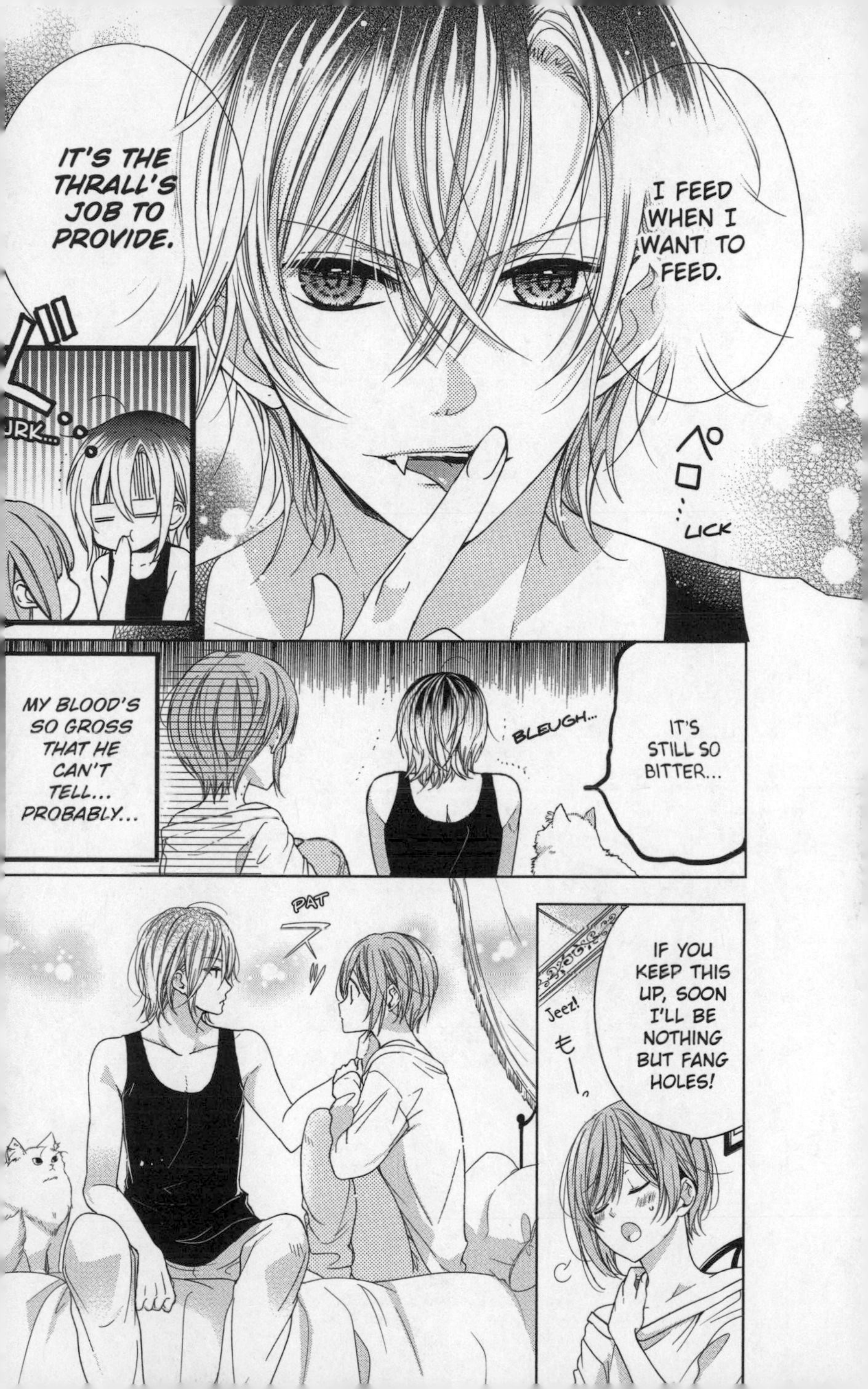
I FEED WHEN I WANT TO FEED.
IT'S THE THRALL'S JOB TO PROVIDE.
ペロ
LICK
URK...
IT'S STILL SO BITTER...
BLEUGH...
MY BLOOD'S SO GROSS THAT HE CAN'T TELL... PROBABLY...
IF YOU KEEP THIS UP, SOON I'LL BE NOTHING BUT FANG HOLES!
もー。
Jeez!
ス
PAT

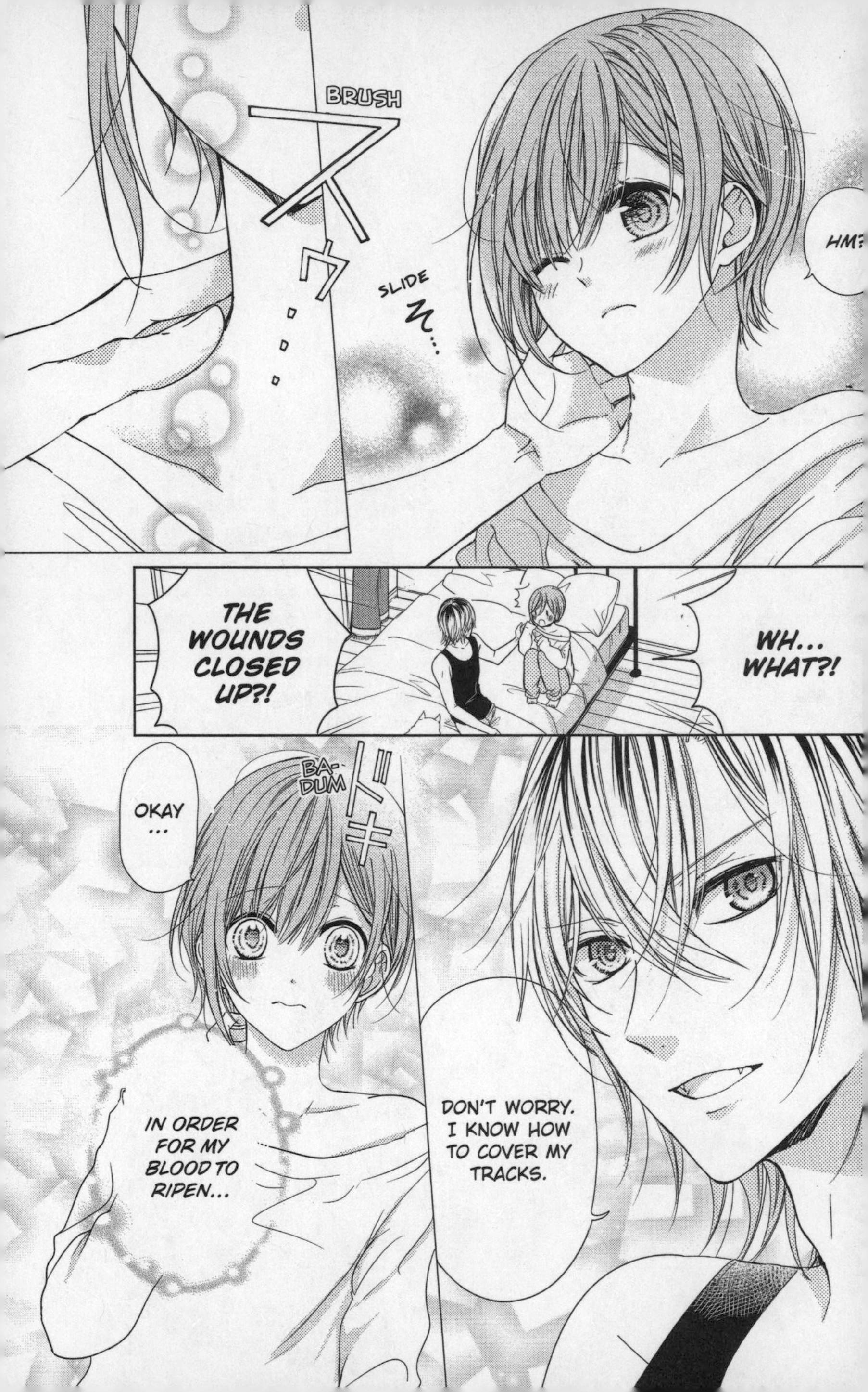
HM?
BRUSH
SLIDE
WH... WHAT?!
THE WOUNDS CLOSED UP?!
DON'T WORRY. I KNOW HOW TO COVER MY TRACKS.
BA-DUM
OKAY ...
IN ORDER FOR MY BLOOD TO RIPEN...

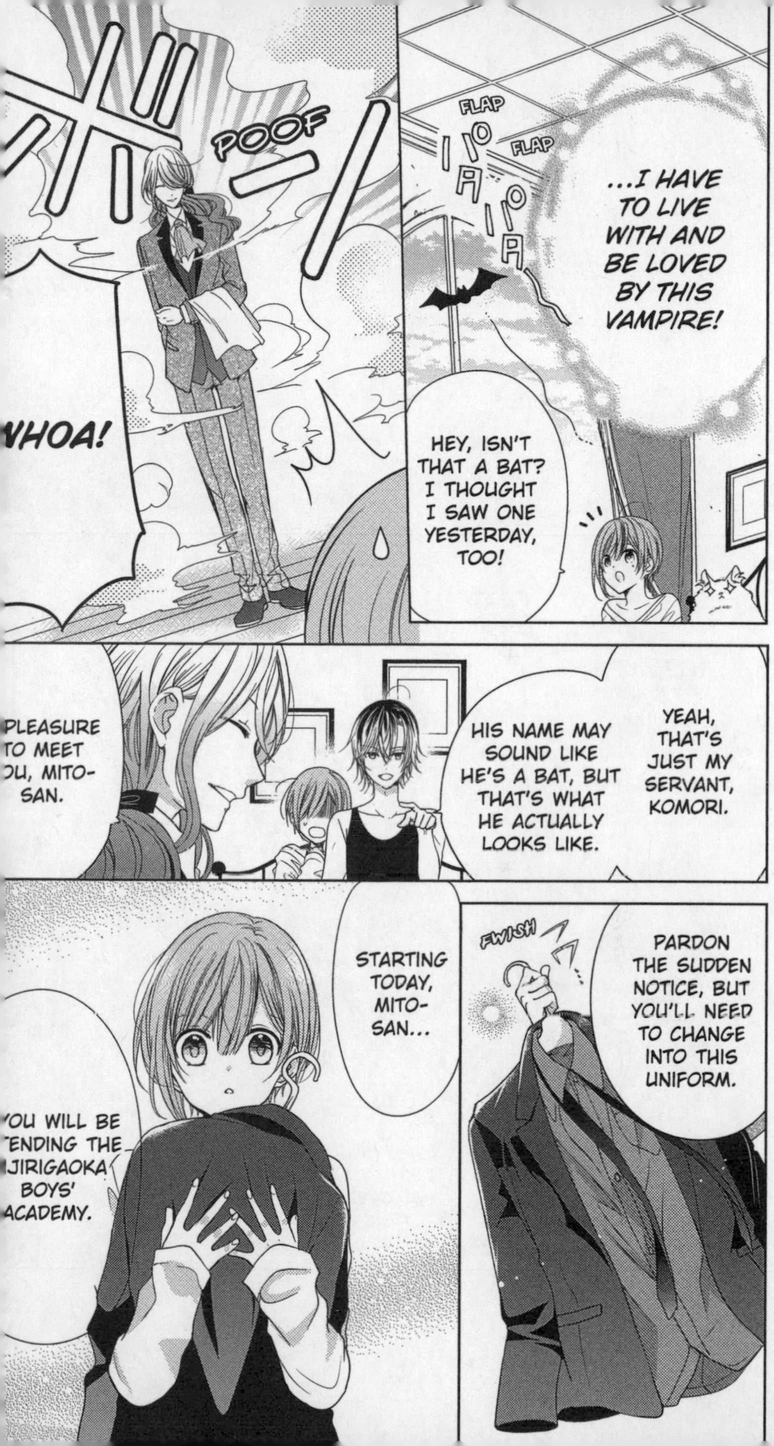
FLAP
FLAP
...I HAVE TO LIVE WITH AND BE LOVED BY THIS VAMPIRE!
HEY, ISN'T THAT A BAT? I THOUGHT I SAW ONE YESTERDAY, TOO!
POOF
WHOA!
YEAH, THAT'S JUST MY SERVANT, KOMORI.
HIS NAME MAY SOUND LIKE HE'S A BAT, BUT THAT'S WHAT HE ACTUALLY LOOKS LIKE.
PLEASURE TO MEET OU, MITO-SAN.
FWISH
PARDON THE SUDDEN NOTICE, BUT YOU'LL NEED TO CHANGE INTO THIS UNIFORM.
STARTING TODAY, MITO-SAN...
OU WILL BE TENDING THE JIRIGAOKA BOYS' ACADEMY.

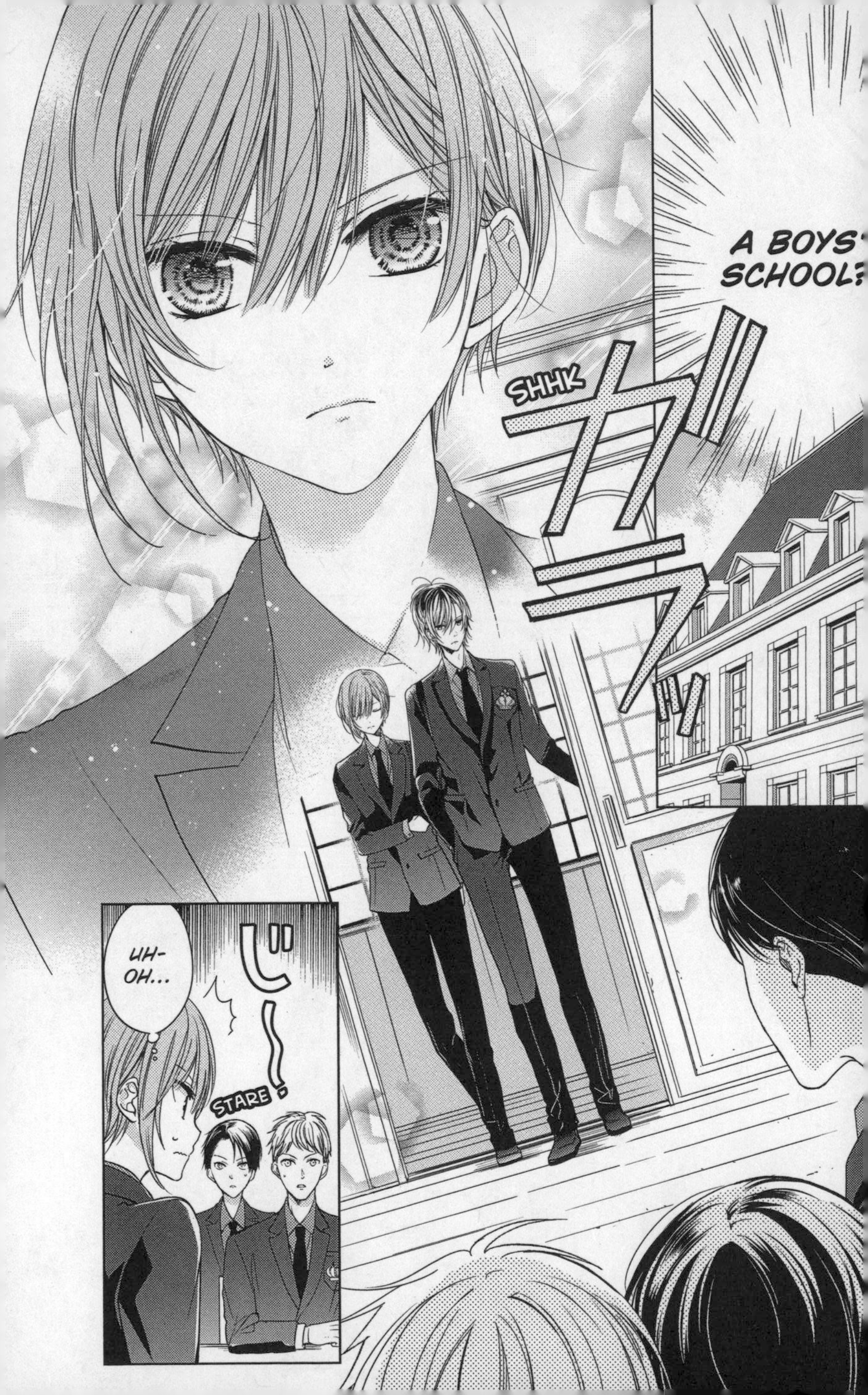
A BOYS' SCHOOL!?
SHHK
ガラッ
UH-OH...
じー
STARE

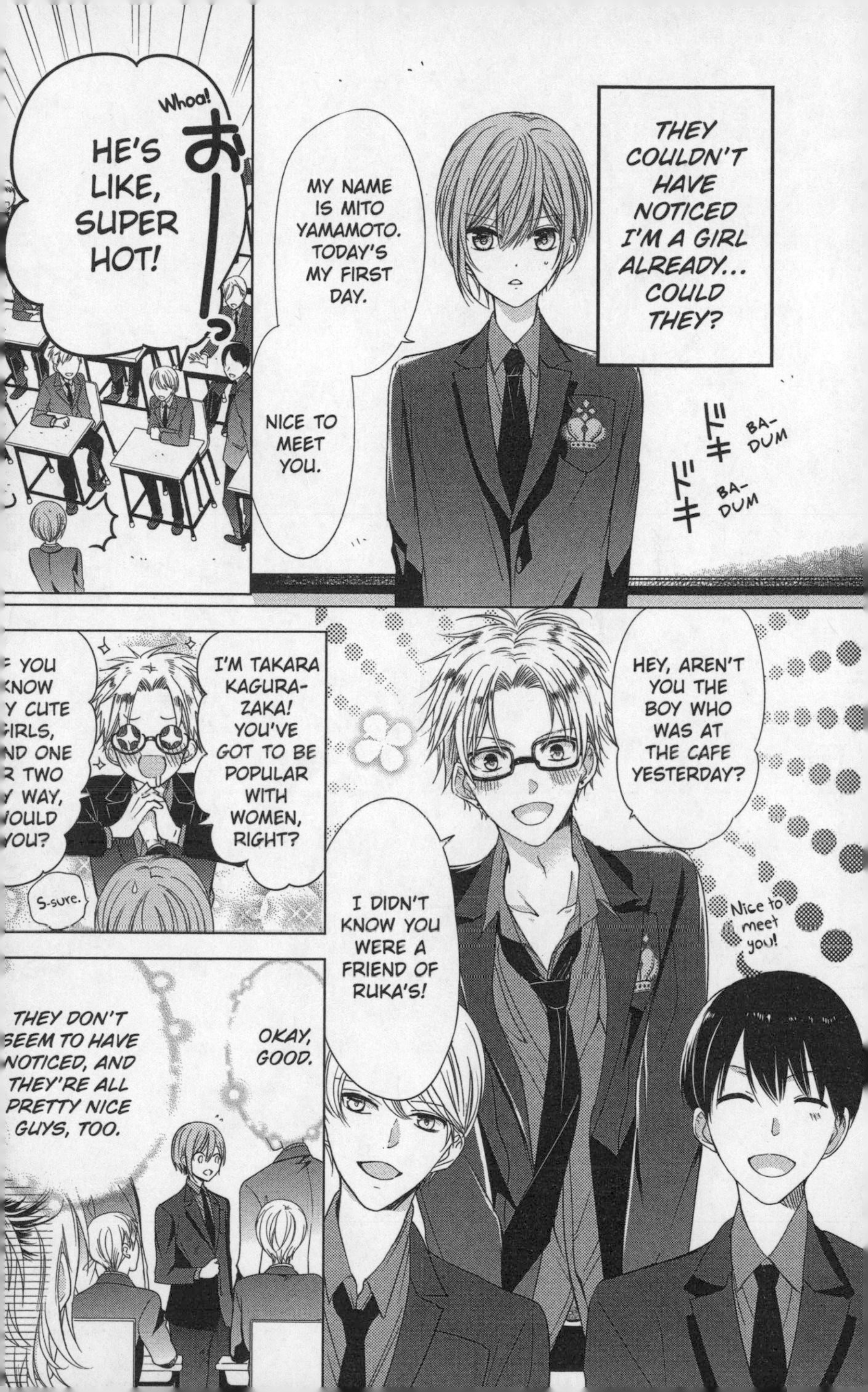
THEY COULDN'T HAVE NOTICED I'M A GIRL ALREADY... COULD THEY?
ドキ BA-DUM
ドキ BA-DUM
MY NAME IS MITO YAMAMOTO. TODAY'S MY FIRST DAY.
NICE TO MEET YOU.
おーっ
Whoa!
HE'S LIKE, SUPER HOT!
HEY, AREN'T YOU THE BOY WHO WAS AT THE CAFE YESTERDAY?
Nice to meet you!
I DIDN'T KNOW YOU WERE A FRIEND OF RUKA'S!
I'M TAKARA KAGURA-ZAKA! YOU'VE GOT TO BE POPULAR WITH WOMEN, RIGHT?
F YOU KNOW Y CUTE GIRLS, ND ONE R TWO Y WAY, OULD YOU?
S-sure.
OKAY, GOOD.
THEY DON'T SEEM TO HAVE NOTICED, AND THEY'RE ALL PRETTY NICE GUYS, TOO.

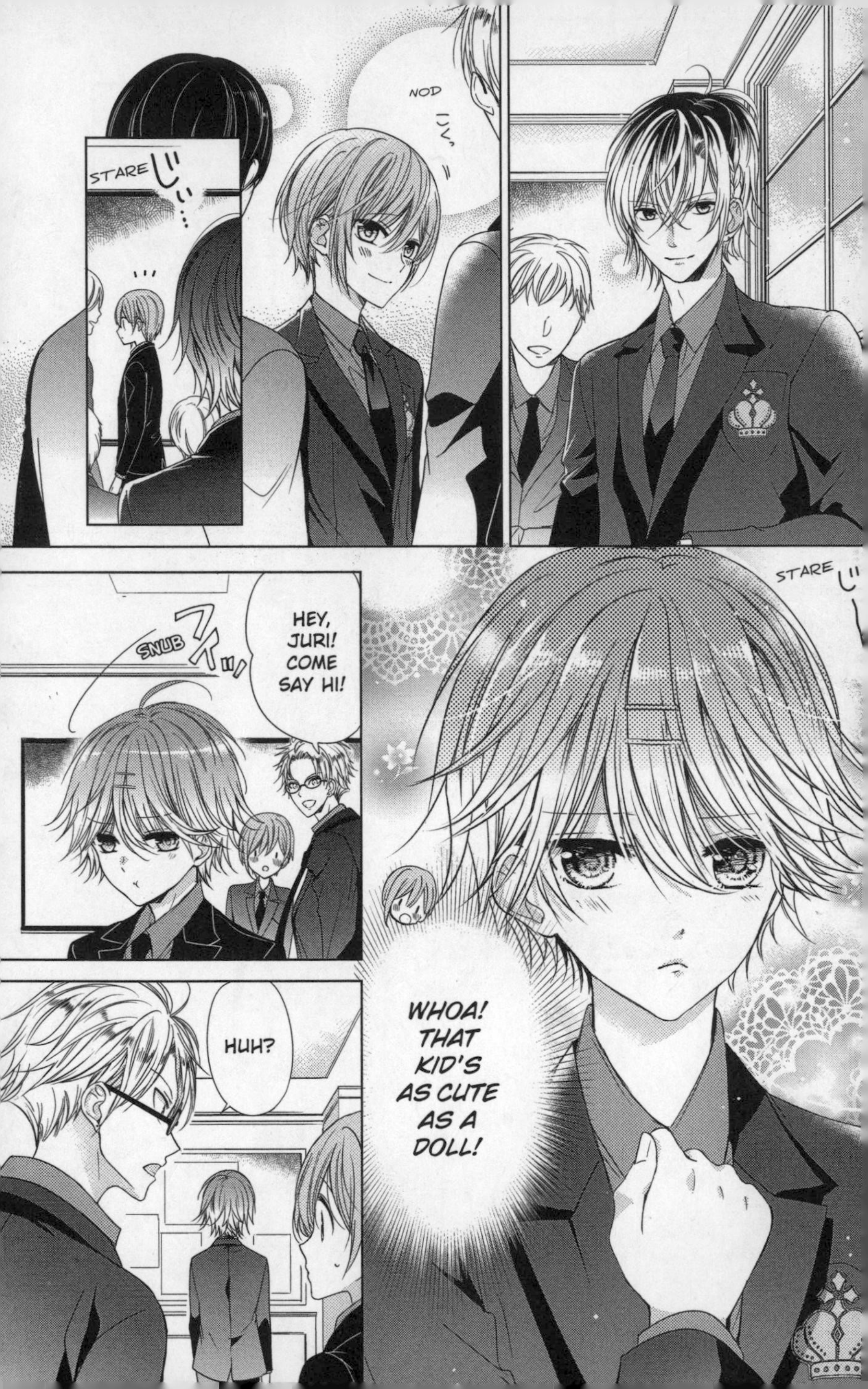
NOD
STARE
STARE
WHOA! THAT KID'S AS CUTE AS A DOLL!
HEY, JURI! COME SAY HI!
SNUB
HUH?

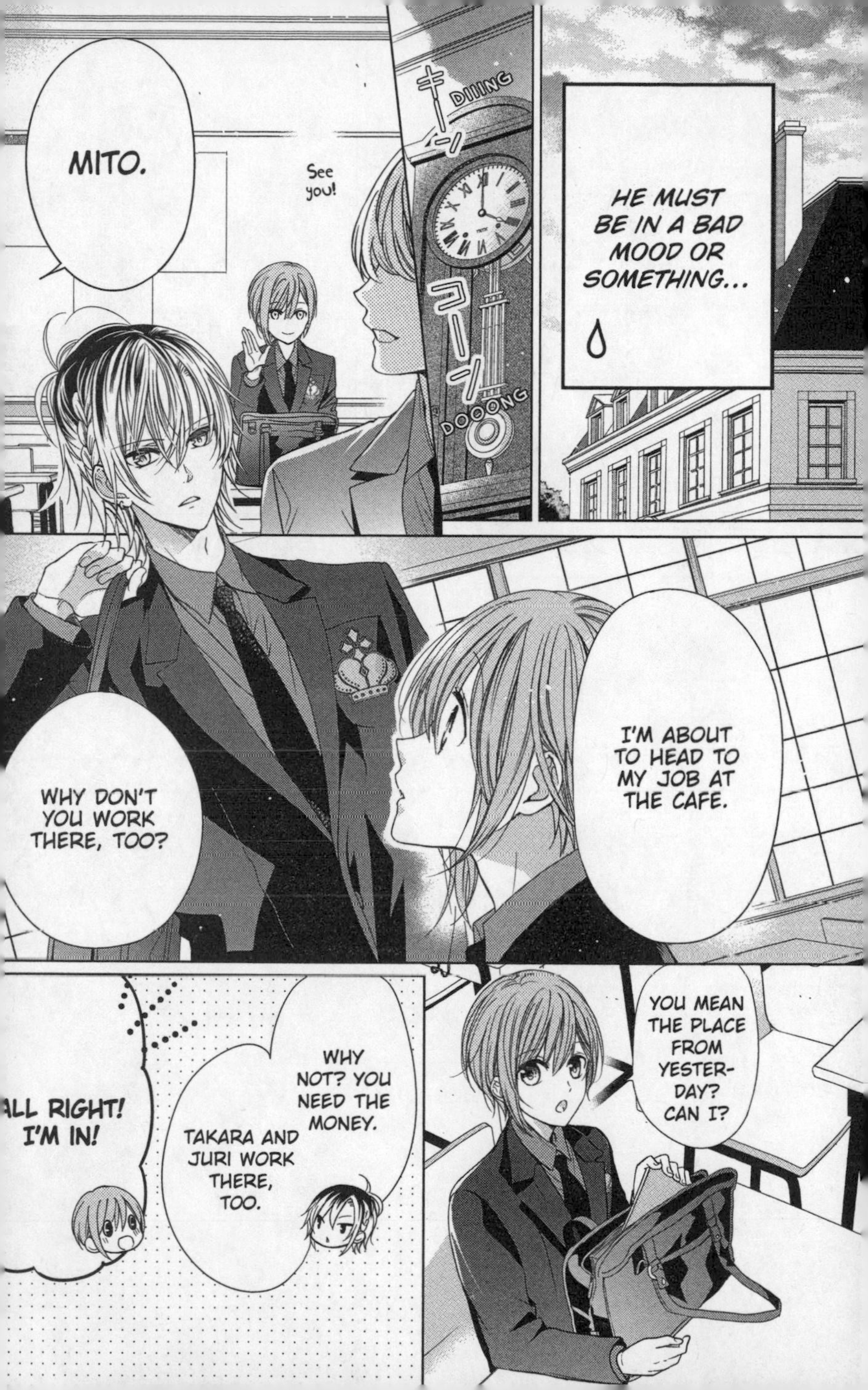
HE MUST BE IN A BAD MOOD OR SOMETHING...
キーン
DIIING
コーン
DOOONG
See you!
MITO.
I'M ABOUT TO HEAD TO MY JOB AT THE CAFE.
WHY DON'T YOU WORK THERE, TOO?
YOU MEAN THE PLACE FROM YESTER-DAY? CAN I?
WHY NOT? YOU NEED THE MONEY.
TAKARA AND JURI WORK THERE, TOO.
ALL RIGHT! I'M IN!

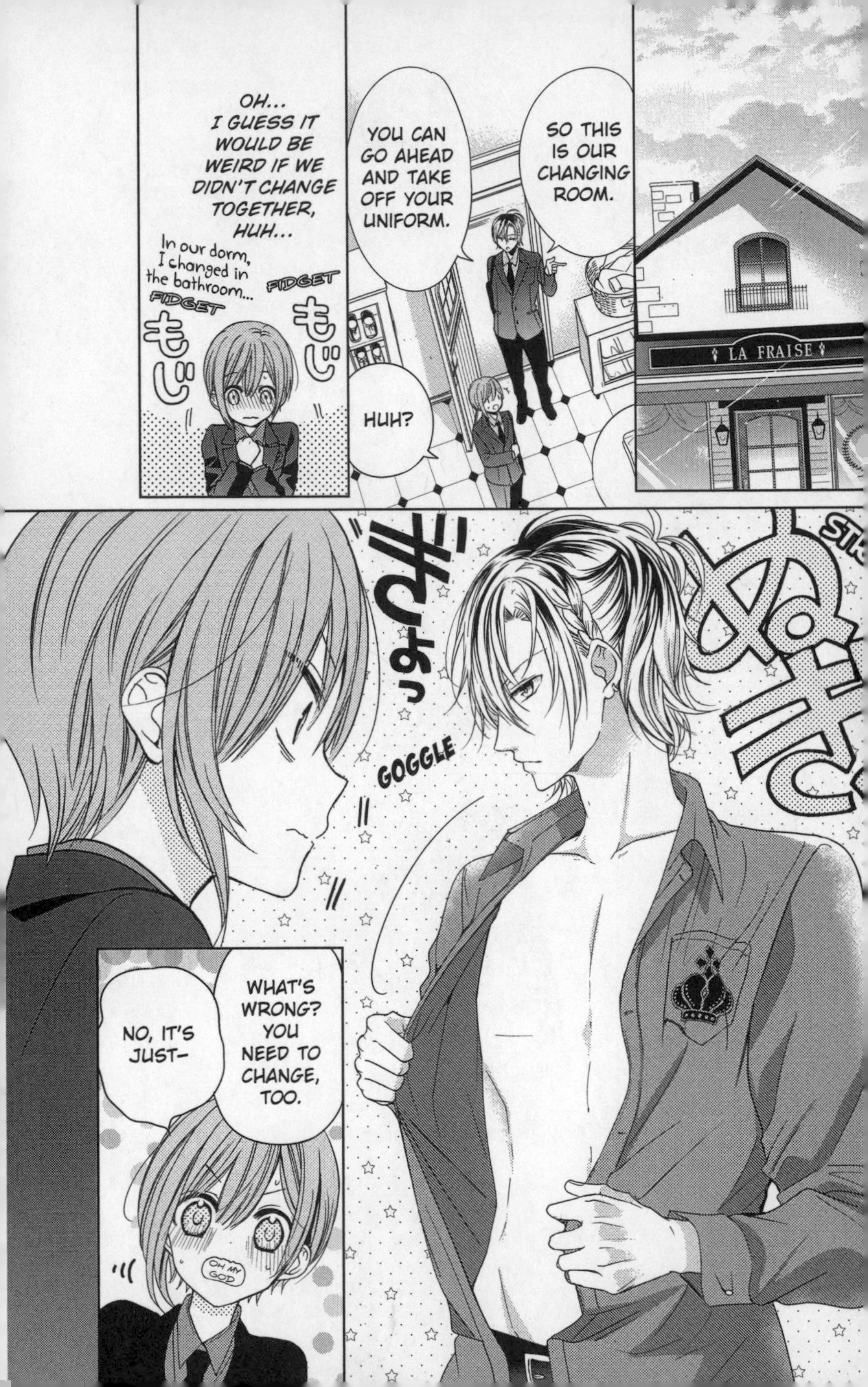
LA FRAISE
SO THIS IS OUR CHANGING ROOM.
YOU CAN GO AHEAD AND TAKE OFF YOUR UNIFORM.
HUH?
OH... I GUESS IT WOULD BE WEIRD IF WE DIDN'T CHANGE TOGETHER, HUH...
In our dorm, I changed in the bathroom...
FIDGET
もじ
FIDGET
もじ
ぎょっ
GOGGLE
WHAT'S WRONG? YOU NEED TO CHANGE, TOO.
NO, IT'S JUST-
OH MY GOD

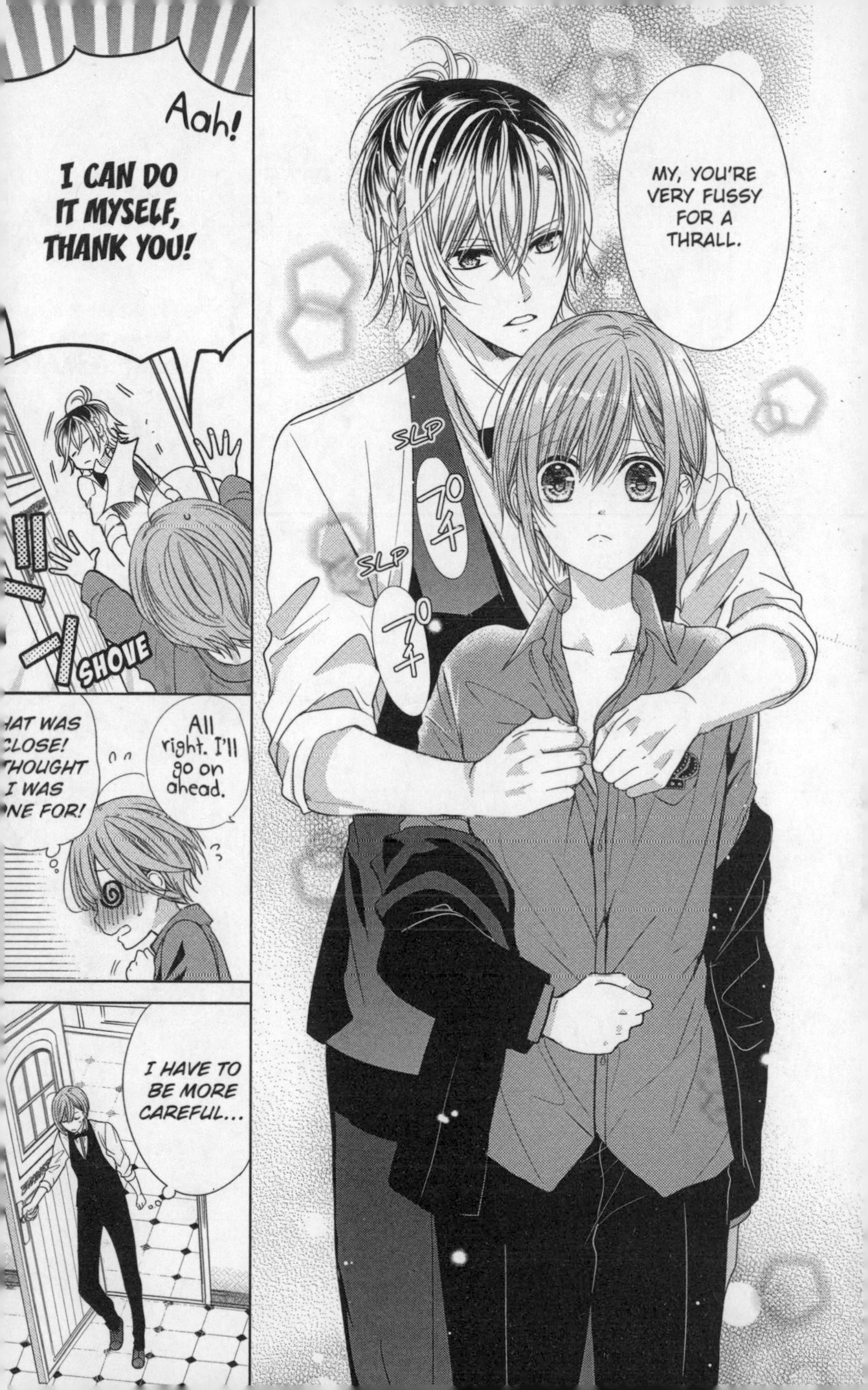
MY, YOU'RE VERY FUSSY FOR A THRALL.
SLP
プチ
SLP
プチ
Aah!
I CAN DO IT MYSELF, THANK YOU!
SHOVE
All right. I'll go on ahead.
HAT WAS CLOSE! THOUGHT I WAS NE FOR!
I HAVE TO BE MORE CAREFUL...

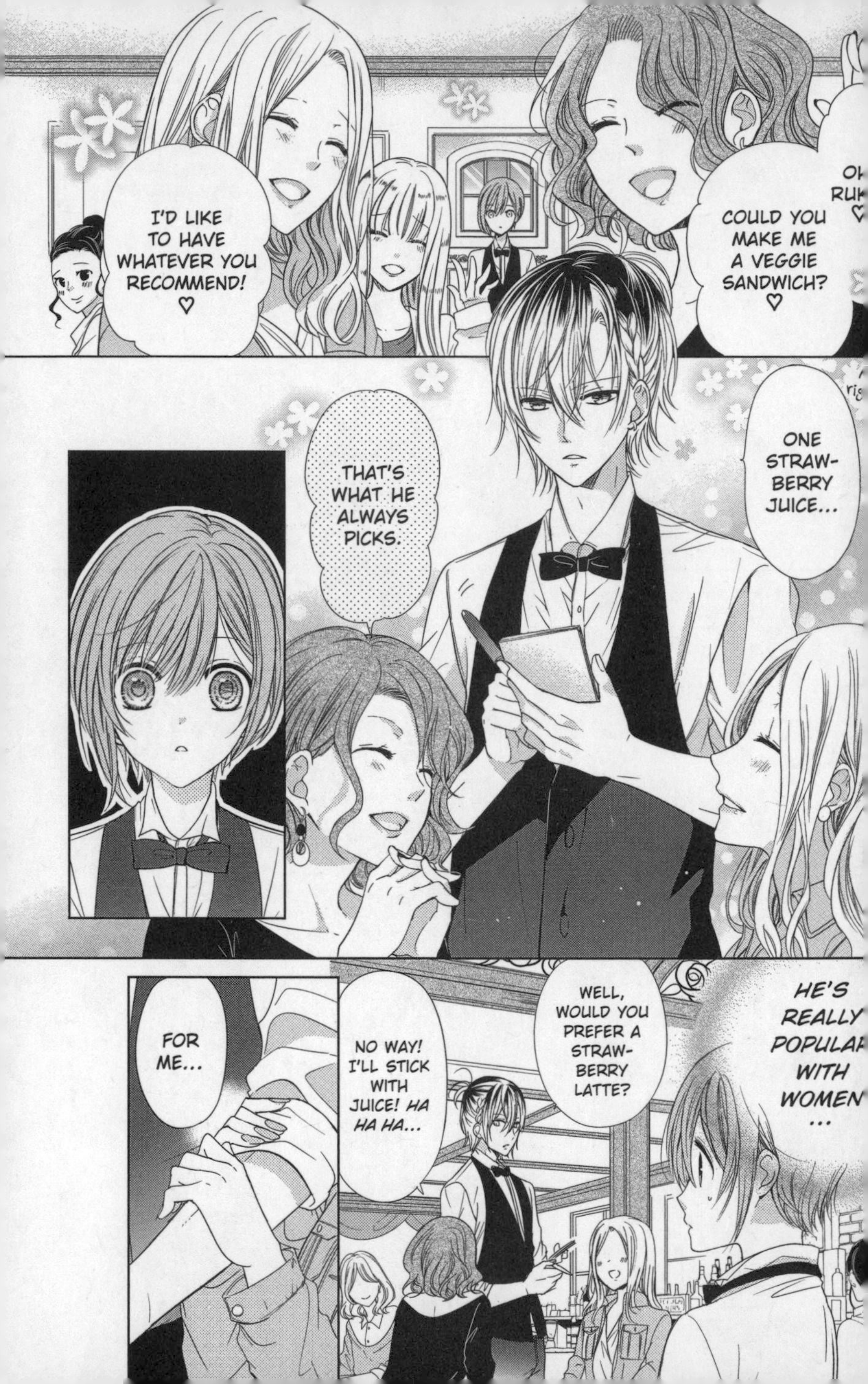
COULD YOU MAKE ME A VEGGIE SANDWICH? ♡
I'D LIKE TO HAVE WHATEVER YOU RECOMMEND! ♡
ONE STRAW-BERRY JUICE...
THAT'S WHAT HE ALWAYS PICKS.
HE'S REALLY POPULA WITH WOMEN ...
WELL, WOULD YOU PREFER A STRAW-BERRY LATTE?
NO WAY! I'LL STICK WITH JUICE! *HA HA HA...*
FOR ME...

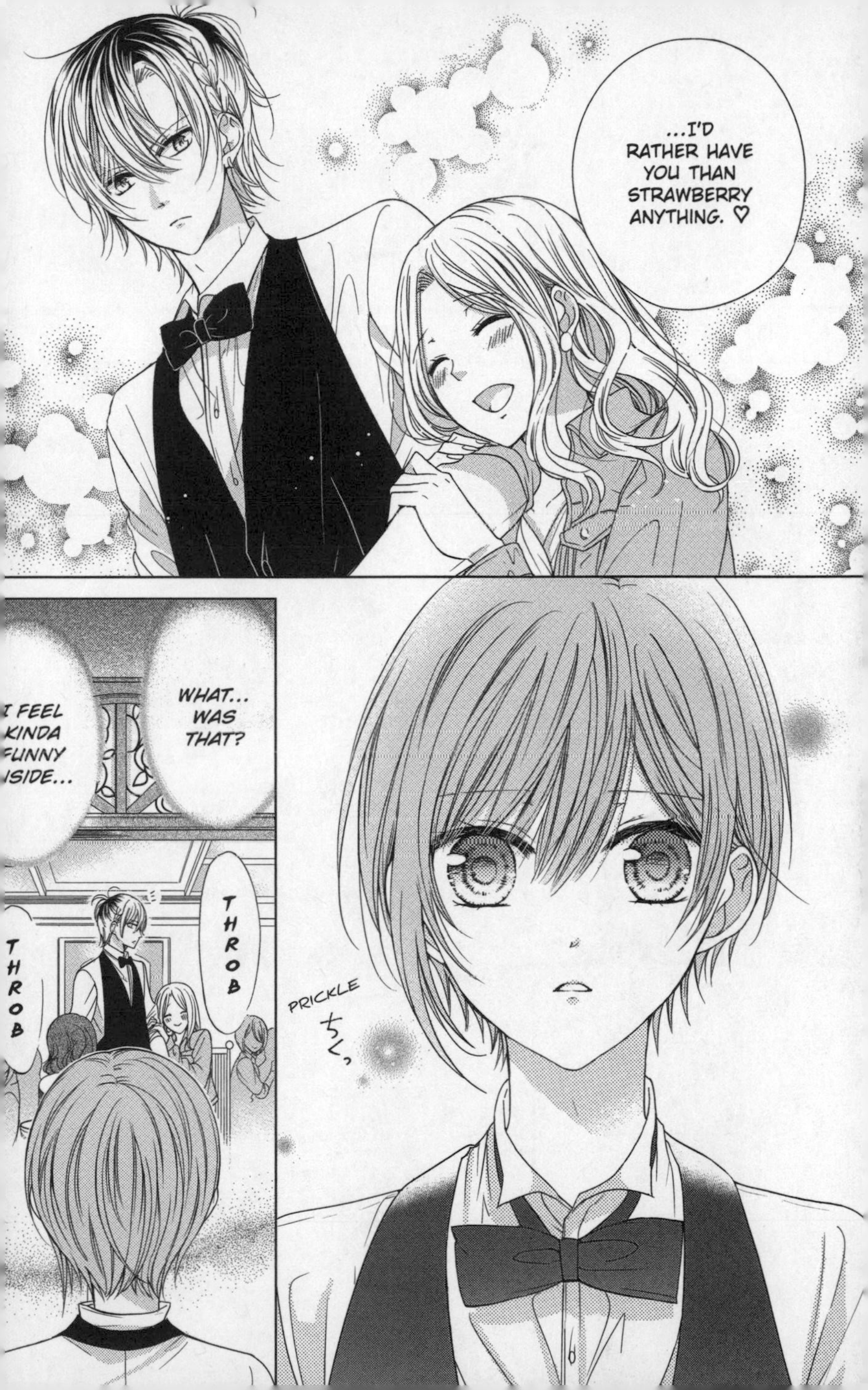
...I'D RATHER HAVE YOU THAN STRAWBERRY ANYTHING. ♡
PRICKLE
ちくっ
WHAT... WAS THAT?
I FEEL KINDA FUNNY INSIDE...
THROB
THROB

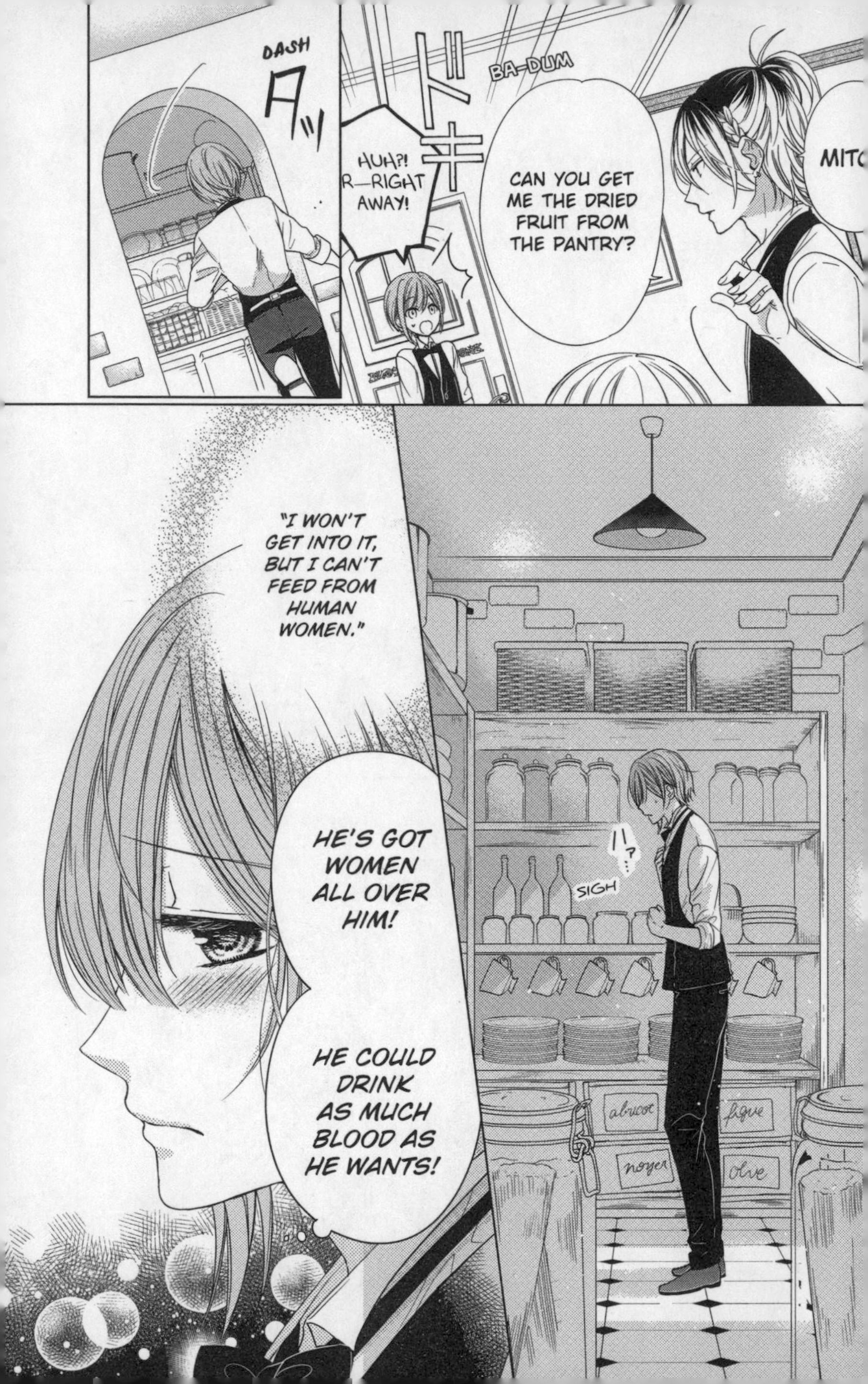
MITC
BA-DUM
CAN YOU GET ME THE DRIED FRUIT FROM THE PANTRY?
HUH?! R—RIGHT AWAY!
DASH
SIGH
abricot
figue
noyer
olive
"I WON'T GET INTO IT, BUT I CAN'T FEED FROM HUMAN WOMEN."
HE'S GOT WOMEN ALL OVER HIM!
HE COULD DRINK AS MUCH BLOOD AS HE WANTS!

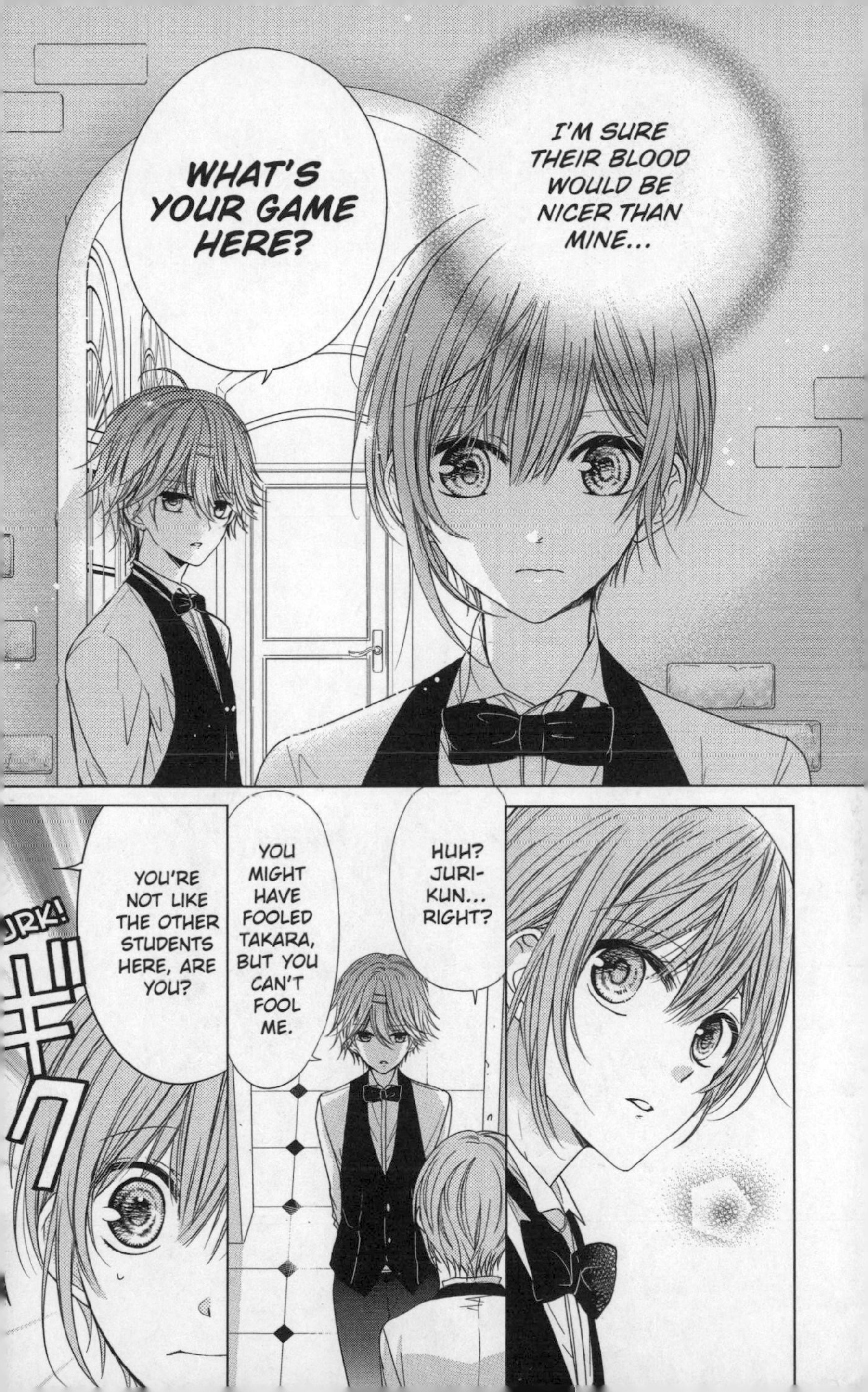
I'M SURE THEIR BLOOD WOULD BE NICER THAN MINE...
WHAT'S YOUR GAME HERE?
HUH? JURI-KUN... RIGHT?
YOU MIGHT HAVE FOOLED TAKARA, BUT YOU CAN'T FOOL ME.
YOU'RE NOT LIKE THE OTHER STUDENTS HERE, ARE YOU?
URK!

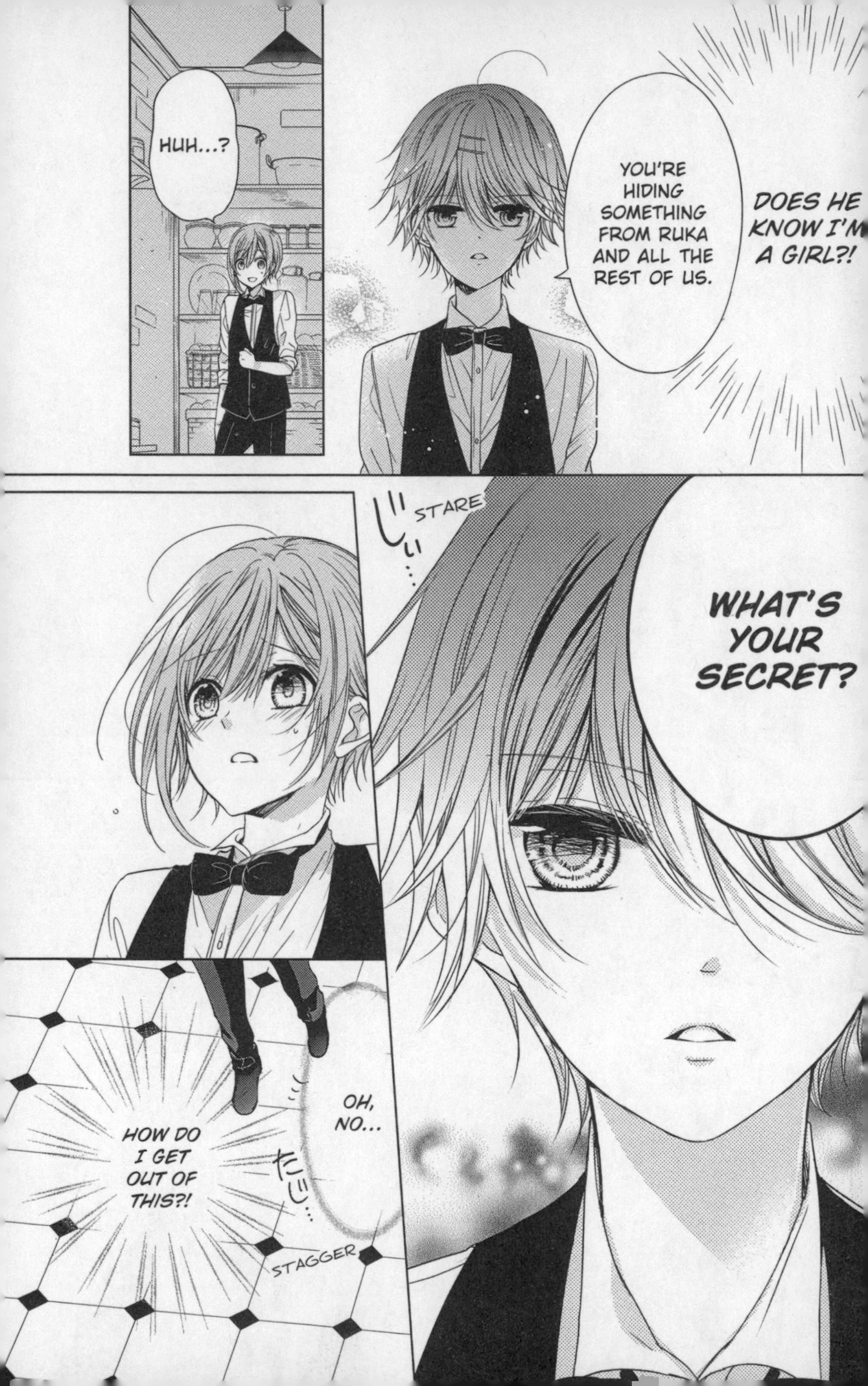

YOU'RE HIDING SOMETHING FROM RUKA AND ALL THE REST OF US.
DOES HE KNOW I'M A GIRL?!
HUH...?
WHAT'S YOUR SECRET?
じい…
STARE
OH, NO...
HOW DO I GET OUT OF THIS?!
たじ…
STAGGER

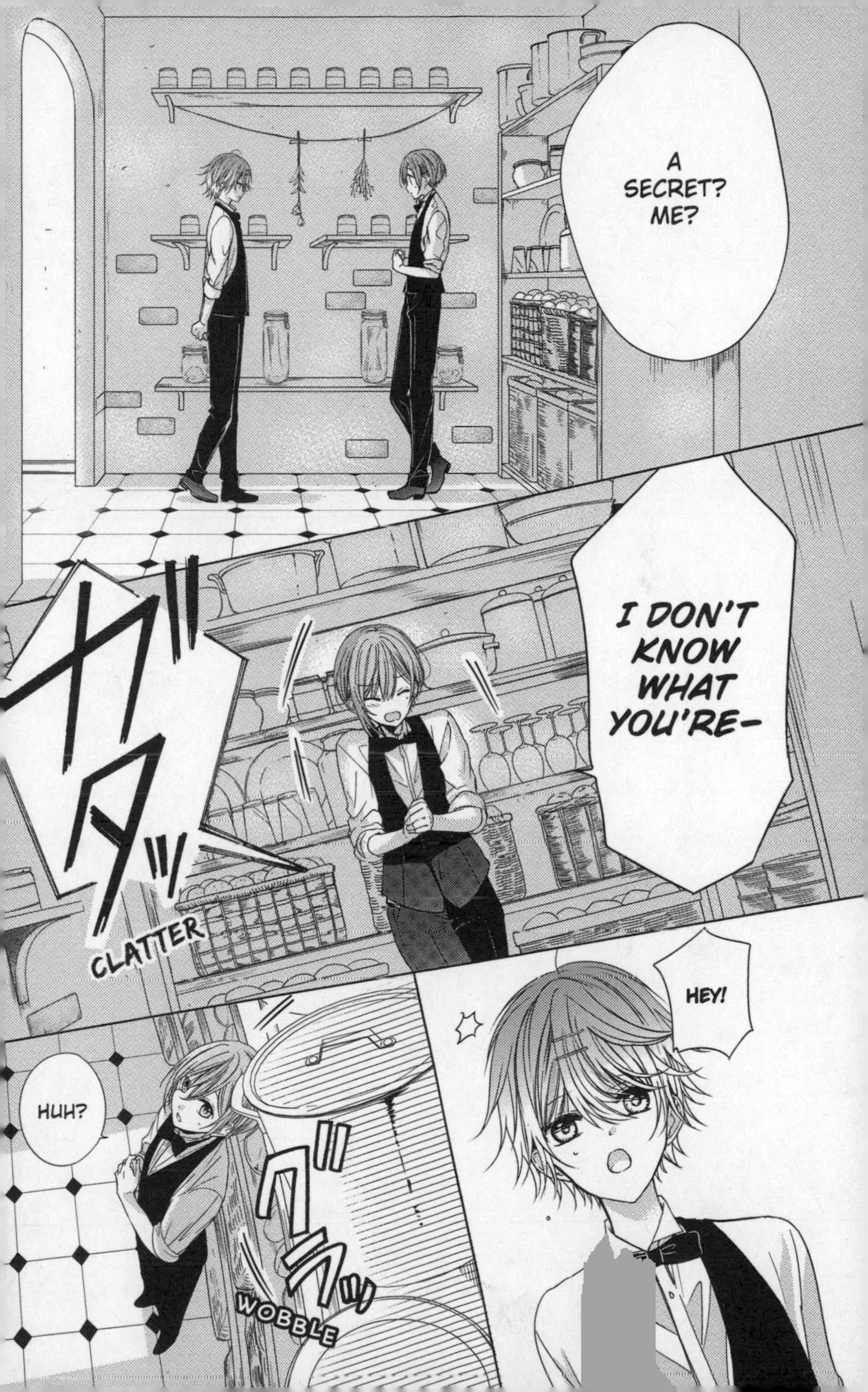
A SECRET? ME?
I DON'T KNOW WHAT YOU'RE–
CLATTER
HEY!
HUH?
WOBBLE

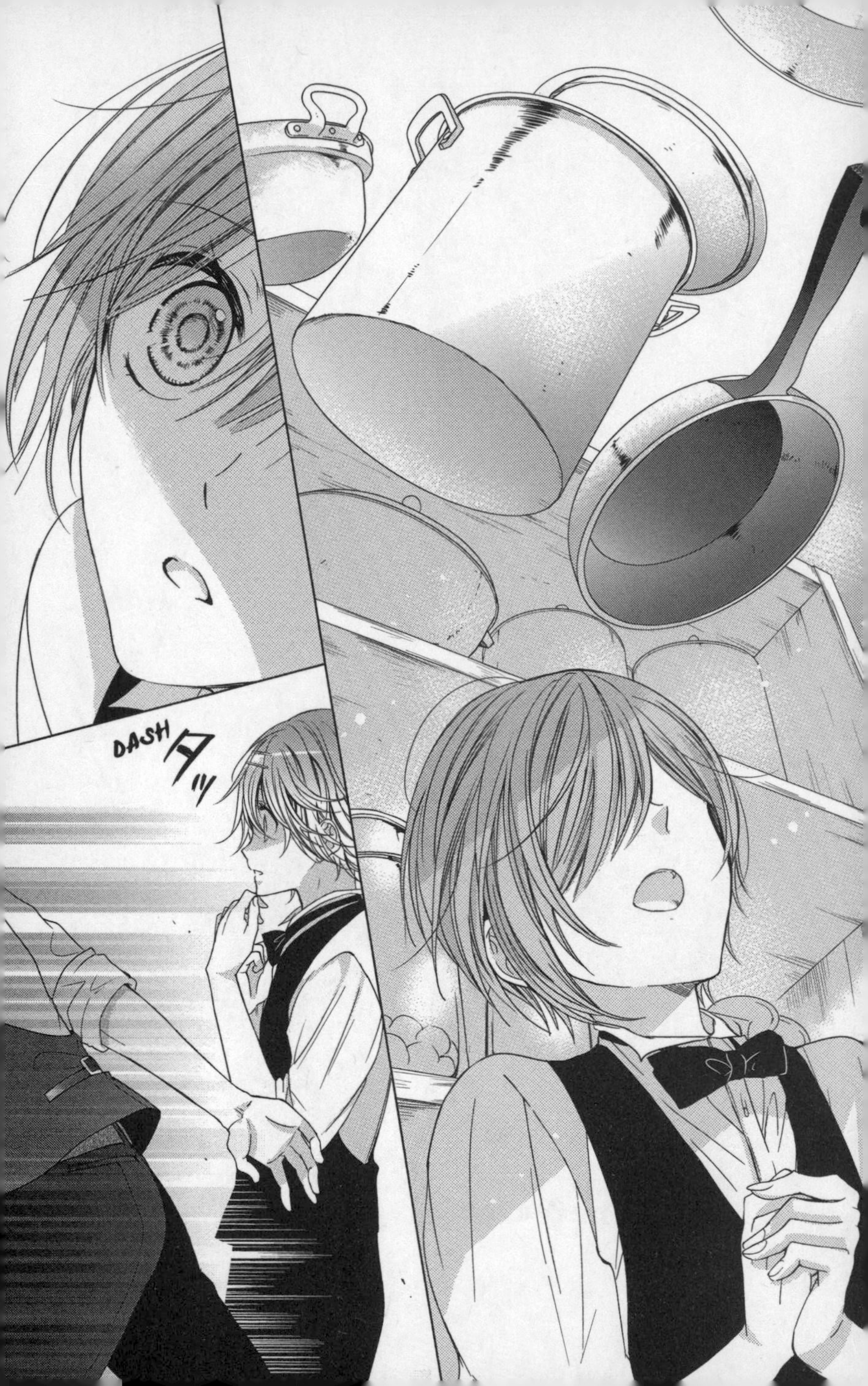
DASH

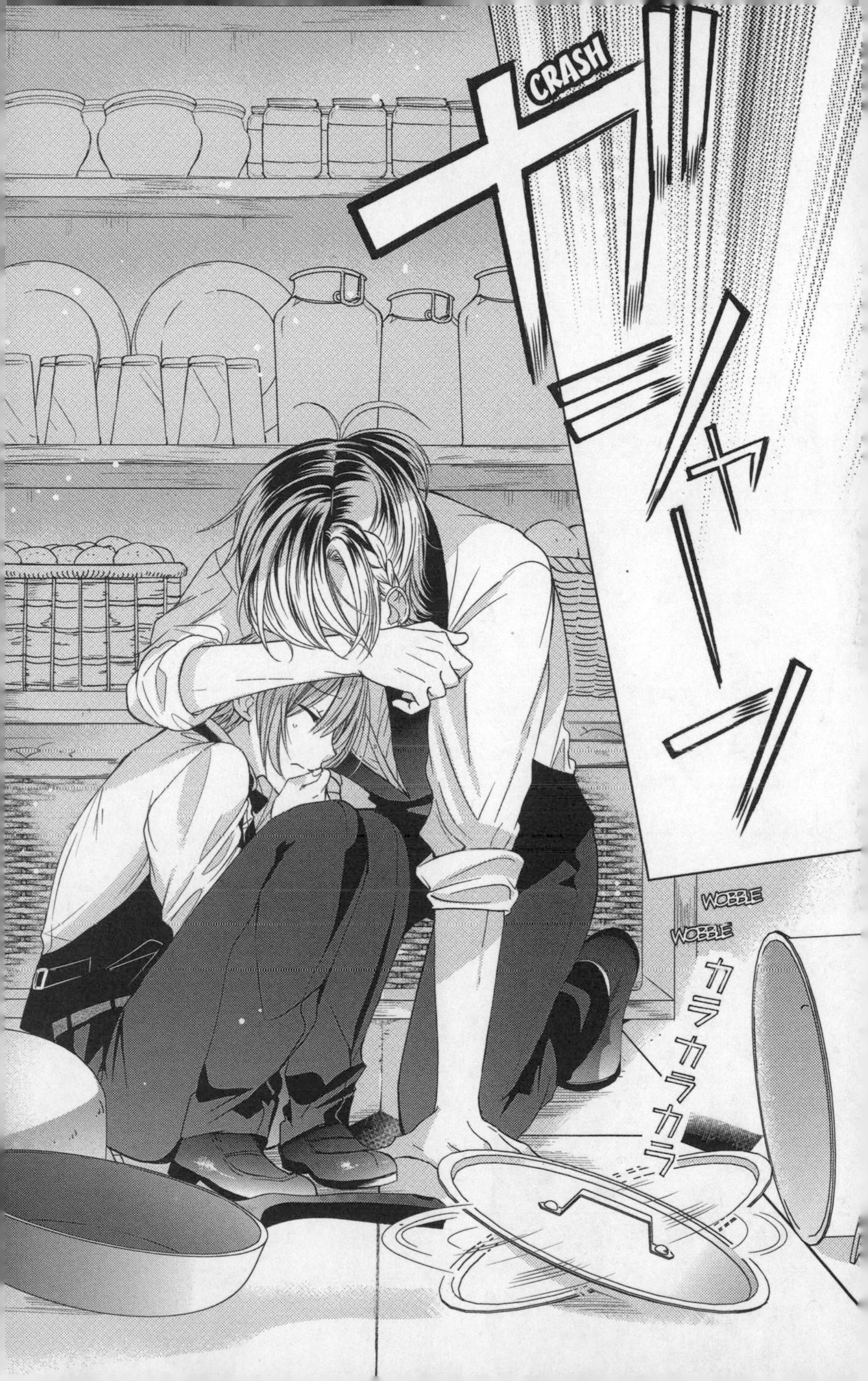
CRASH
ガシャーン
WOBBLE
WOBBLE
カラカラカラ

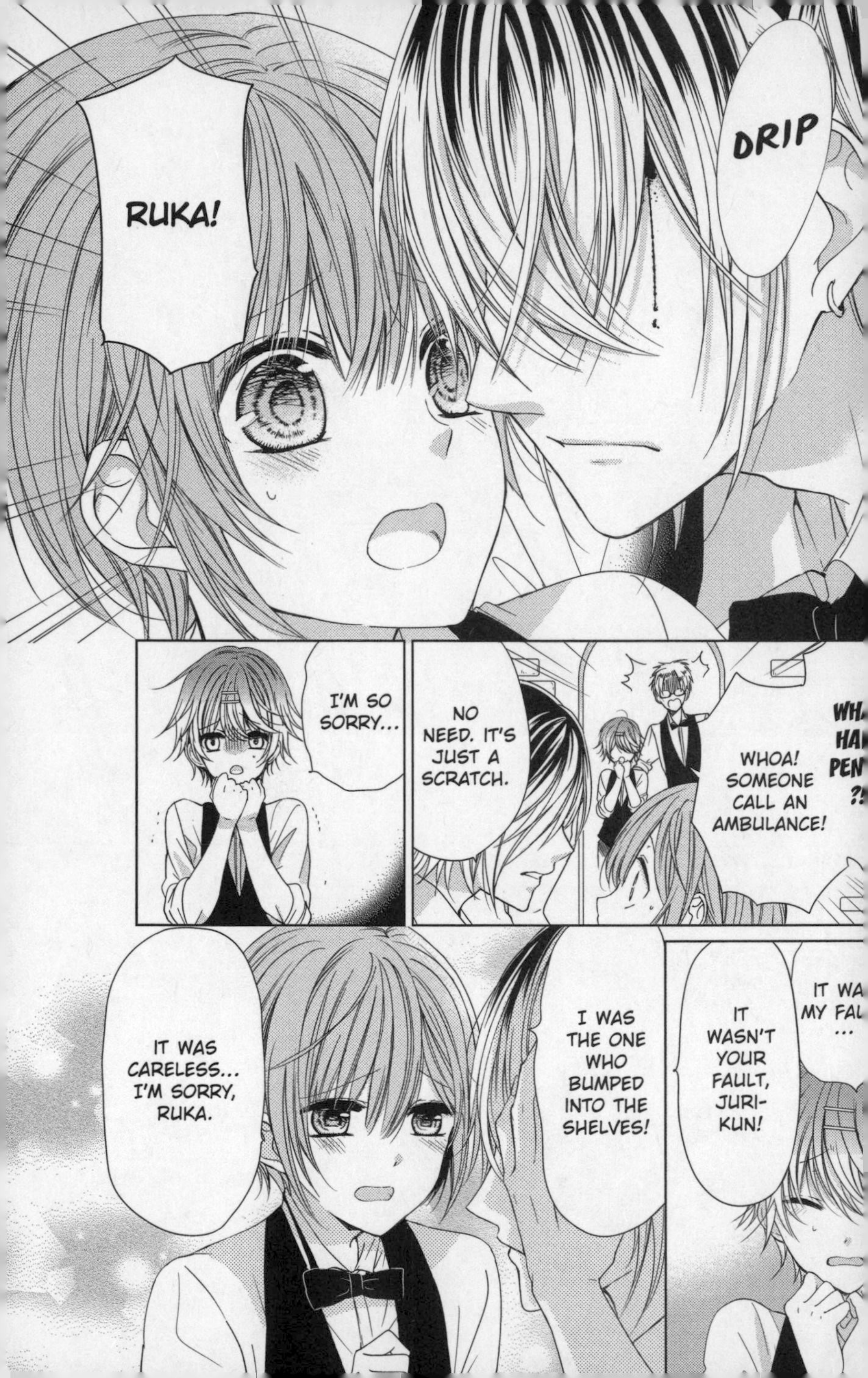
DRIP
RUKA!
WHA HAP PEN ?!
WHOA! SOMEONE CALL AN AMBULANCE!
NO NEED. IT'S JUST A SCRATCH.
I'M SO SORRY...
IT WA MY FAL ...
IT WASN'T YOUR FAULT, JURI-KUN!
I WAS THE ONE WHO BUMPED INTO THE SHELVES!
IT WAS CARELESS... I'M SORRY, RUKA.

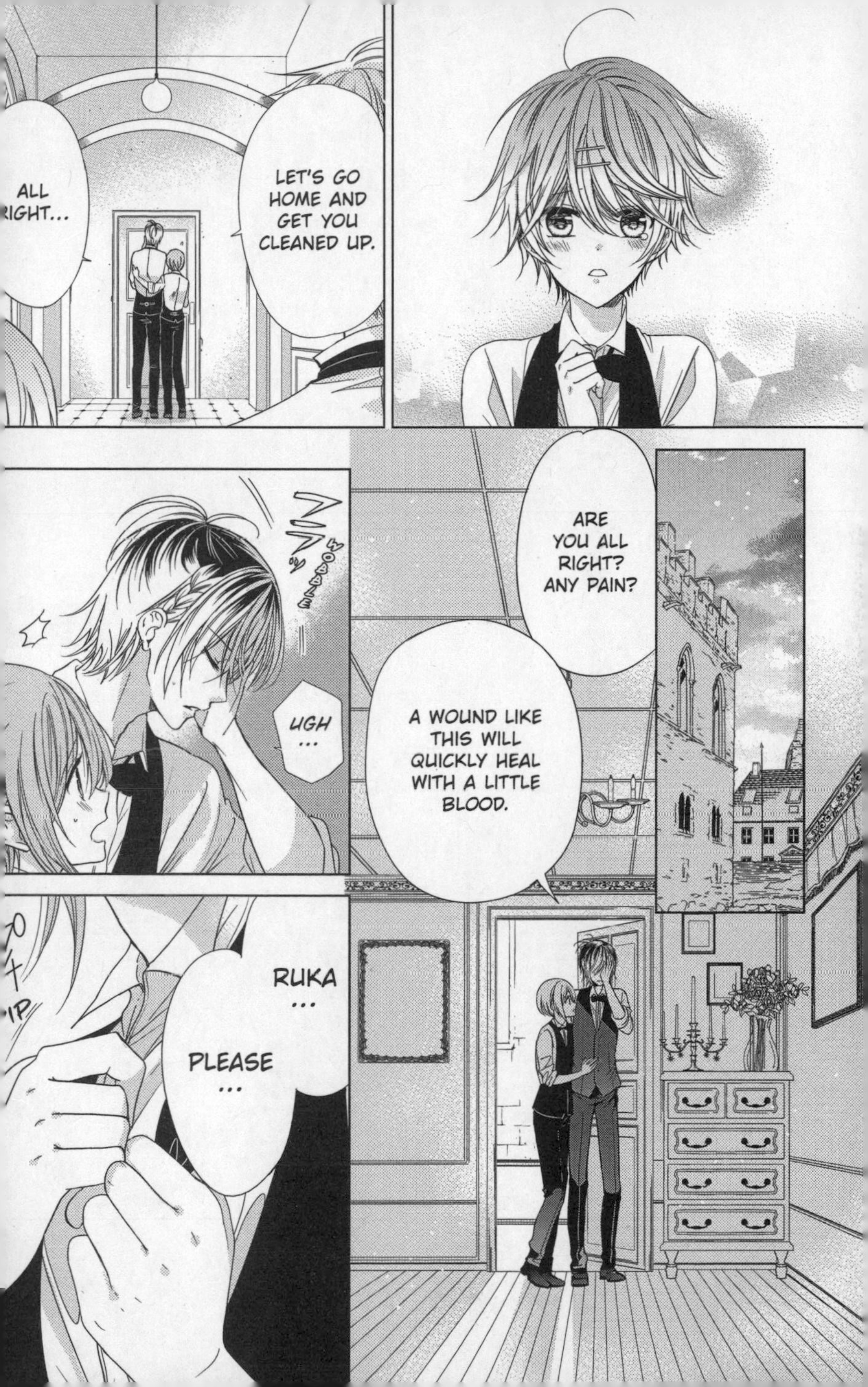
LET'S GO HOME AND GET YOU CLEANED UP.
ALL RIGHT...
ARE YOU ALL RIGHT? ANY PAIN?
A WOUND LIKE THIS WILL QUICKLY HEAL WITH A LITTLE BLOOD.
WOBBLE
UGH ...
RUKA ...
PLEASE ...
RIP

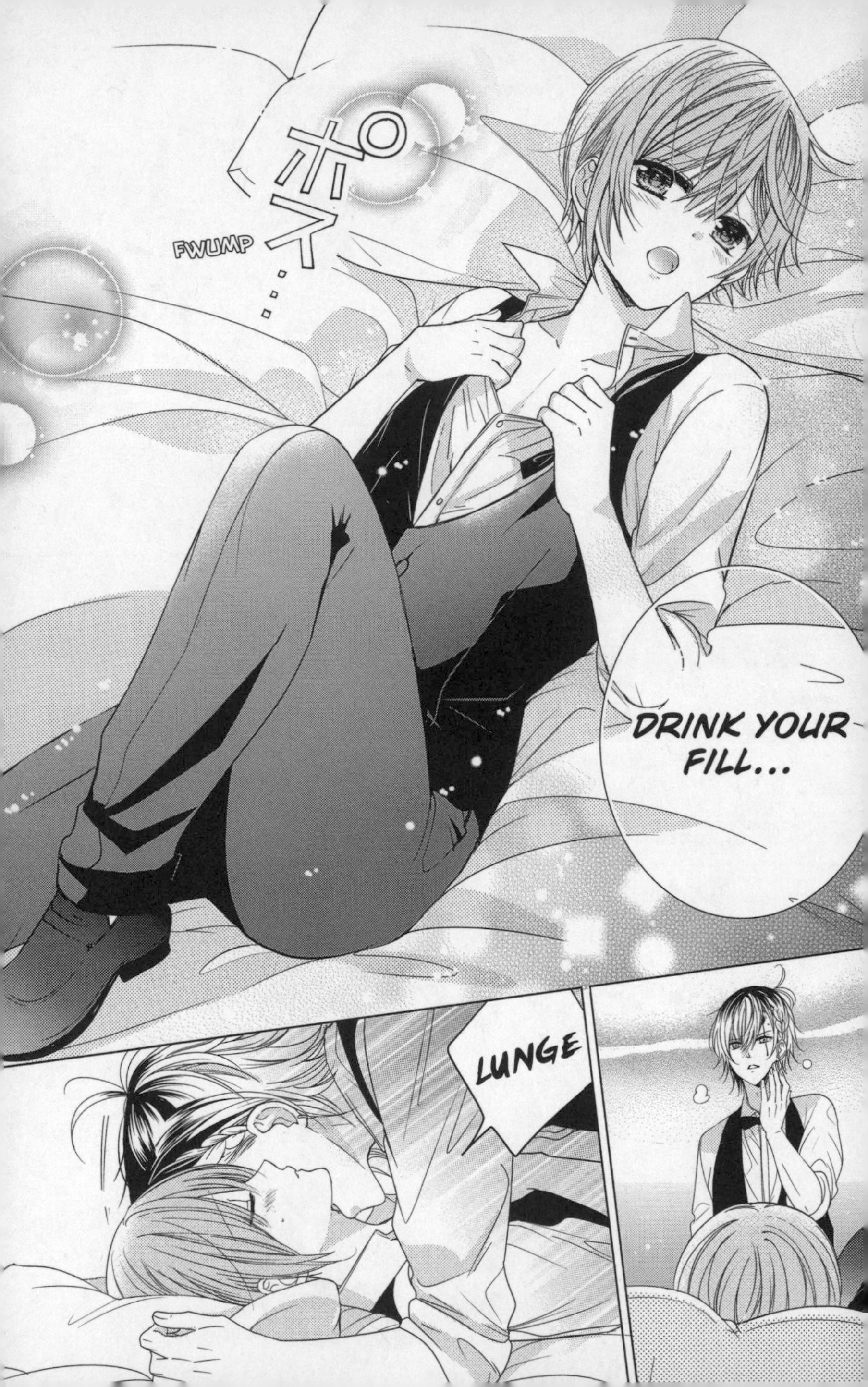
ポフ…
FWUMP
DRINK YOUR FILL...
LUNGE

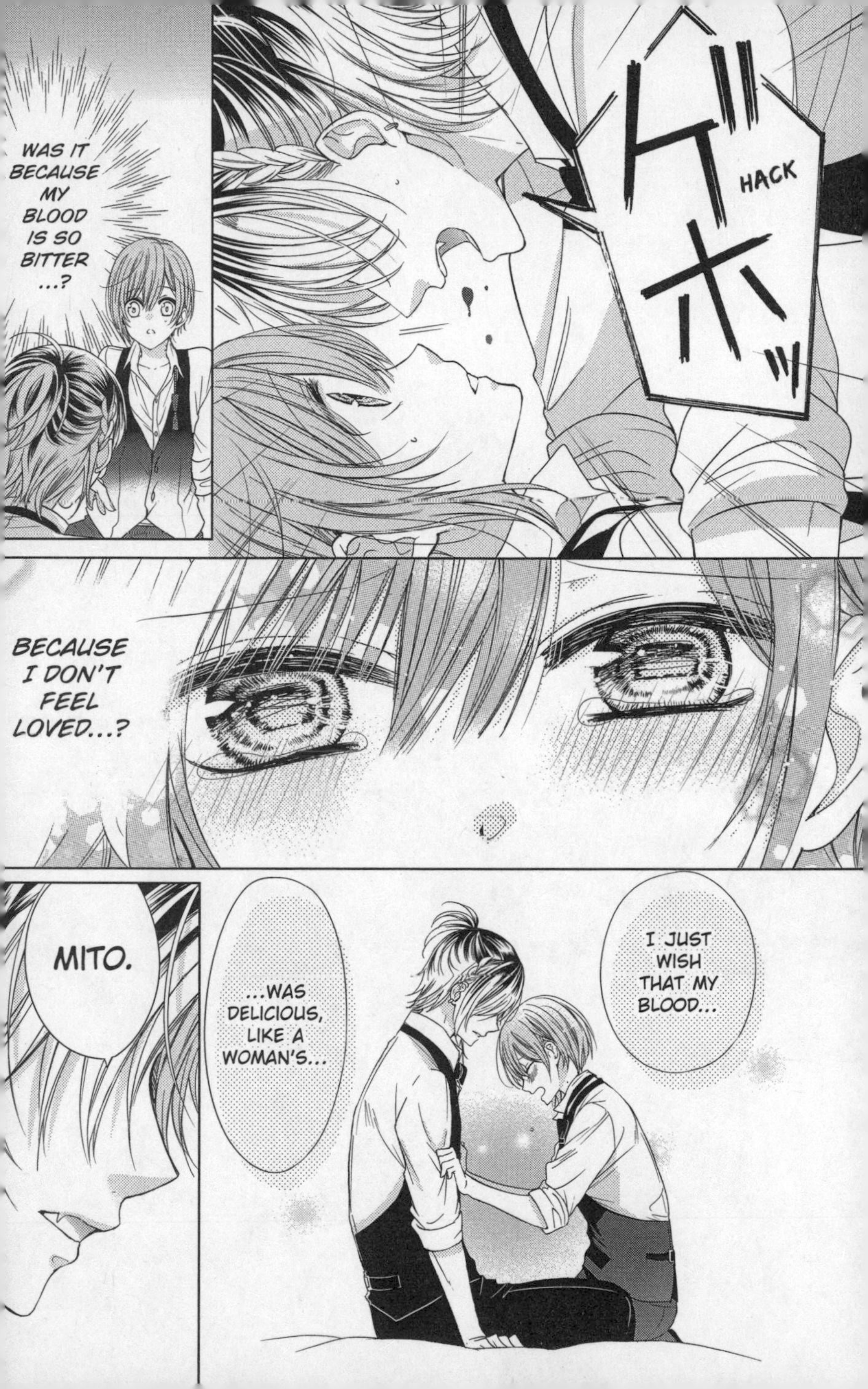
ゲホッ
HACK
WAS IT BECAUSE MY BLOOD IS SO BITTER ...?
BECAUSE I DON'T FEEL LOVED...?
I JUST WISH THAT MY BLOOD...
...WAS DELICIOUS, LIKE A WOMAN'S...
MITO.

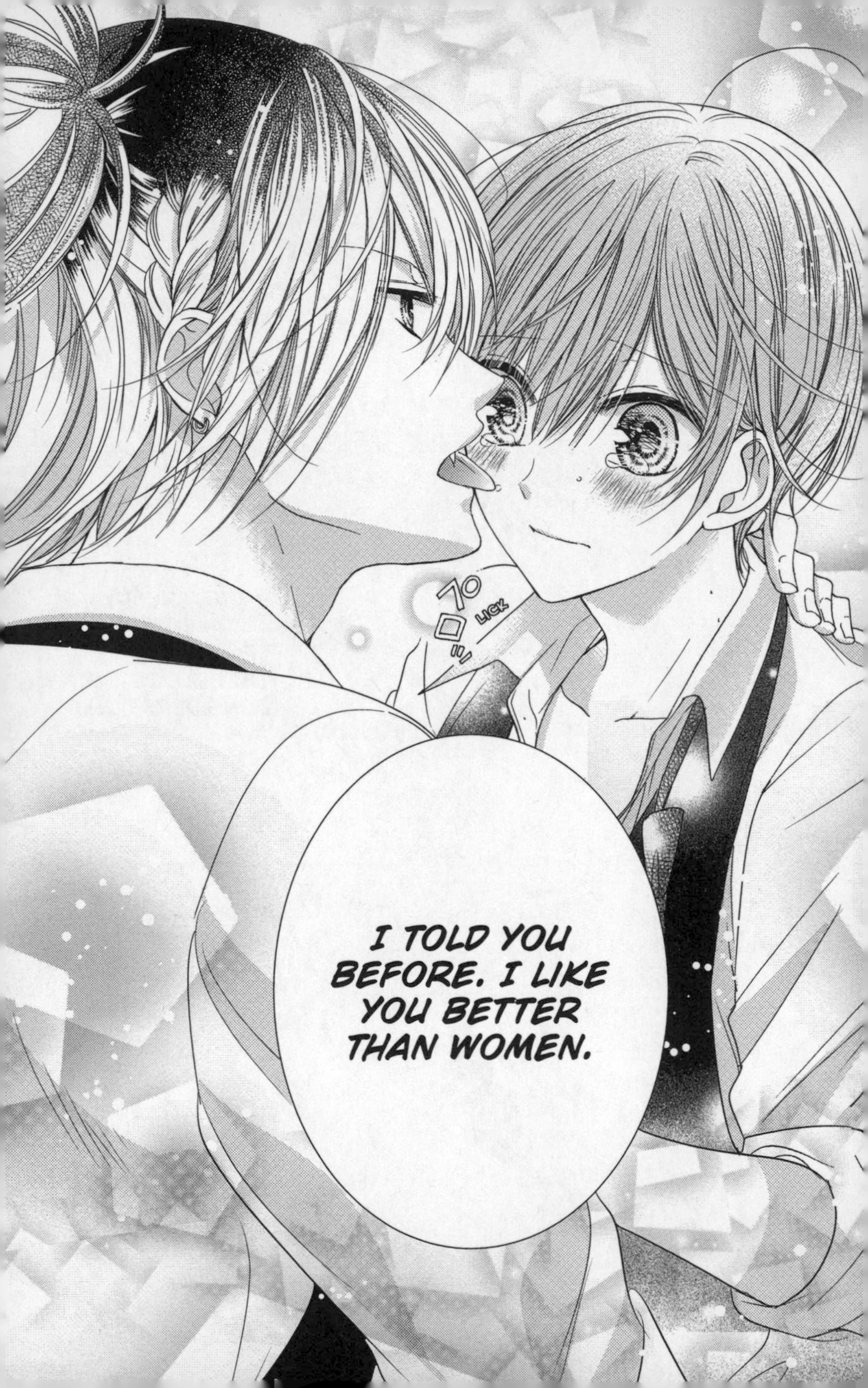
LICK
I TOLD YOU BEFORE. I LIKE YOU BETTER THAN WOMEN.

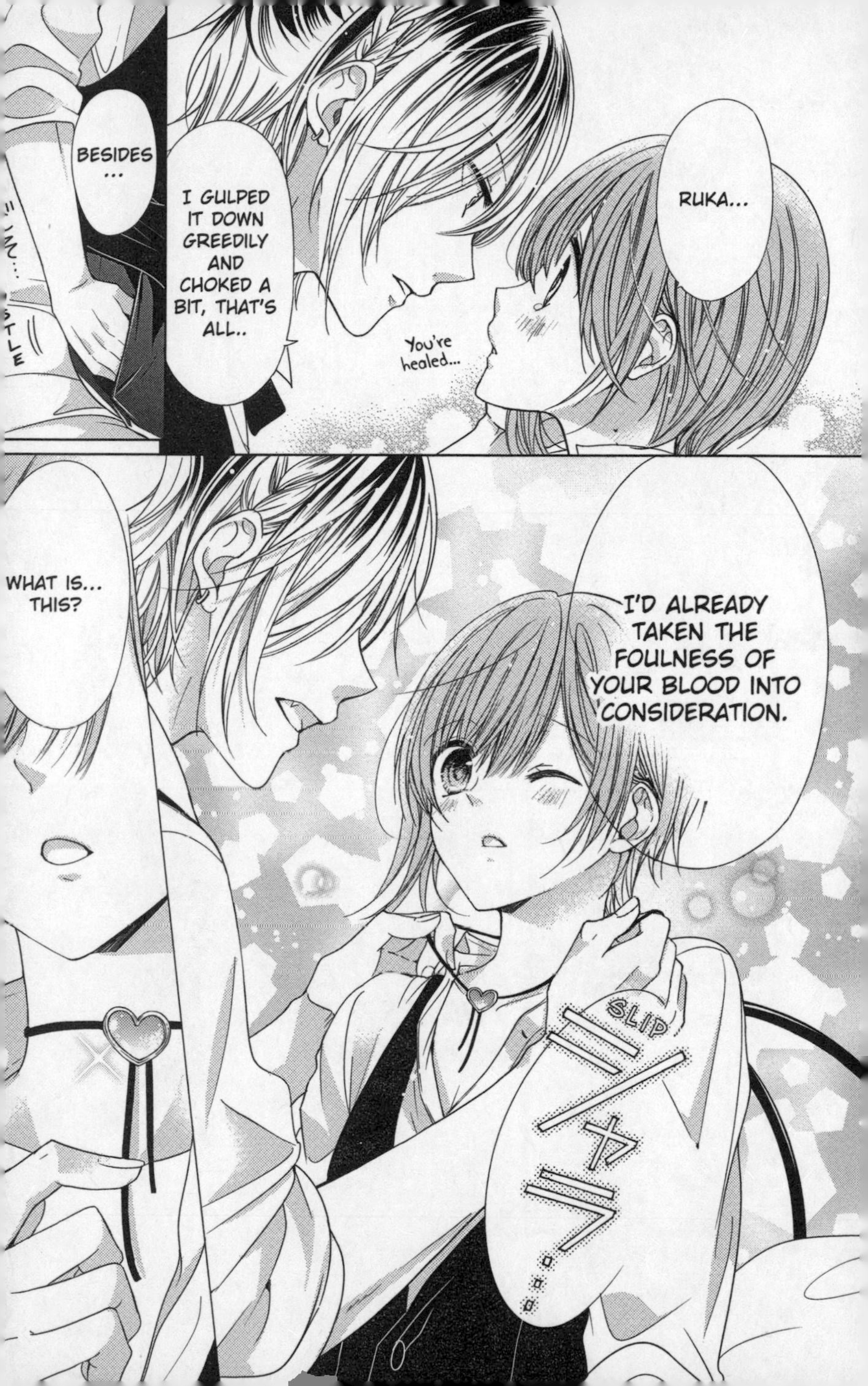
RUKA...
You're healed...
I GULPED IT DOWN GREEDILY AND CHOKED A BIT, THAT'S ALL..
BESIDES...
I'D ALREADY TAKEN THE FOULNESS OF YOUR BLOOD INTO CONSIDERATION.
SLIP
WHAT IS... THIS?

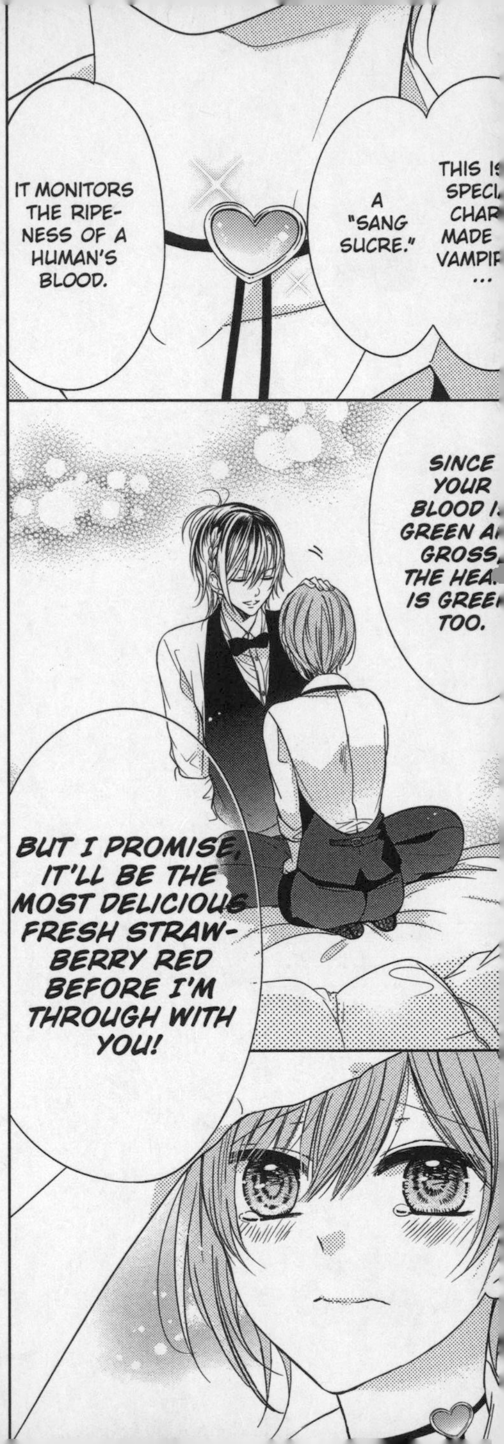
THIS IS SPECI CHAR MADE VAMPIR ...
A "SANG SUCRE."
IT MONITORS THE RIPE-NESS OF A HUMAN'S BLOOD.
SINCE YOUR BLOOD I GREEN A GROSS, THE HEA IS GREE TOO.
BUT I PROMISE, IT'LL BE THE MOST DELICIOUS FRESH STRAW-BERRY RED BEFORE I'M THROUGH WITH YOU!

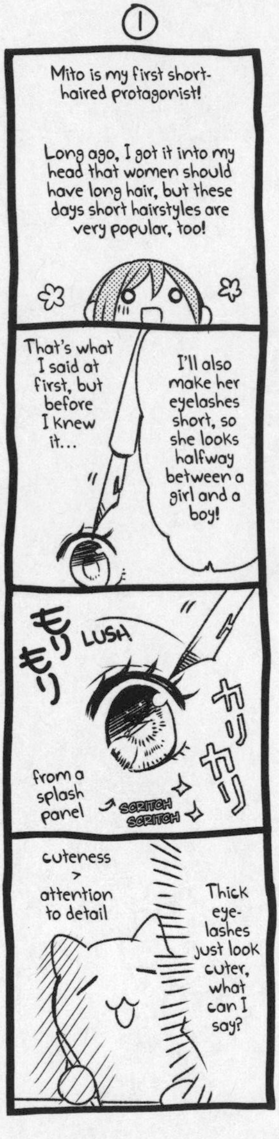
1
Mito is my first short-haired protagonist!
Long ago, I got it into my head that women should have long hair, but these days short hairstyles are very popular, too!
I'll also make her eyelashes short, so she looks halfway between a girl and a boy!
That's what I said at first, but before I knew it...
モリモリ
LUSH
カリカリ
from a splash panel
SCRITCH SCRITCH
cuteness > attention to detail
Thick eye-lashes just look cuter, what can I say?

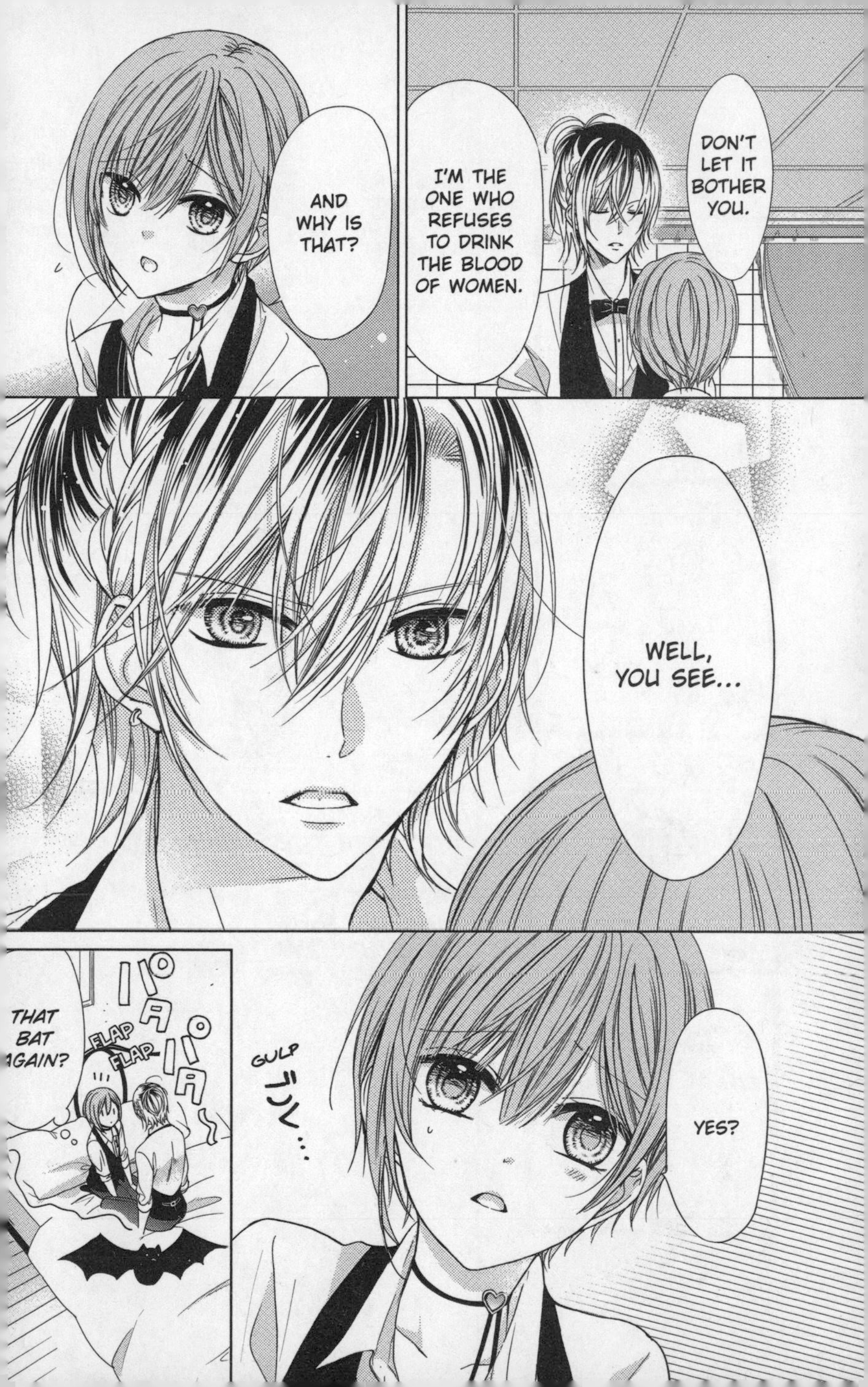
DON'T LET IT BOTHER YOU.
I'M THE ONE WHO REFUSES TO DRINK THE BLOOD OF WOMEN.
AND WHY IS THAT?
WELL, YOU SEE...
YES?
GULP
FLAP FLAP
THAT BAT AGAIN?

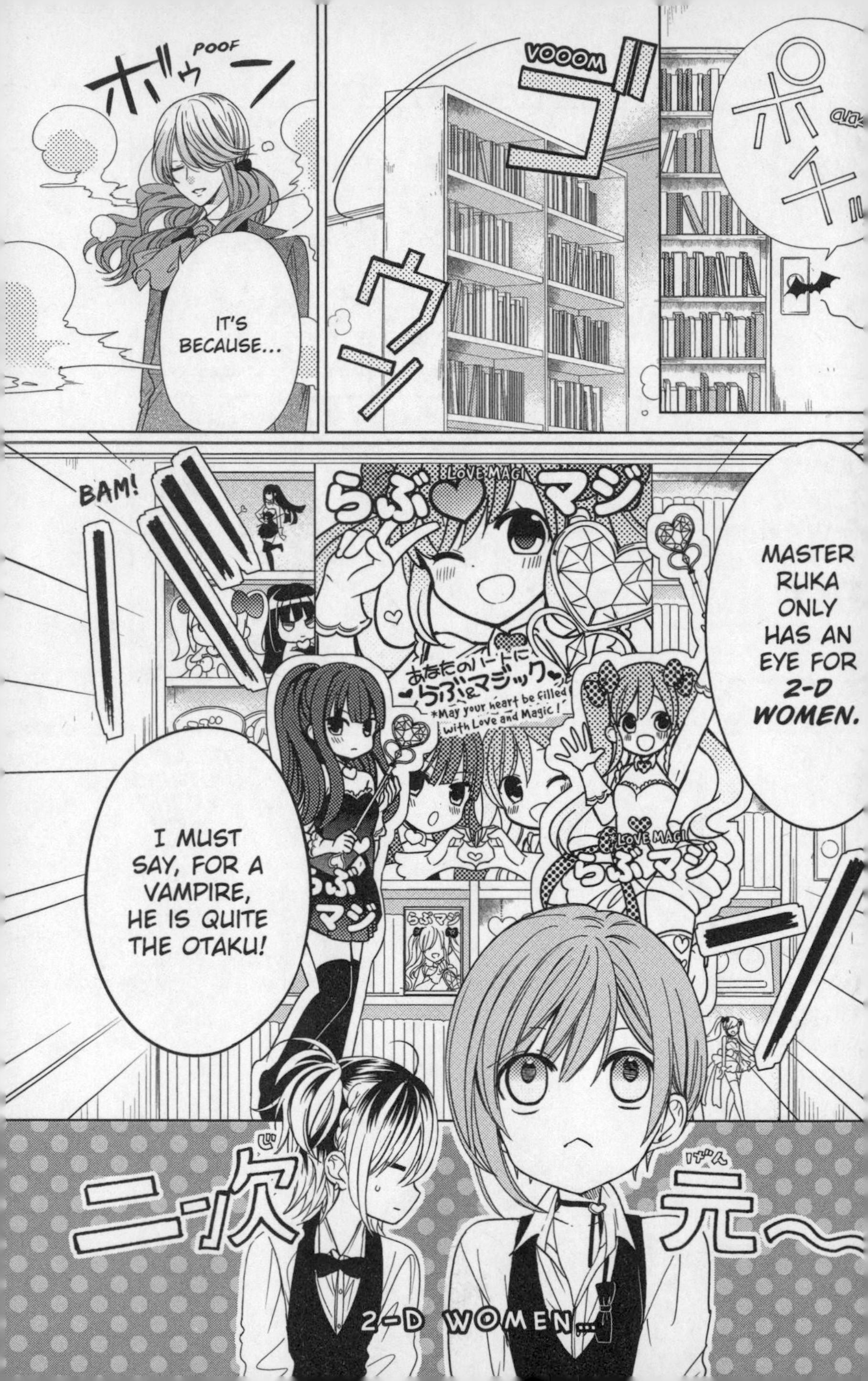
ポギ
VOOOM
ゴウン
POOF
ボヴゥーン
IT'S BECAUSE...
MASTER RUKA ONLY HAS AN EYE FOR 2-D WOMEN.
LOVE MAGI
らぶ♡マジ
あなたのハートに らぶ&マジック
*May your heart be filled with Love and Magic!
BAM!
バーン
I MUST SAY, FOR A VAMPIRE, HE IS QUITE THE OTAKU!
二次元〜
2-D WOMEN...

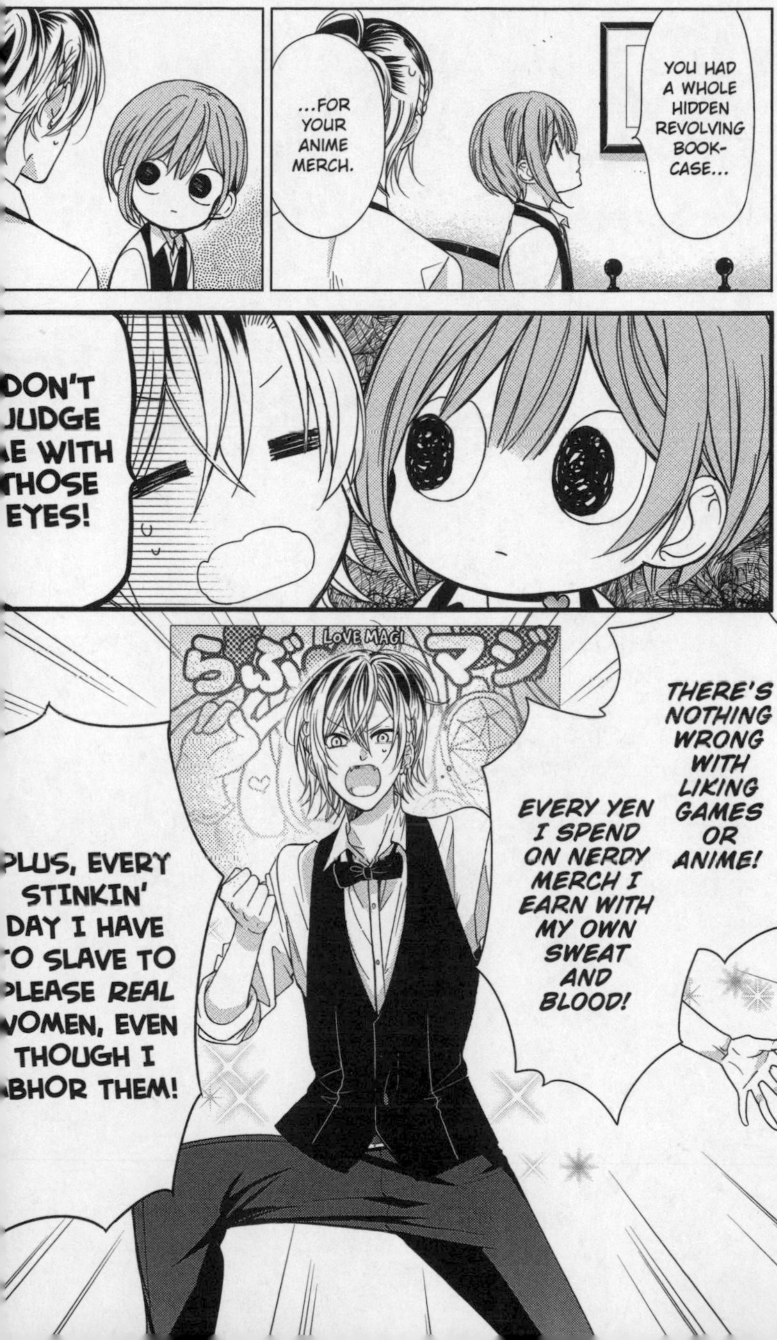
YOU HAD A WHOLE HIDDEN REVOLVING BOOK-CASE...
...FOR YOUR ANIME MERCH.
DON'T JUDGE E WITH THOSE EYES!
LOVE MAGI
THERE'S NOTHING WRONG WITH LIKING GAMES OR ANIME!
EVERY YEN I SPEND ON NERDY MERCH I EARN WITH MY OWN SWEAT AND BLOOD!
LUS, EVERY STINKIN' DAY I HAVE O SLAVE TO LEASE *REAL* OMEN, EVEN THOUGH I BHOR THEM!

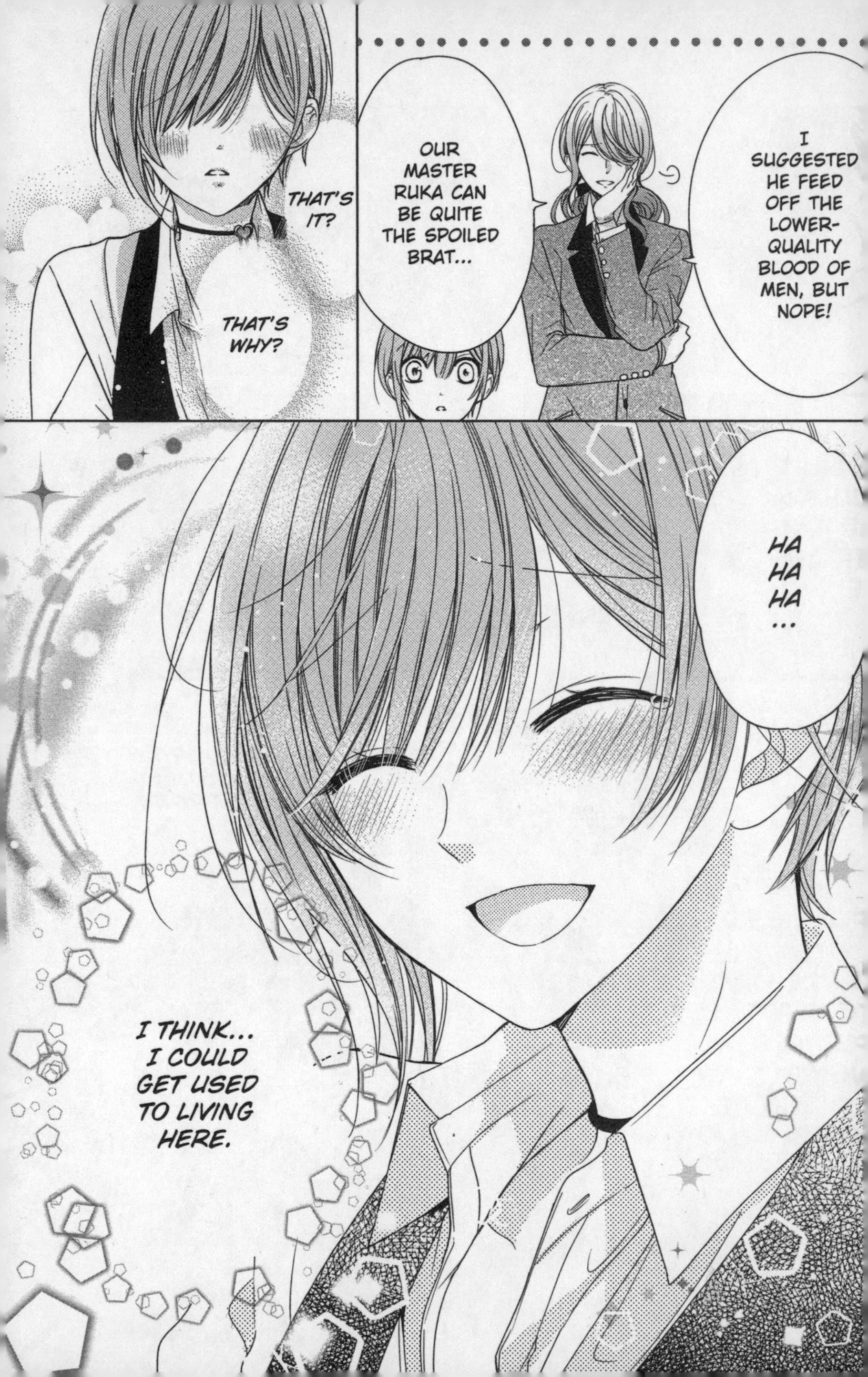
I SUGGESTED HE FEED OFF THE LOWER-QUALITY BLOOD OF MEN, BUT NOPE!
OUR MASTER RUKA CAN BE QUITE THE SPOILED BRAT...
THAT'S IT?
THAT'S WHY?
HA HA HA ...
I THINK... I COULD GET USED TO LIVING HERE.

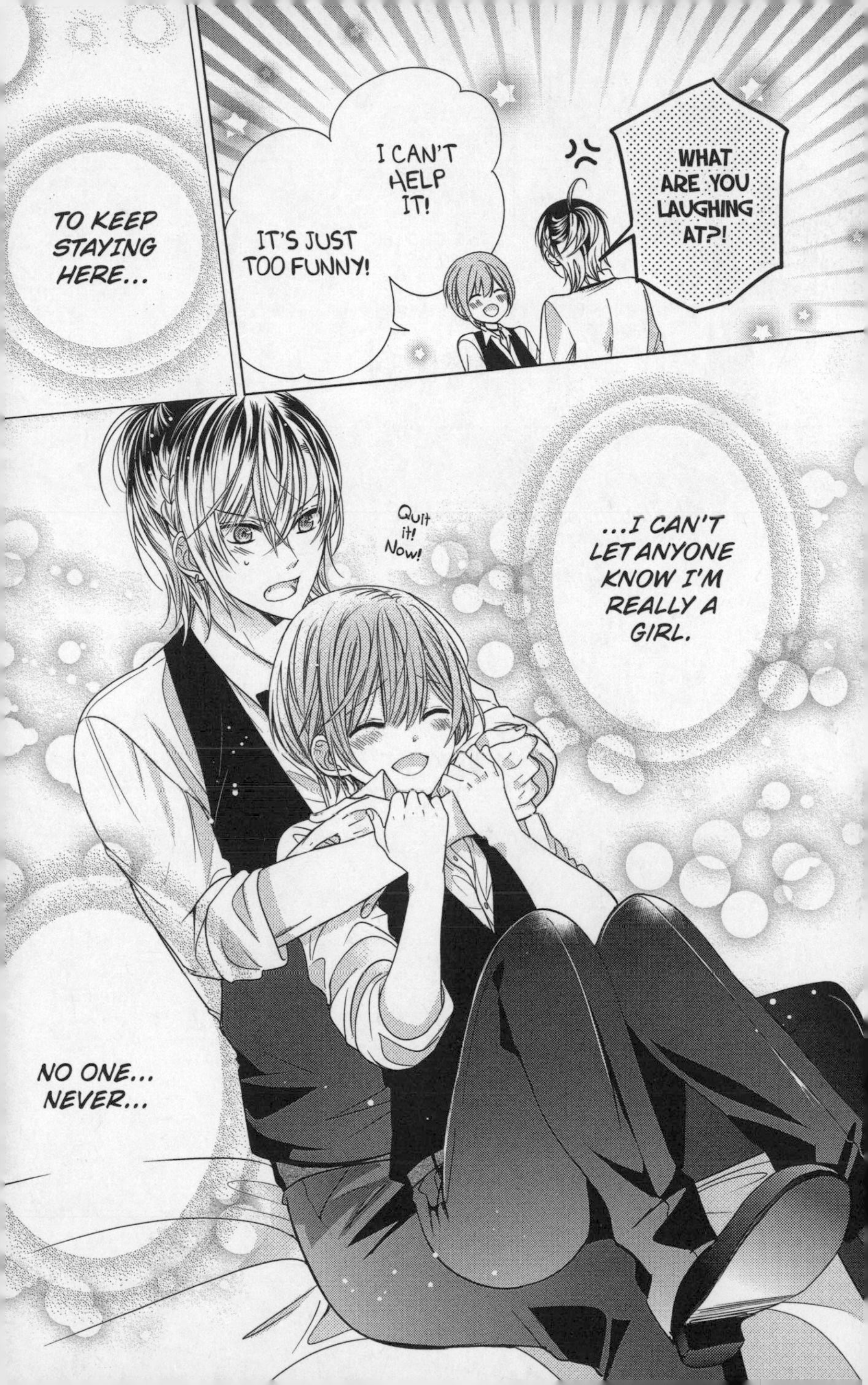
WHAT ARE YOU LAUGHING AT?!
I CAN'T HELP IT!
IT'S JUST TOO FUNNY!
TO KEEP STAYING HERE...
...I CAN'T LETANYONE KNOW I'M REALLY A GIRL.
Quit it! Now!
NO ONE... NEVER...

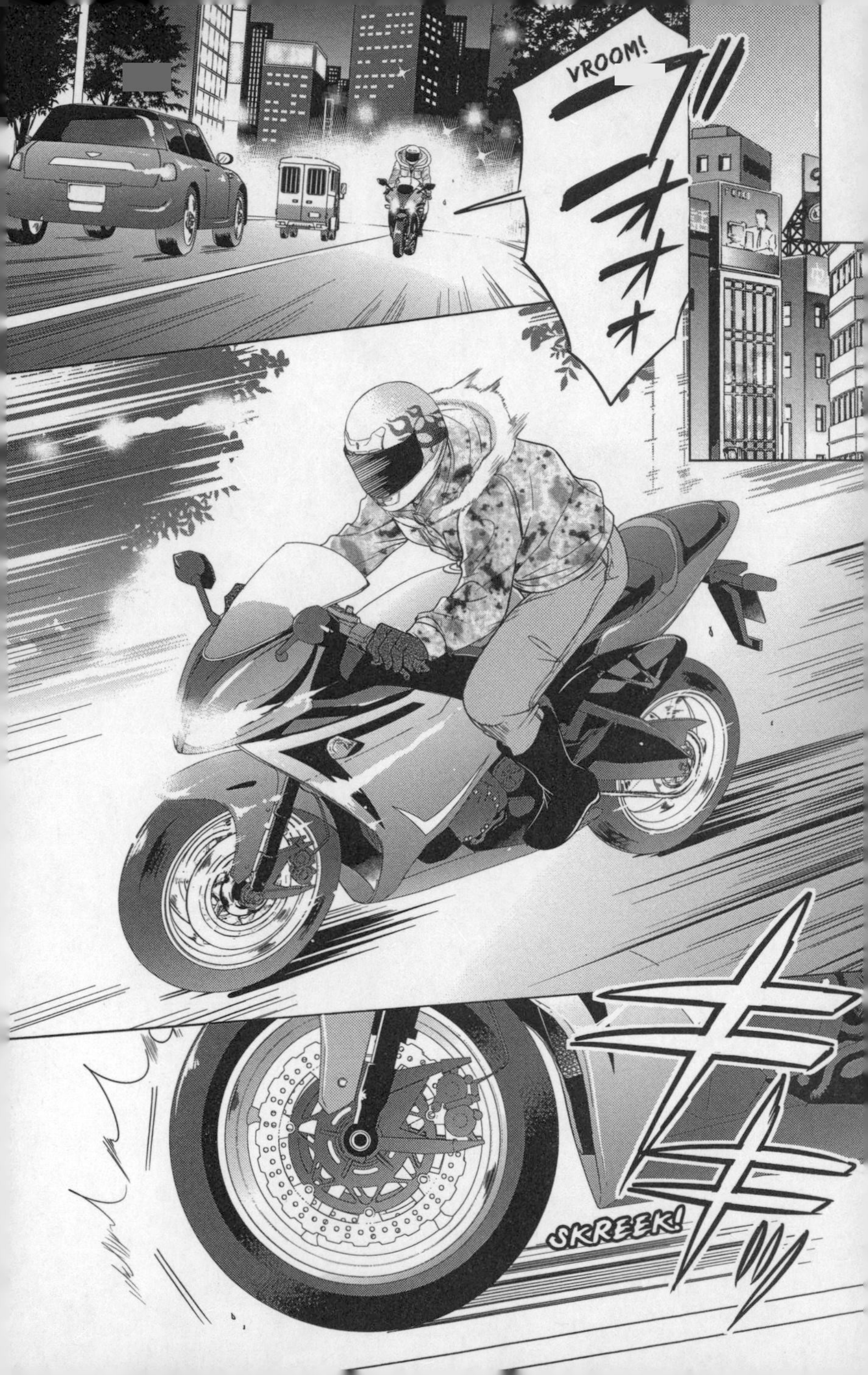
VROOM!
ブオオォォ
キキキッ
SKREEK!

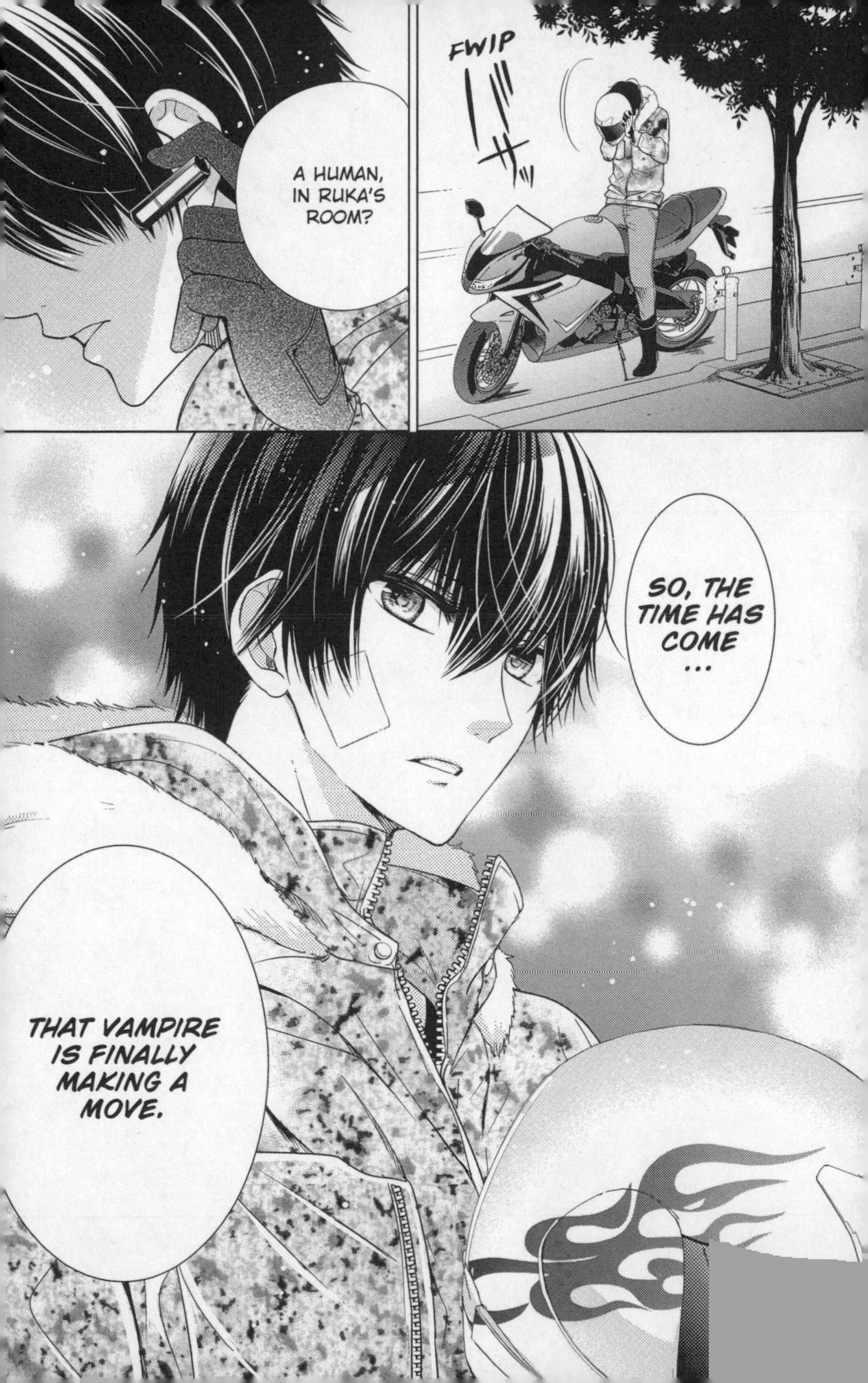
FWIP
A HUMAN, IN RUKA'S ROOM?
SO, THE TIME HAS COME ...
THAT VAMPIRE IS FINALLY MAKING A MOVE.

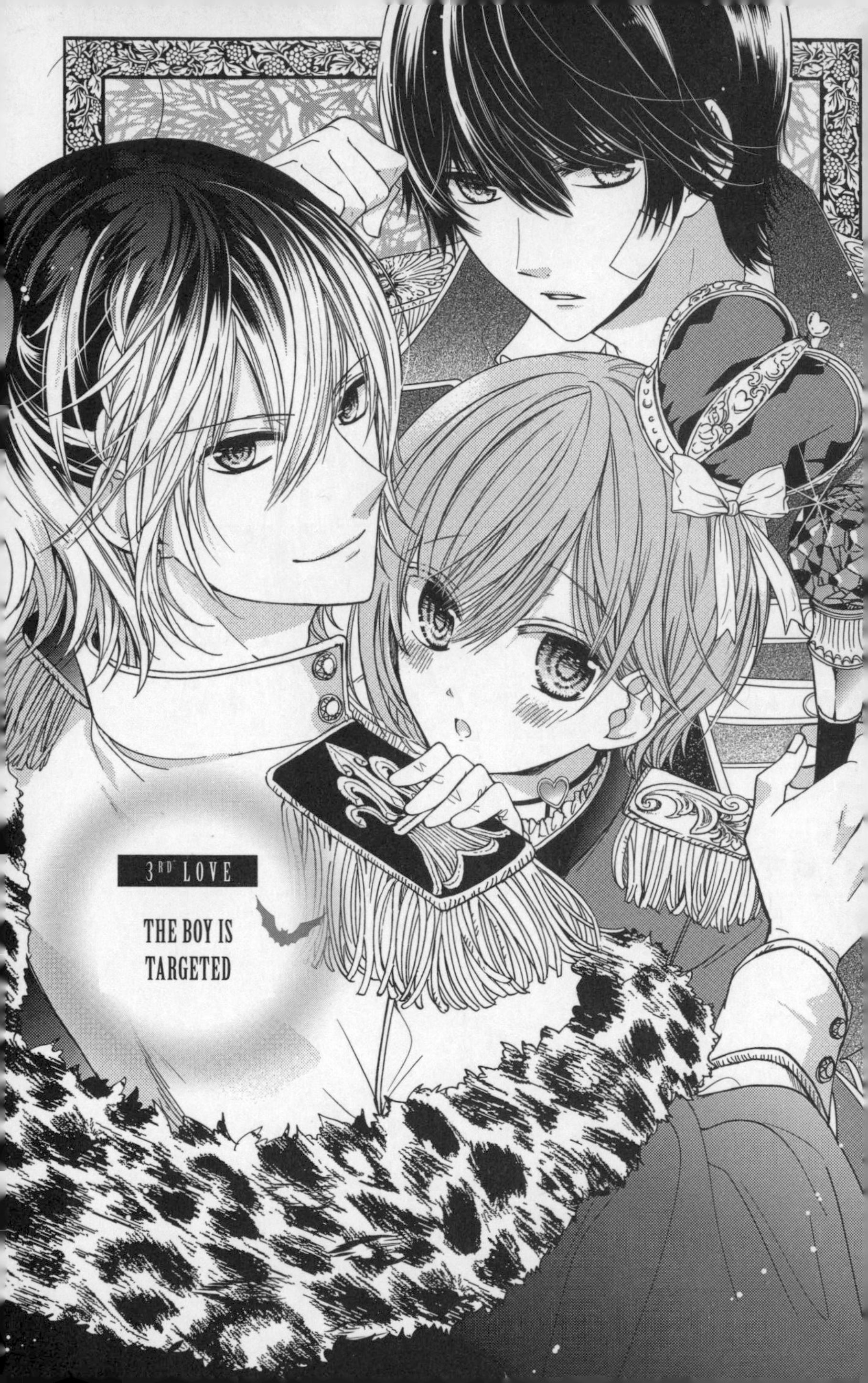
3RD LOVE
THE BOY IS TARGETED

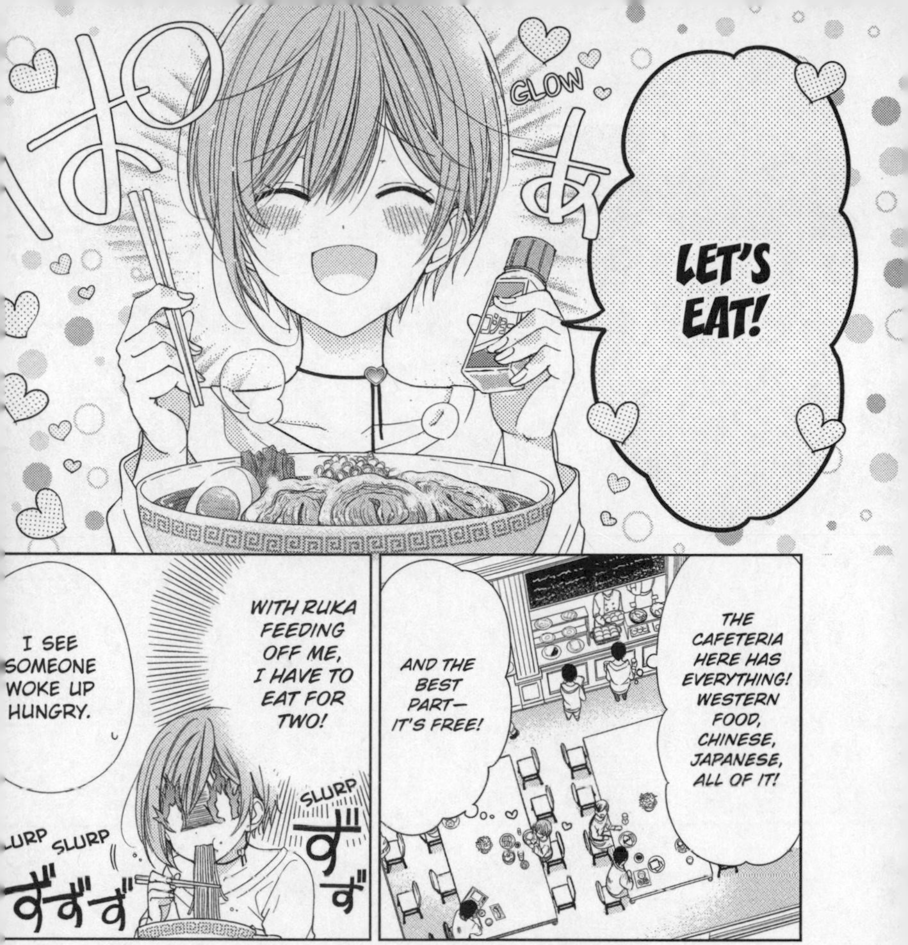
GLOW
LET'S EAT!
THE CAFETERIA HERE HAS EVERYTHING! WESTERN FOOD, CHINESE, JAPANESE, ALL OF IT!
AND THE BEST PART— IT'S FREE!
WITH RUKA FEEDING OFF ME, I HAVE TO EAT FOR TWO!
I SEE SOMEONE WOKE UP HUNGRY.
SLURP
ずず
SLURP SLURP
ずずず

Vampire Dormitory

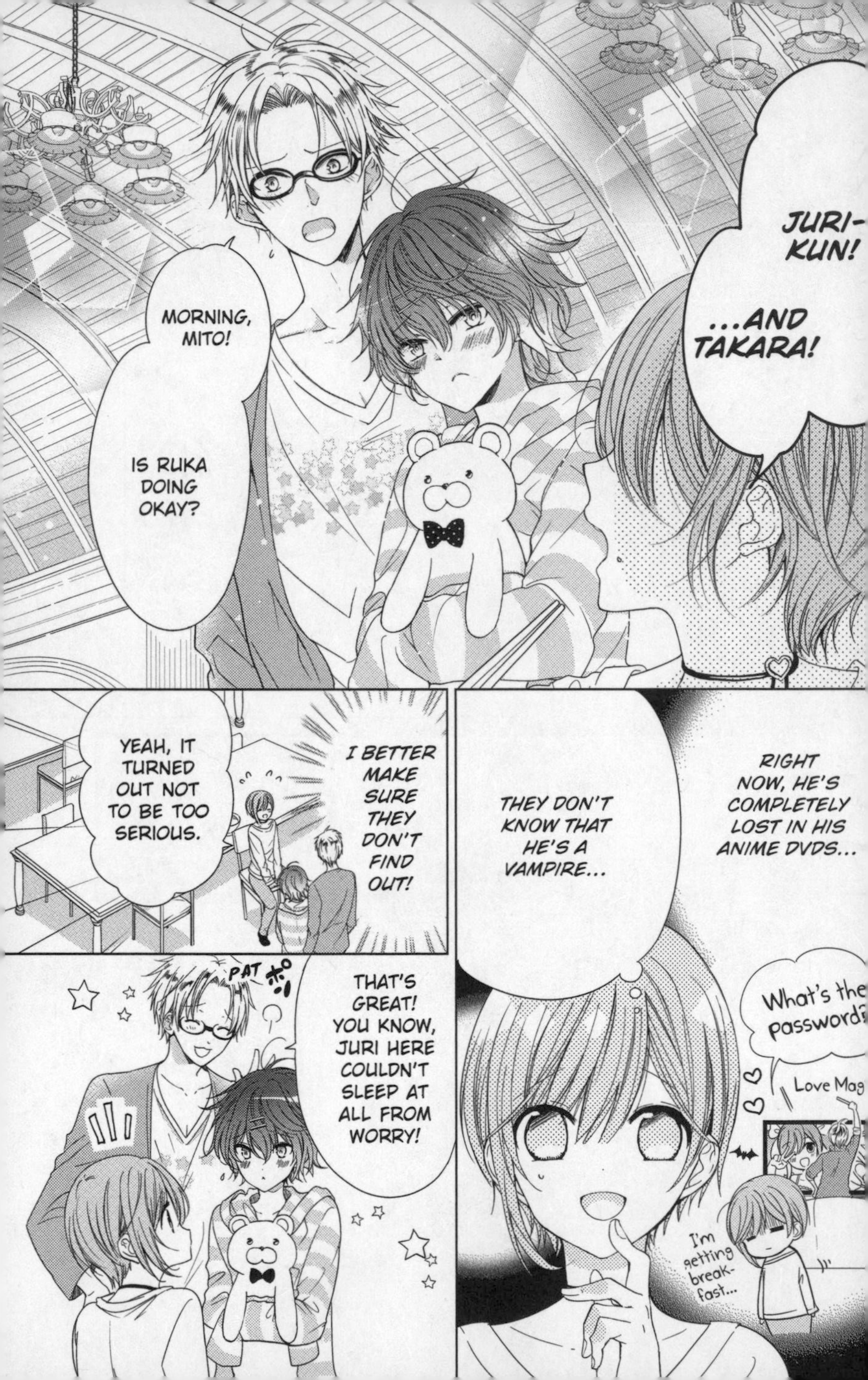
JURI-KUN!
...AND TAKARA!
MORNING, MITO!
IS RUKA DOING OKAY?
RIGHT NOW, HE'S COMPLETELY LOST IN HIS ANIME DVDS...
THEY DON'T KNOW THAT HE'S A VAMPIRE...
What's the password?
Love Mag
I'm getting break-fast...
YEAH, IT TURNED OUT NOT TO BE TOO SERIOUS.
I BETTER MAKE SURE THEY DON'T FIND OUT!
PAT
THAT'S GREAT! YOU KNOW, JURI HERE COULDN'T SLEEP AT ALL FROM WORRY!

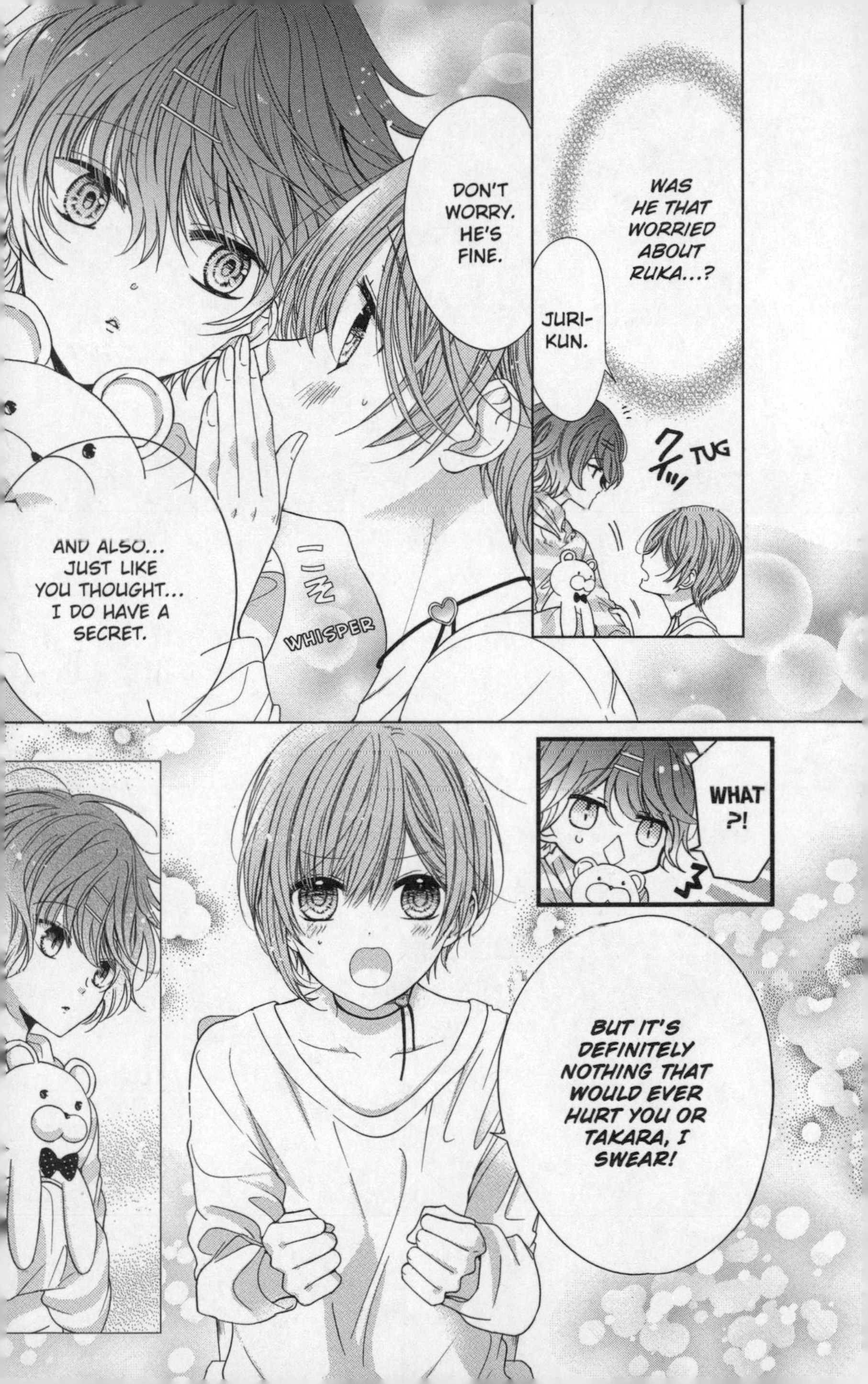
WAS HE THAT WORRIED ABOUT RUKA...?
JURI-KUN.
TUG
DON'T WORRY. HE'S FINE.
WHISPER
AND ALSO... JUST LIKE YOU THOUGHT... I DO HAVE A SECRET.
WHAT?!
BUT IT'S DEFINITELY NOTHING THAT WOULD EVER HURT YOU OR TAKARA, I SWEAR!

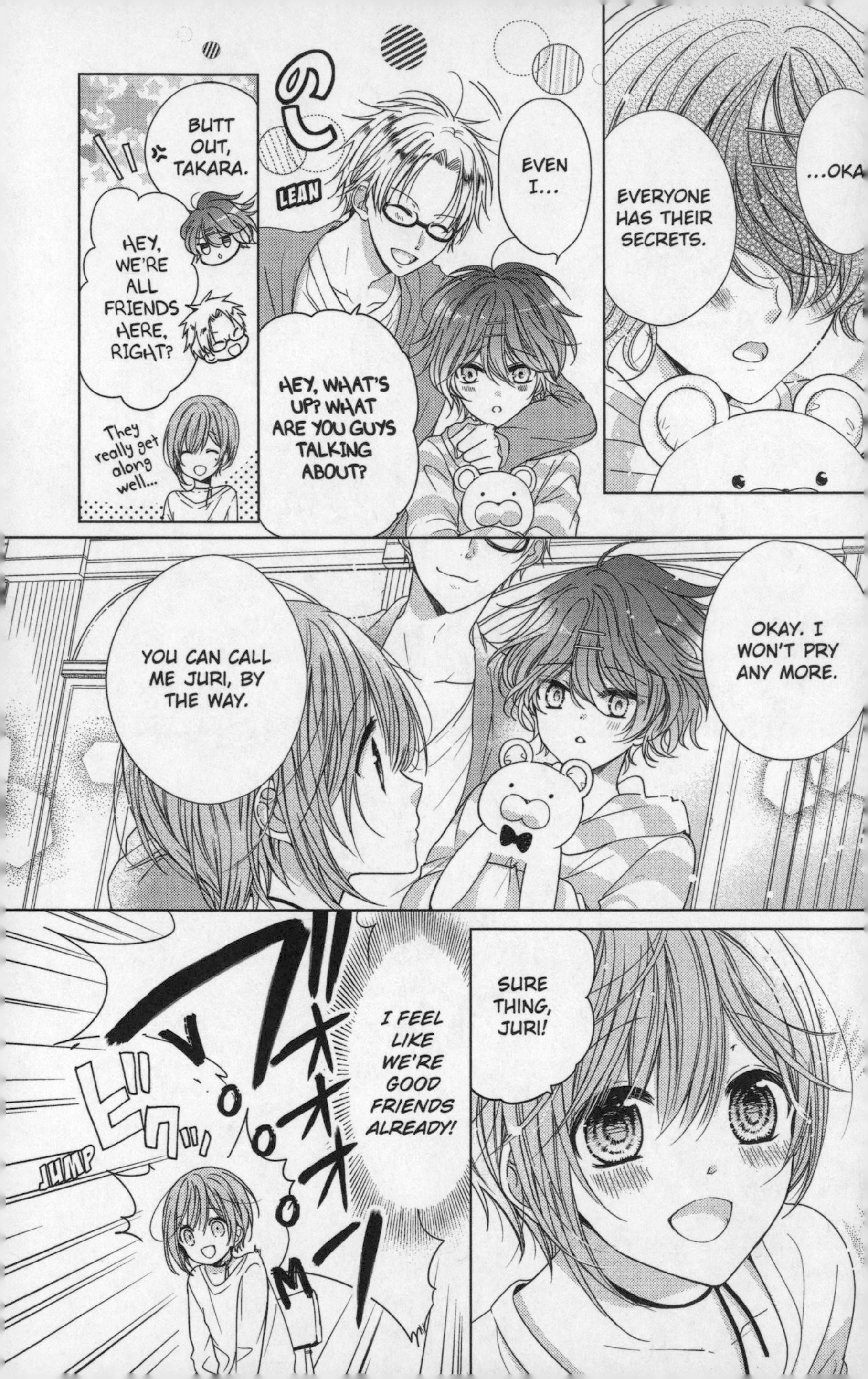

...OKA
EVERYONE HAS THEIR SECRETS.
EVEN I...
のし
LEAN
HEY, WHAT'S UP? WHAT ARE YOU GUYS TALKING ABOUT?
BUTT OUT, TAKARA.
HEY, WE'RE ALL FRIENDS HERE, RIGHT?
They really get along well...
OKAY. I WON'T PRY ANY MORE.
YOU CAN CALL ME JURI, BY THE WAY.
SURE THING, JURI!
I FEEL LIKE WE'RE GOOD FRIENDS ALREADY!
VOOOOOM
ビクッ
JUMP

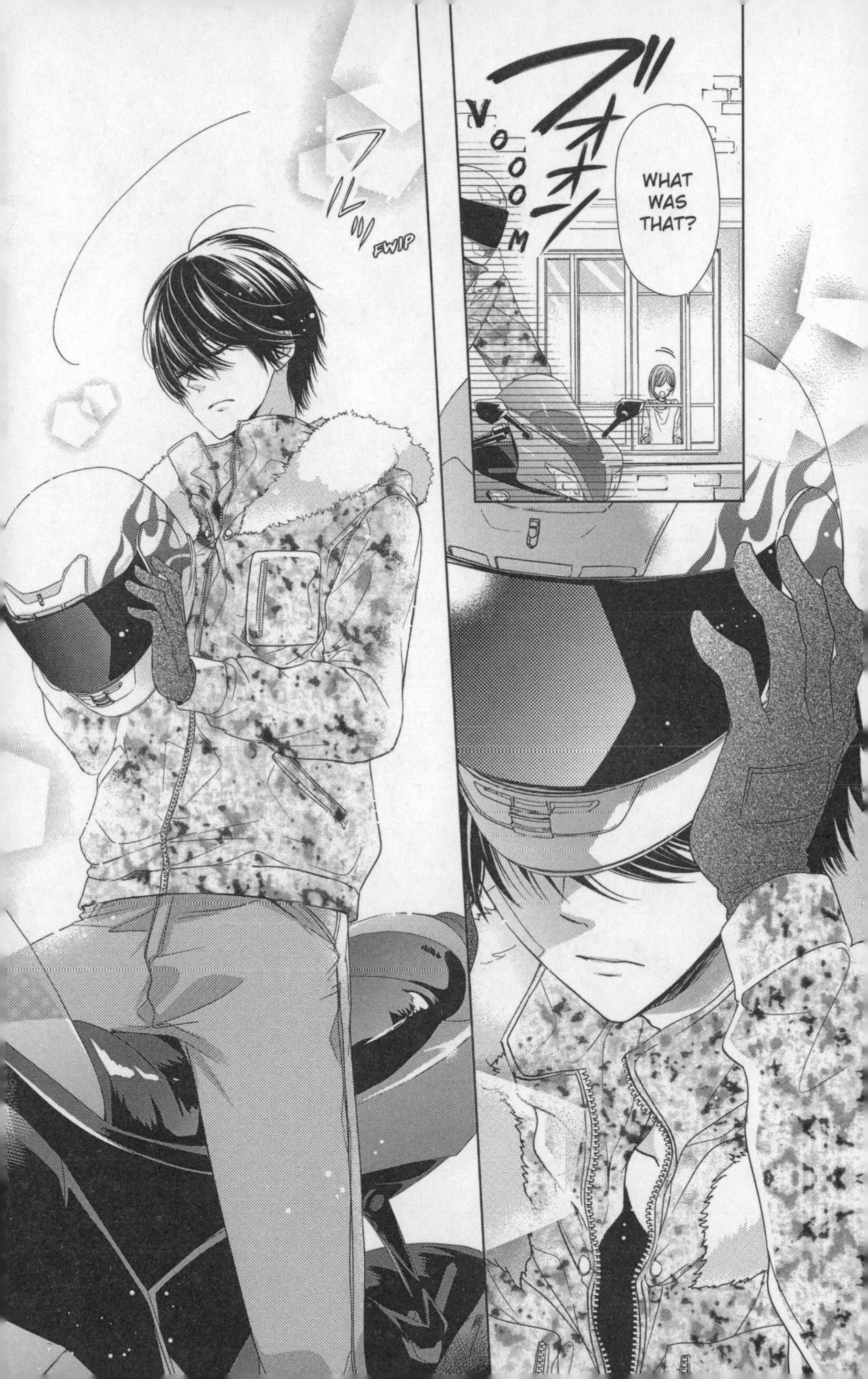
ブォオン
VOOOOM
WHAT WAS THAT?
フルッ
FWIP

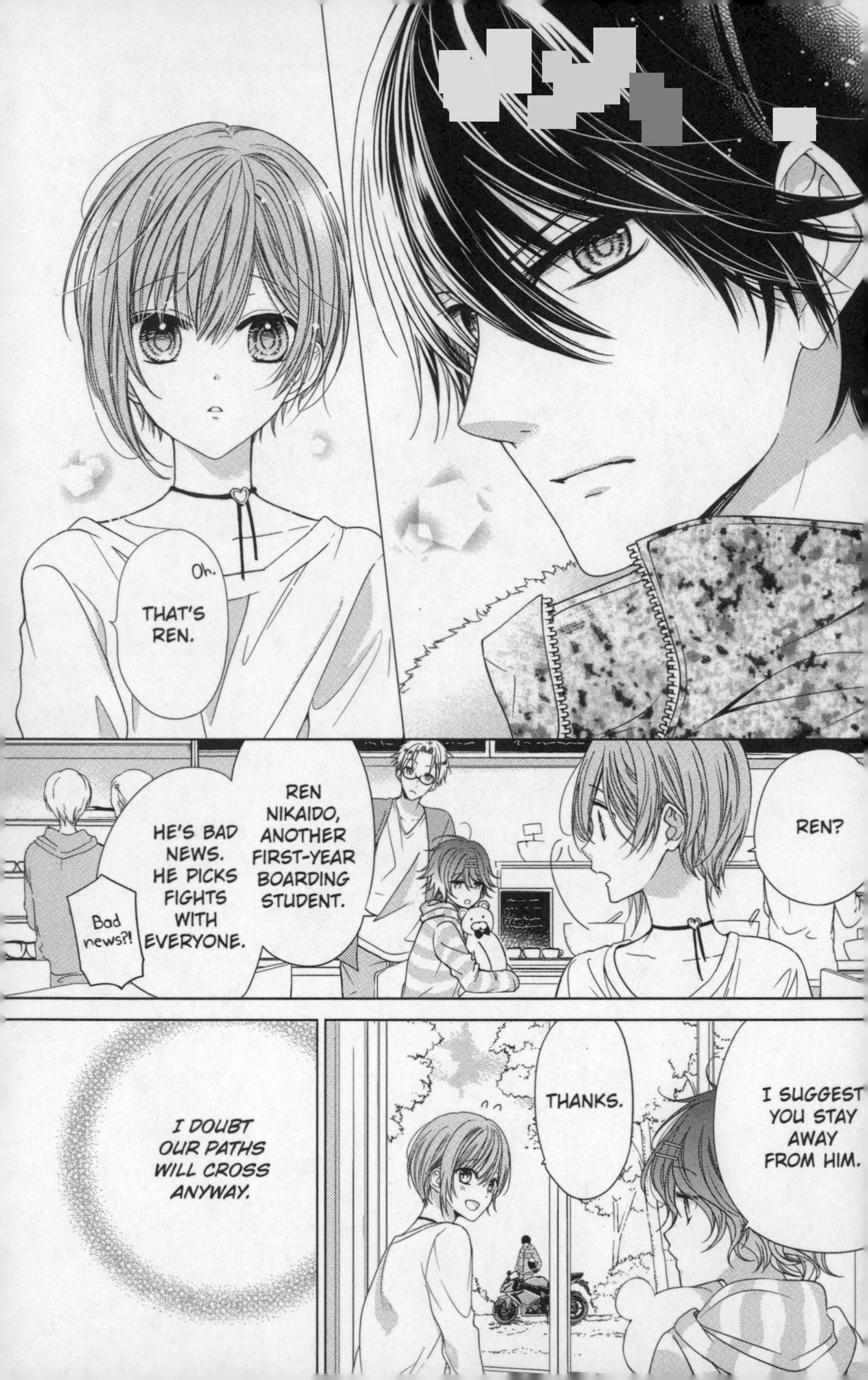
Oh.
THAT'S REN.
REN?
REN NIKAIDO, ANOTHER FIRST-YEAR BOARDING STUDENT.
HE'S BAD NEWS. HE PICKS FIGHTS WITH EVERYONE.
Bad news?!
I SUGGEST YOU STAY AWAY FROM HIM.
THANKS.
I DOUBT OUR PATHS WILL CROSS ANYWAY.

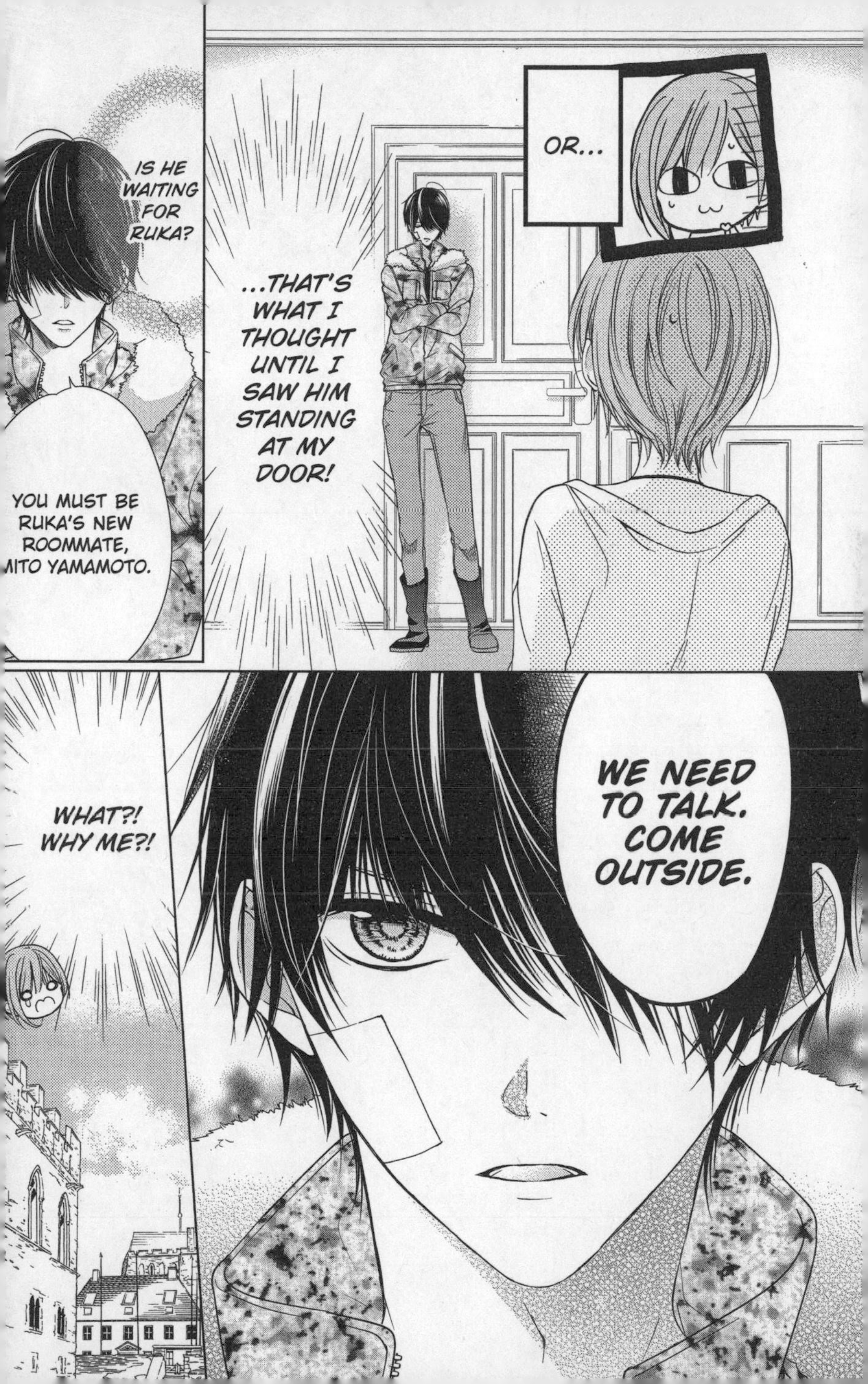
OR...
...THAT'S WHAT I THOUGHT UNTIL I SAW HIM STANDING AT MY DOOR!
IS HE WAITING FOR RUKA?
YOU MUST BE RUKA'S NEW ROOMMATE, MITO YAMAMOTO.
WE NEED TO TALK. COME OUTSIDE.
WHAT?! WHY ME?!

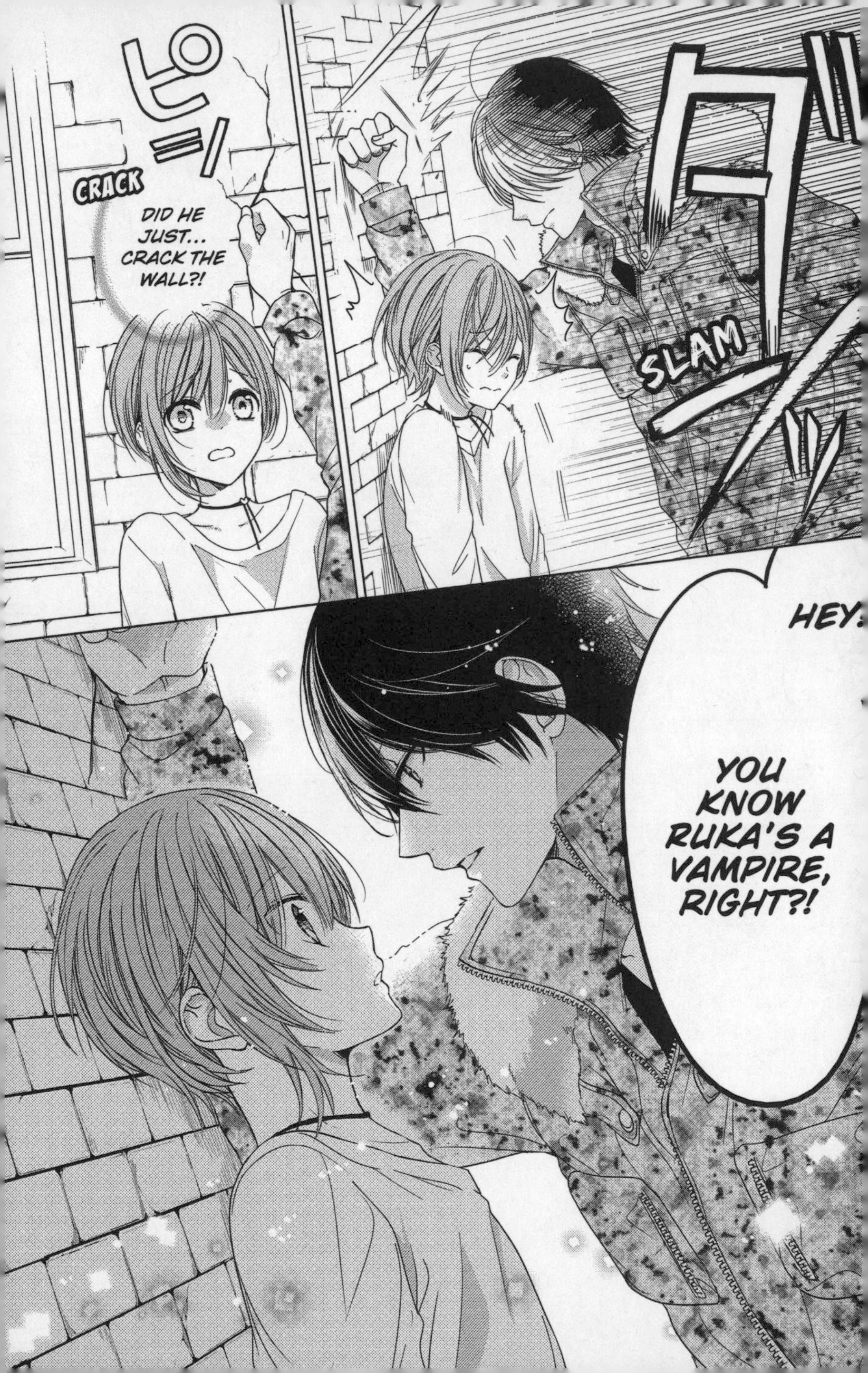
SLAM
CRACK
DID HE JUST... CRACK THE WALL?!
HEY!
YOU KNOW RUKA'S A VAMPIRE, RIGHT?!

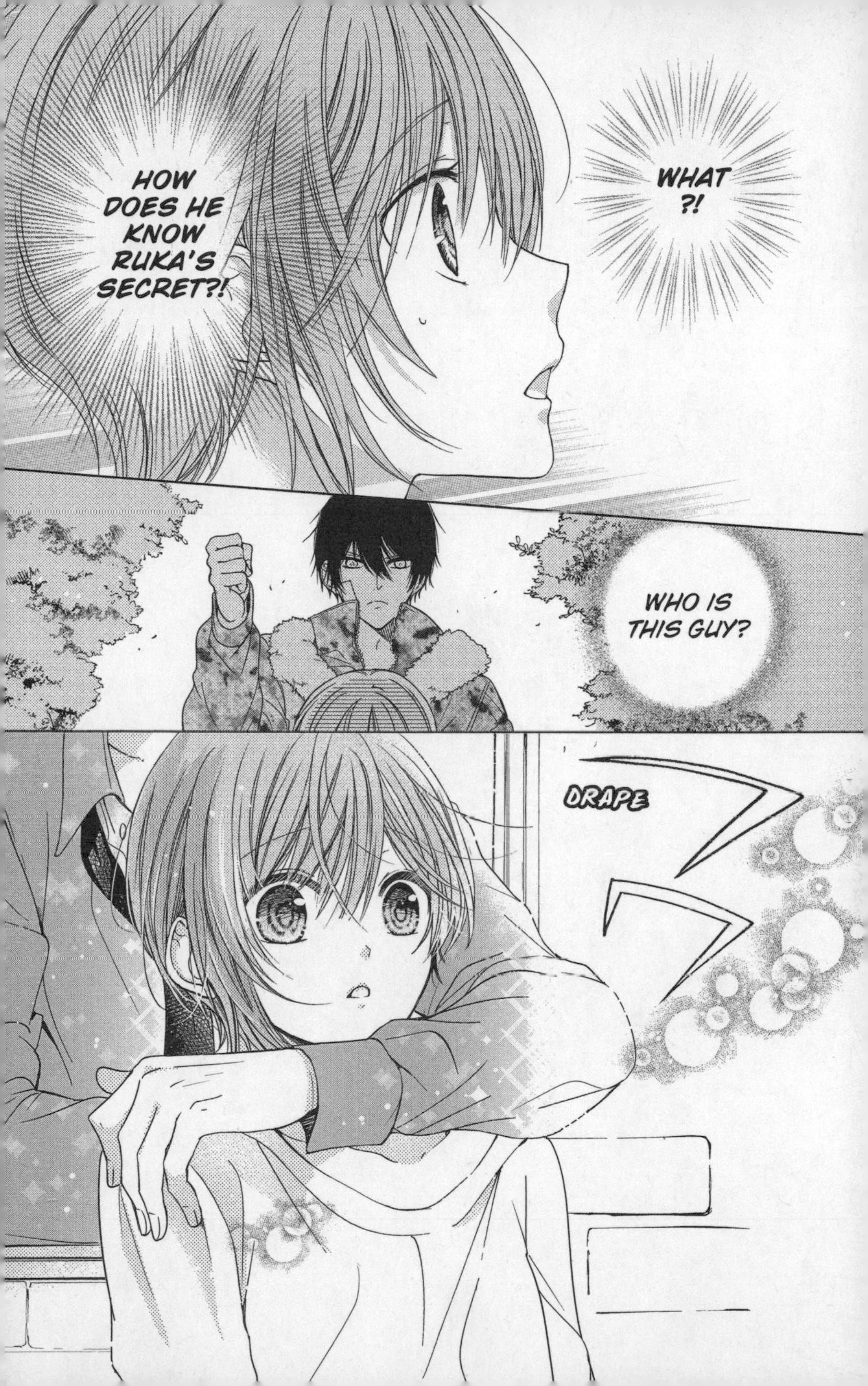
WHAT ?!
HOW DOES HE KNOW RUKA'S SECRET?!
WHO IS THIS GUY?
DRAPE

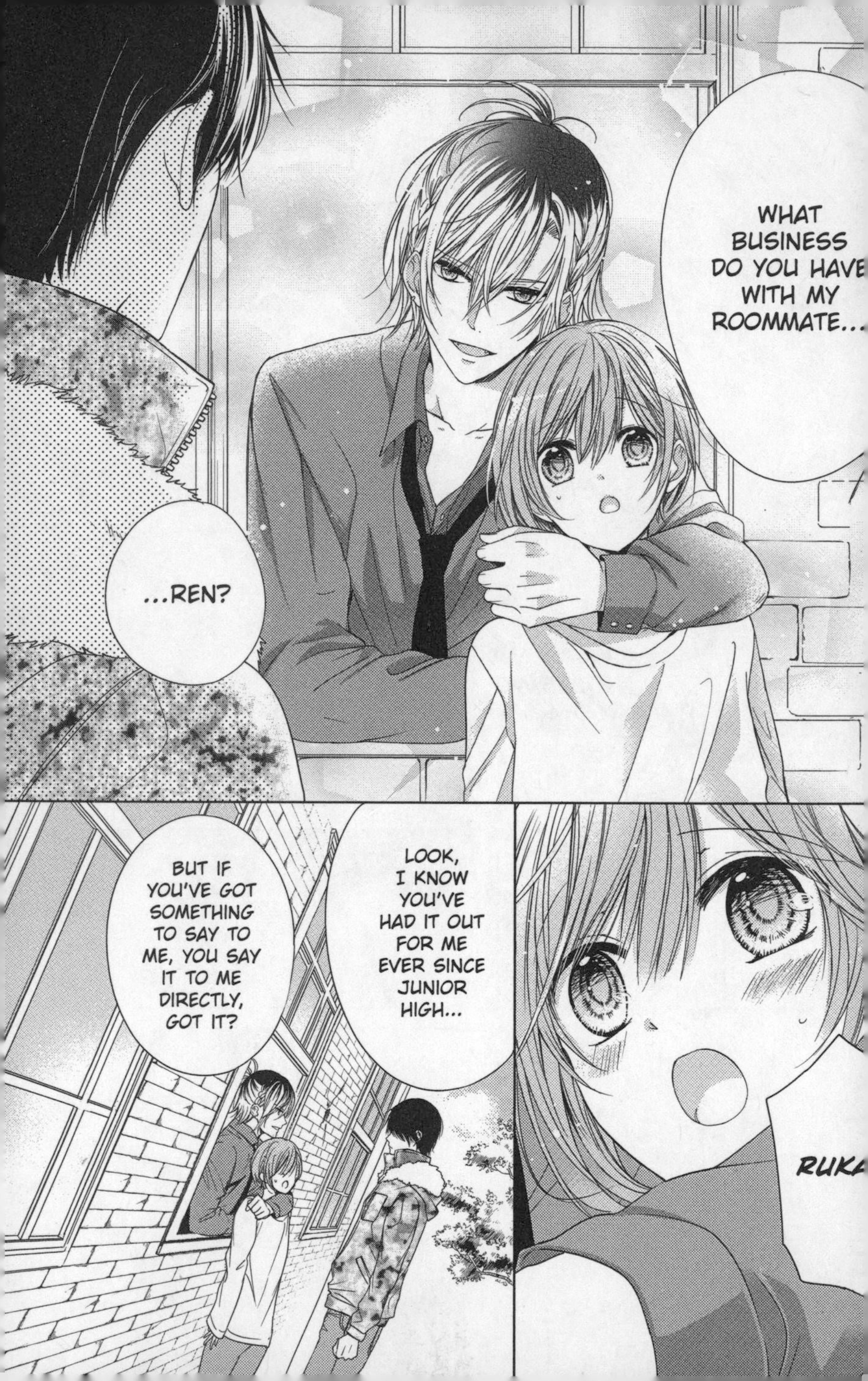
WHAT BUSINESS DO YOU HAVE WITH MY ROOMMATE...
...REN?
RUKA
LOOK, I KNOW YOU'VE HAD IT OUT FOR ME EVER SINCE JUNIOR HIGH...
BUT IF YOU'VE GOT SOMETHING TO SAY TO ME, YOU SAY IT TO ME DIRECTLY, GOT IT?

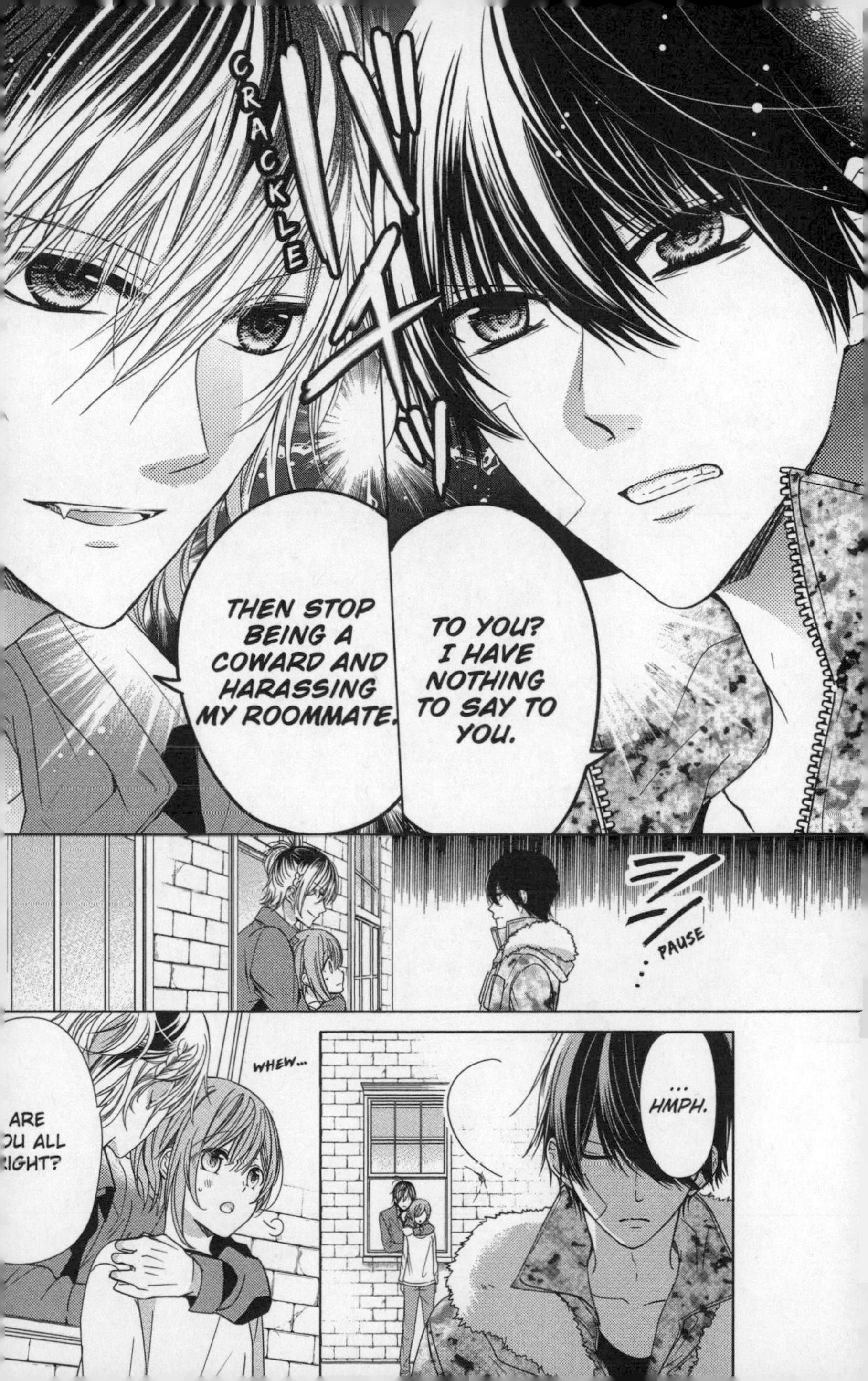
CRACKLE
TO YOU? I HAVE NOTHING TO SAY TO YOU.
THEN STOP BEING A COWARD AND HARASSING MY ROOMMATE.
... PAUSE
... HMPH.
WHEW...
ARE OU ALL IGHT?

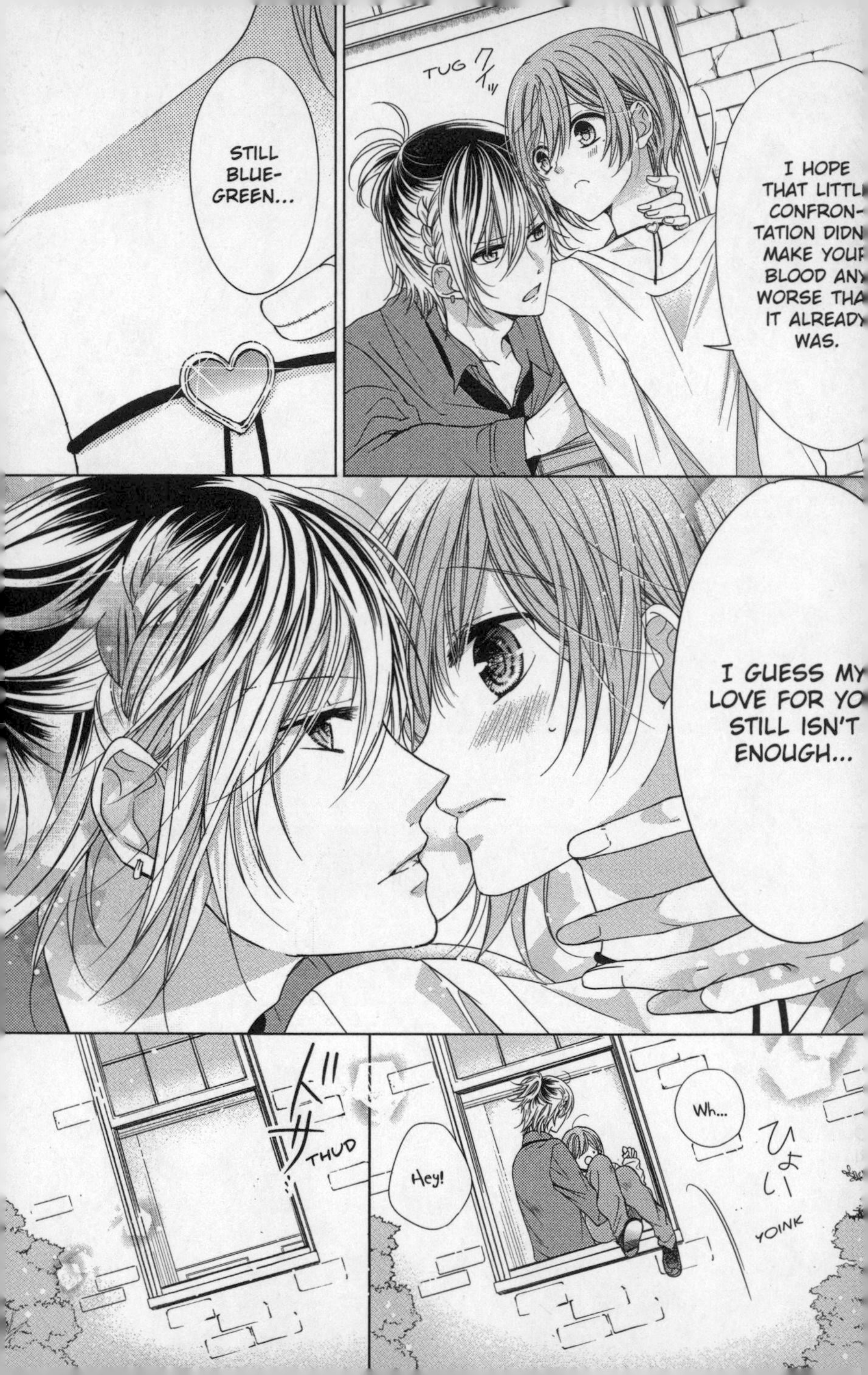
TUG
I HOPE THAT LITTL CONFRON- TATION DIDN MAKE YOUR BLOOD ANY WORSE THA IT ALREADY WAS.
STILL BLUE- GREEN...
I GUESS MY LOVE FOR YO STILL ISN'T ENOUGH...
Wh...
ひょい
YOINK
Hey!
THUD

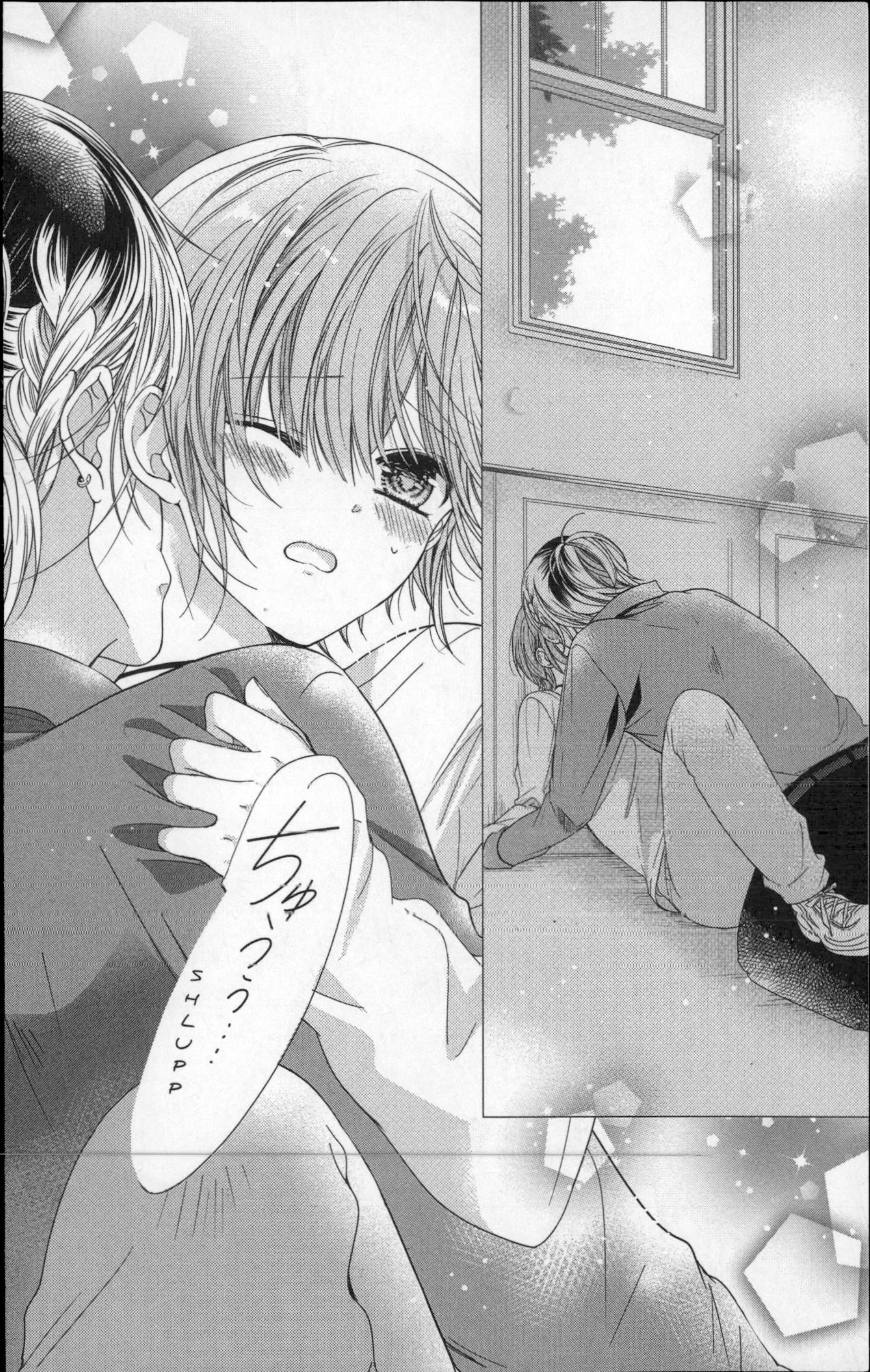

ちゅっっ…
SHLUPP

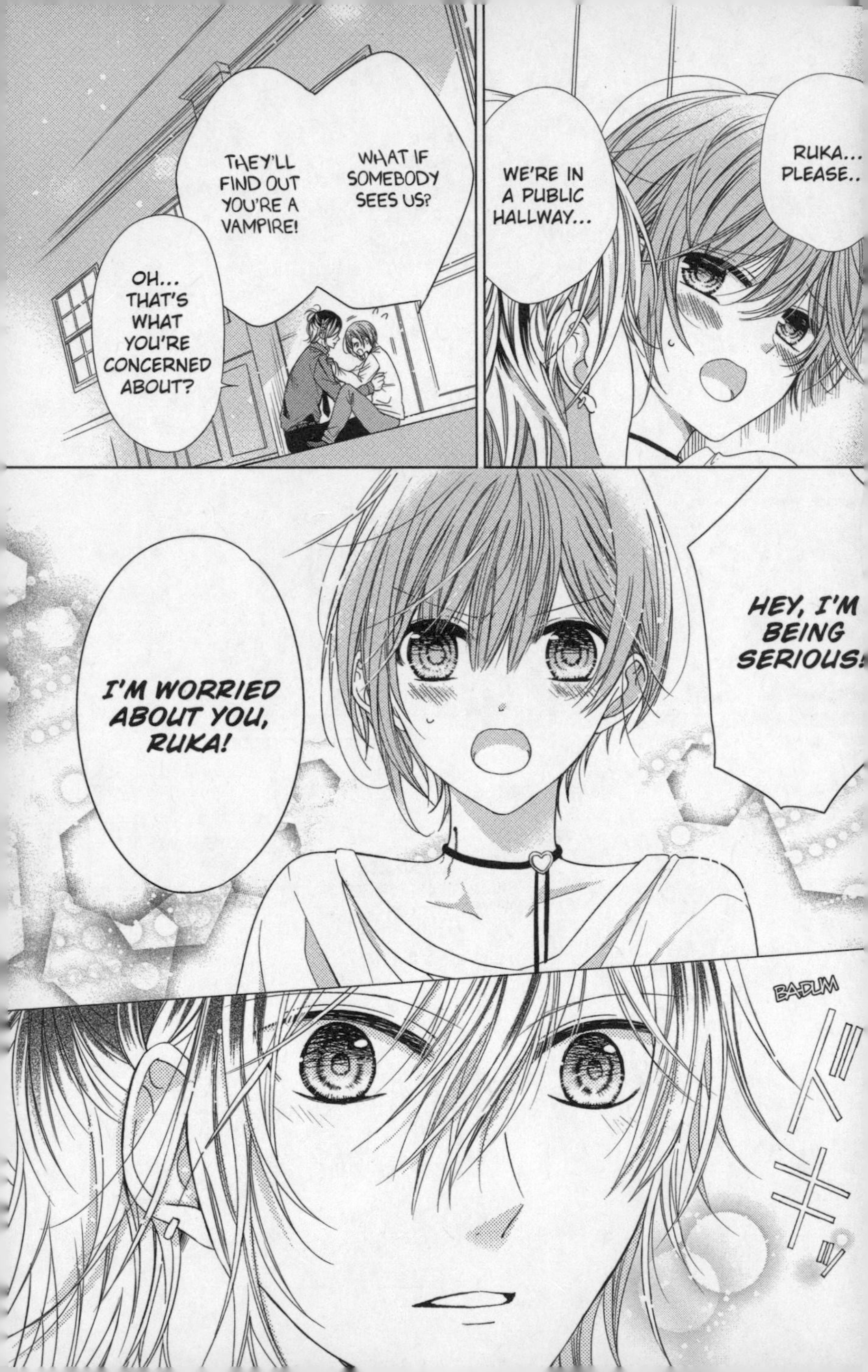
RUKA... PLEASE..
WE'RE IN A PUBLIC HALLWAY...
WHAT IF SOMEBODY SEES US?
THEY'LL FIND OUT YOU'RE A VAMPIRE!
OH... THAT'S WHAT YOU'RE CONCERNED ABOUT?
HEY, I'M BEING SERIOUS!
I'M WORRIED ABOUT YOU, RUKA!
BA-DUM

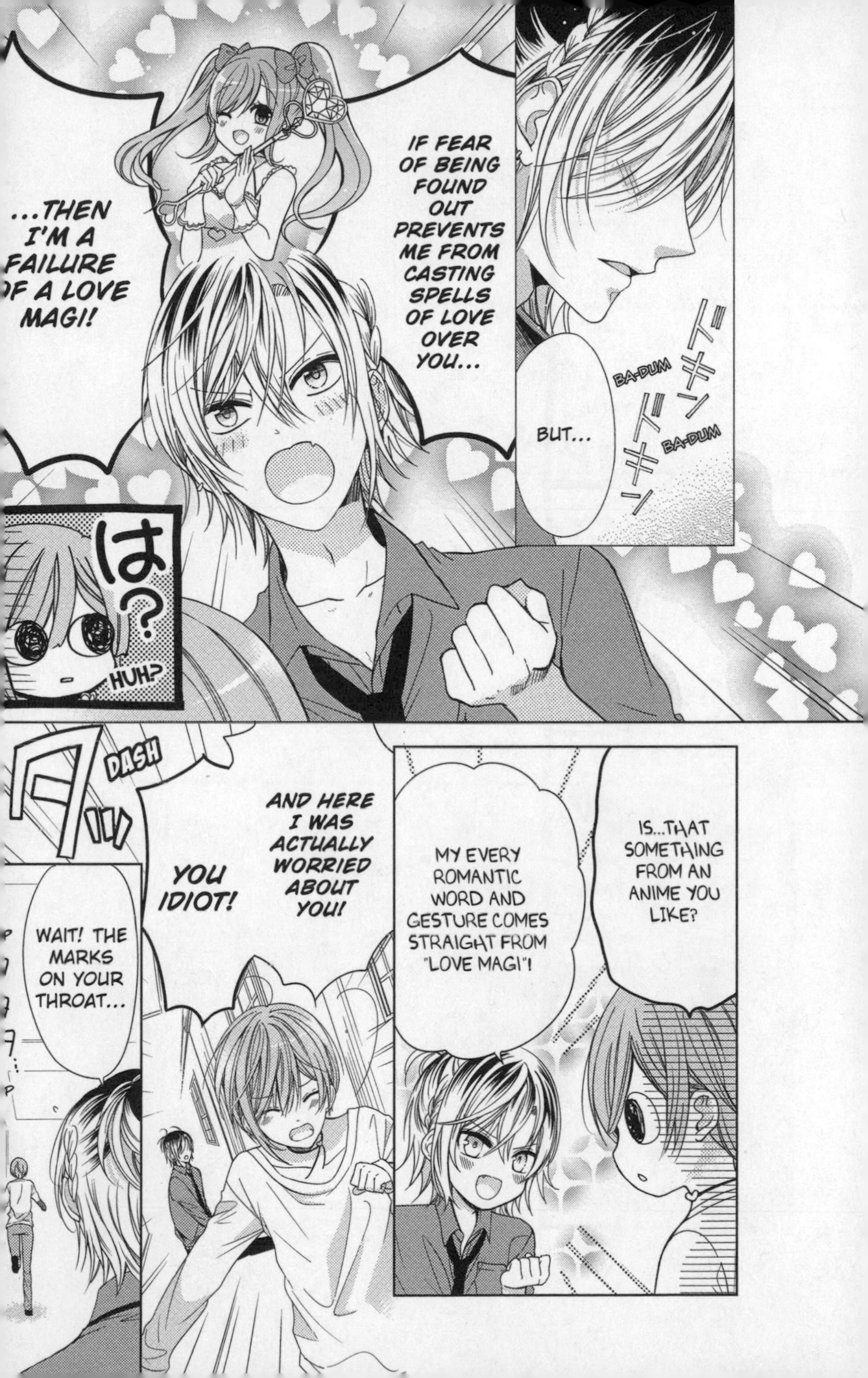
BUT...
ドキン BA-DUM
ドキン BA-DUM
IF FEAR OF BEING FOUND OUT PREVENTS ME FROM CASTING SPELLS OF LOVE OVER YOU...
...THEN I'M A FAILURE OF A LOVE MAGI!
は? HUH?
IS...THAT SOMETHING FROM AN ANIME YOU LIKE?
MY EVERY ROMANTIC WORD AND GESTURE COMES STRAIGHT FROM "LOVE MAGI"!
AND HERE I WAS ACTUALLY WORRIED ABOUT YOU!
YOU IDIOT!
DASH
WAIT! THE MARKS ON YOUR THROAT...

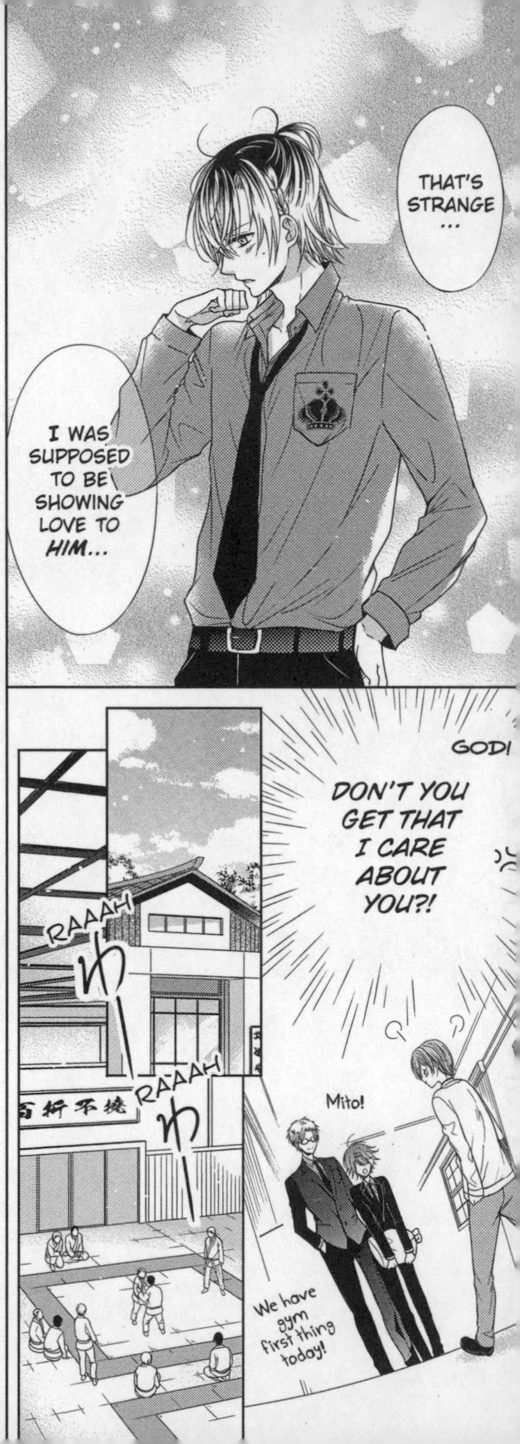
THAT'S STRANGE...
I WAS SUPPOSED TO BE SHOWING LOVE TO HIM...
GODI
DON'T YOU GET THAT I CARE ABOUT YOU?!
Mito!
We have gym first thing today!
RAAAH
RAAAH

②

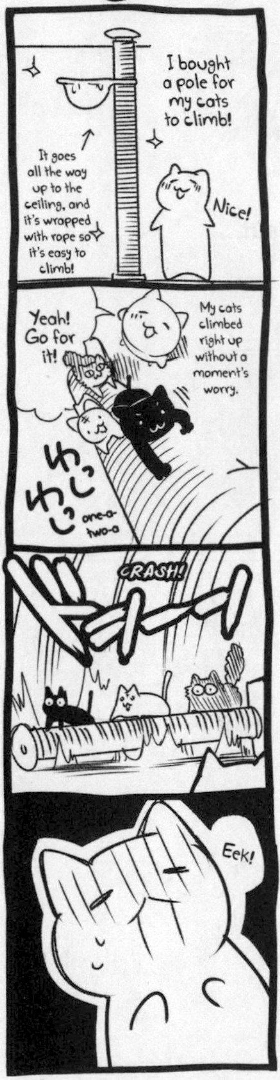
I bought a pole for my cats to climb!
It goes all the way up to the ceiling, and it's wrapped with rope so it's easy to climb!
Nice!
Yeah! Go for it!
My cats climbed right up without a moment's worry.
one-a-two-a
CRASH!
Eek!

I guess they were over the recommended weight...

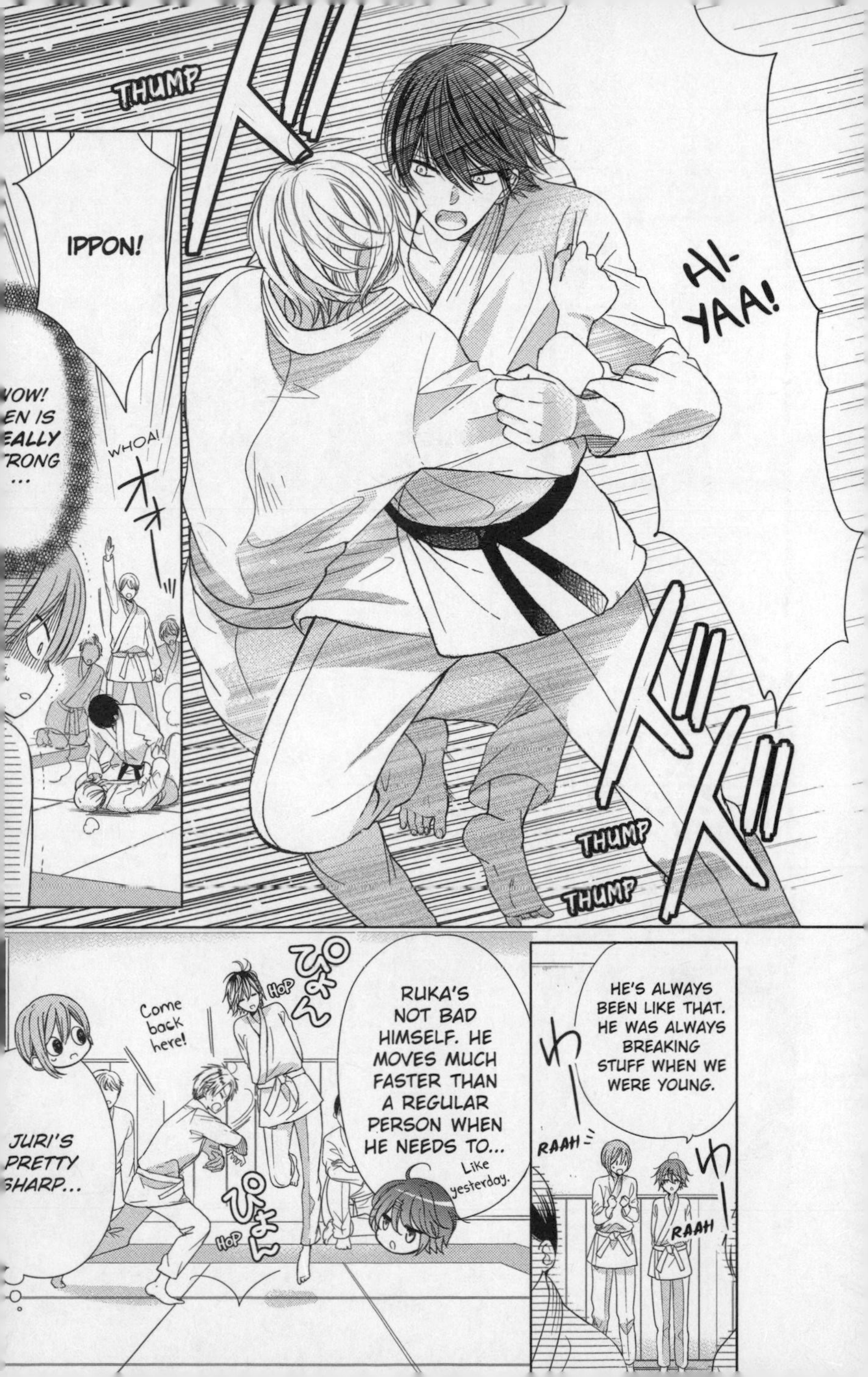
THUMP
HI-YAA!
THUMP
THUMP
IPPON!
WOW! EN IS EALLY TRONG ...
WHOA!
HE'S ALWAYS BEEN LIKE THAT. HE WAS ALWAYS BREAKING STUFF WHEN WE WERE YOUNG.
RAAH
RAAH
RUKA'S NOT BAD HIMSELF. HE MOVES MUCH FASTER THAN A REGULAR PERSON WHEN HE NEEDS TO...
Like yesterday.
HOP
Come back here!
HOP
JURI'S PRETTY SHARP...

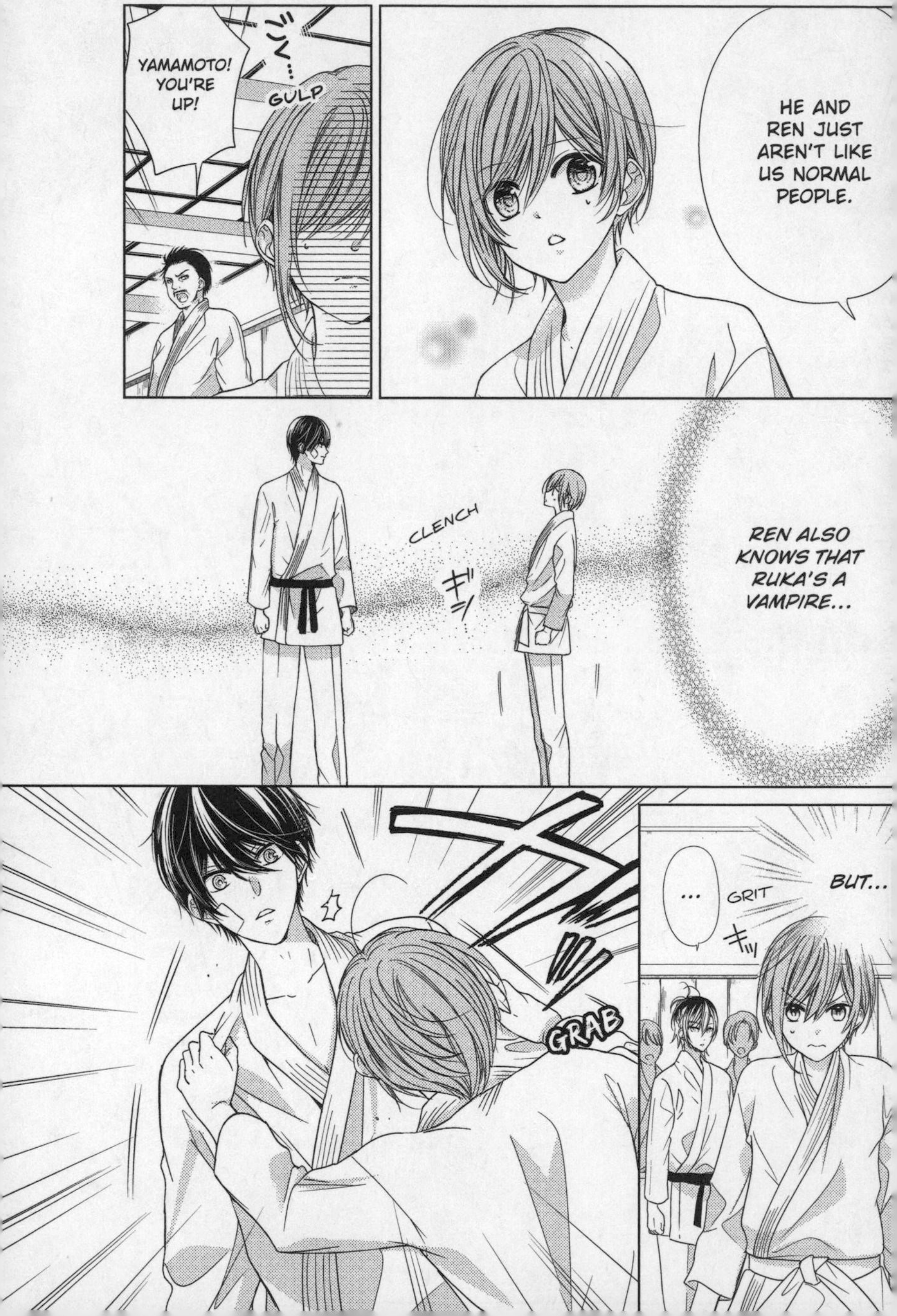
HE AND REN JUST AREN'T LIKE US NORMAL PEOPLE.
GULP
YAMAMOTO! YOU'RE UP!
REN ALSO KNOWS THAT RUKA'S A VAMPIRE...
CLENCH
BUT...
GRIT
...
GRAB

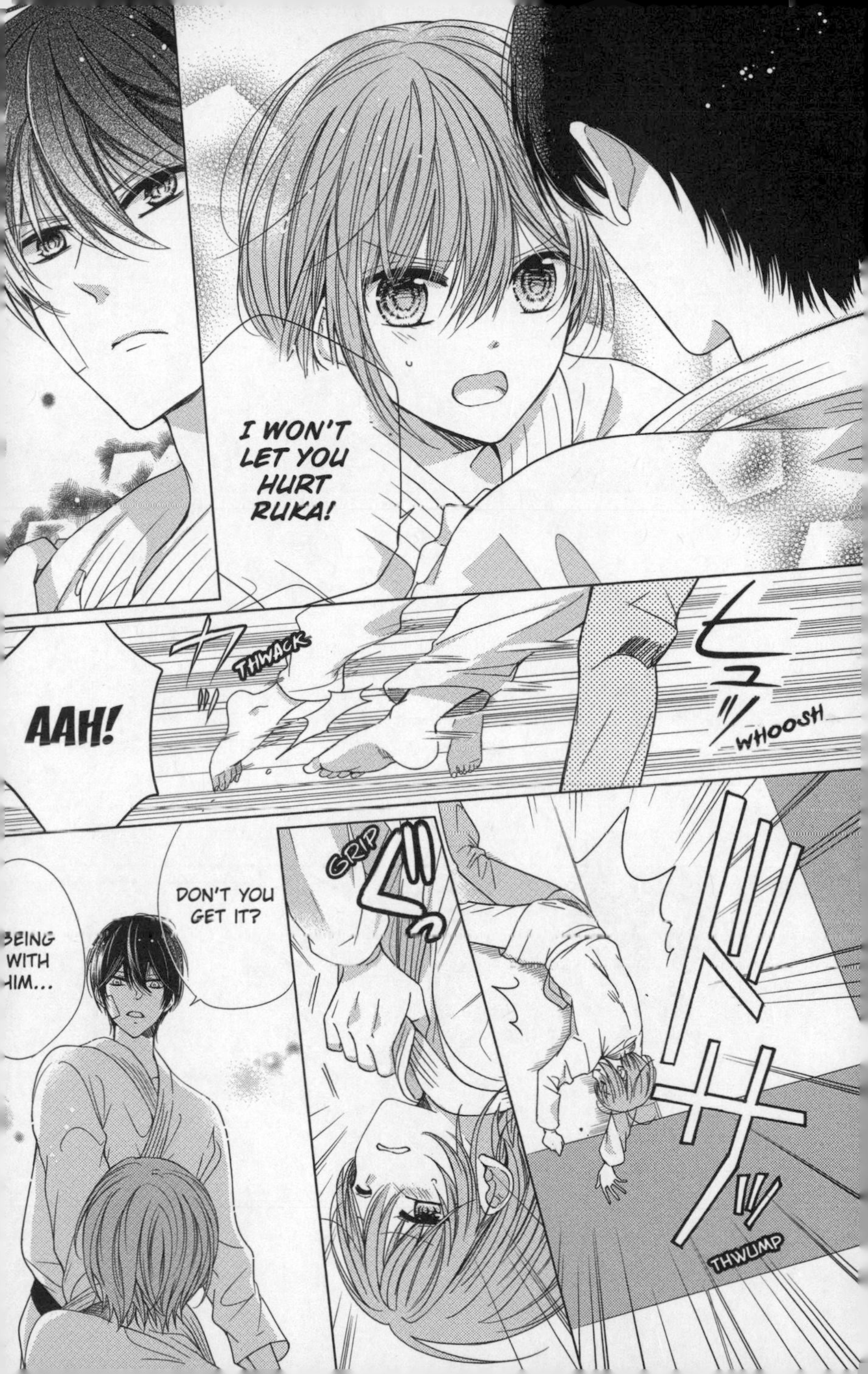
I WON'T LET YOU HURT RUKA!
WHOOSH
THWACK
AAH!
THWUMP
GRIP
DON'T YOU GET IT?
BEING WITH HIM...

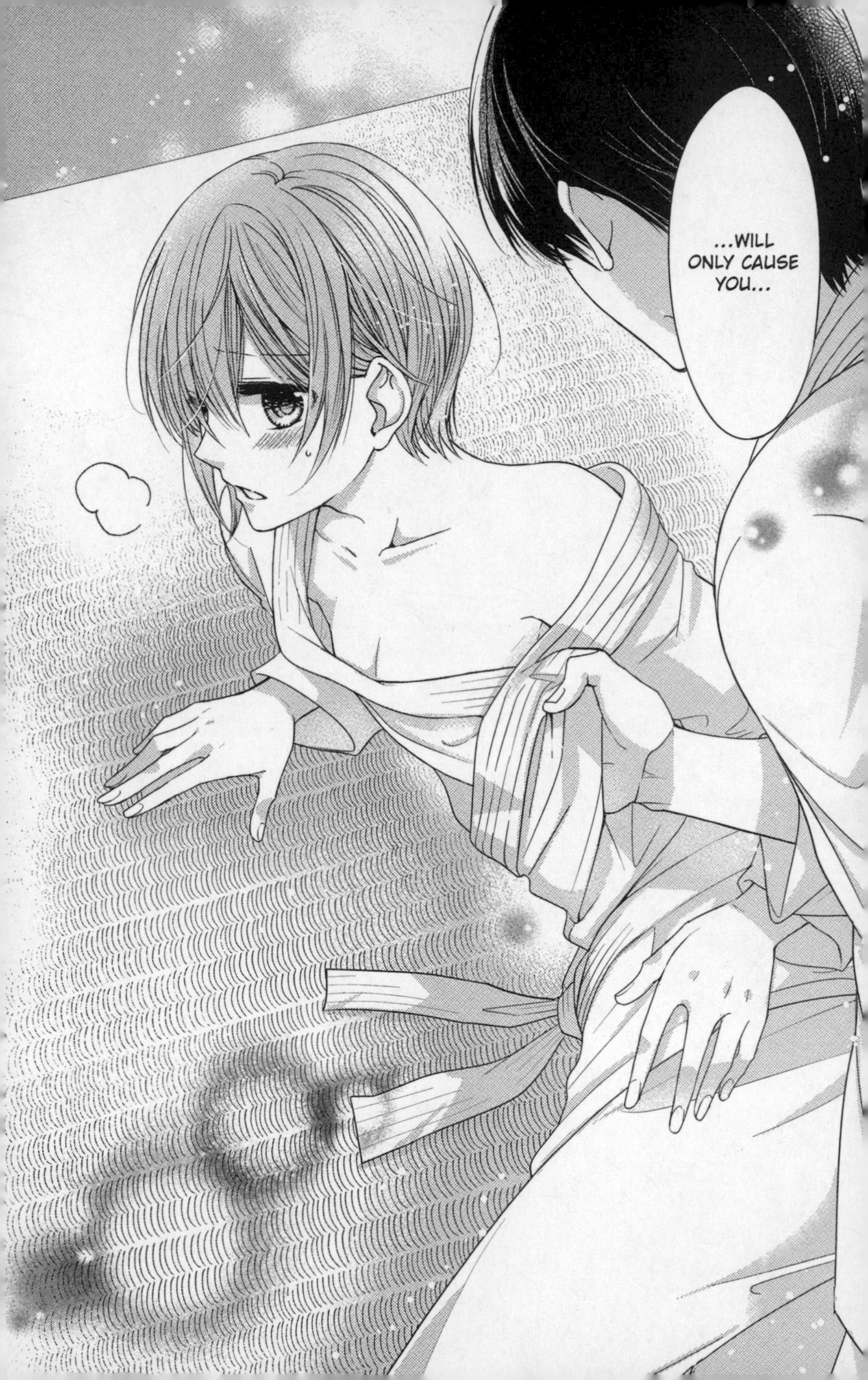
...WILL ONLY CAUSE YOU...

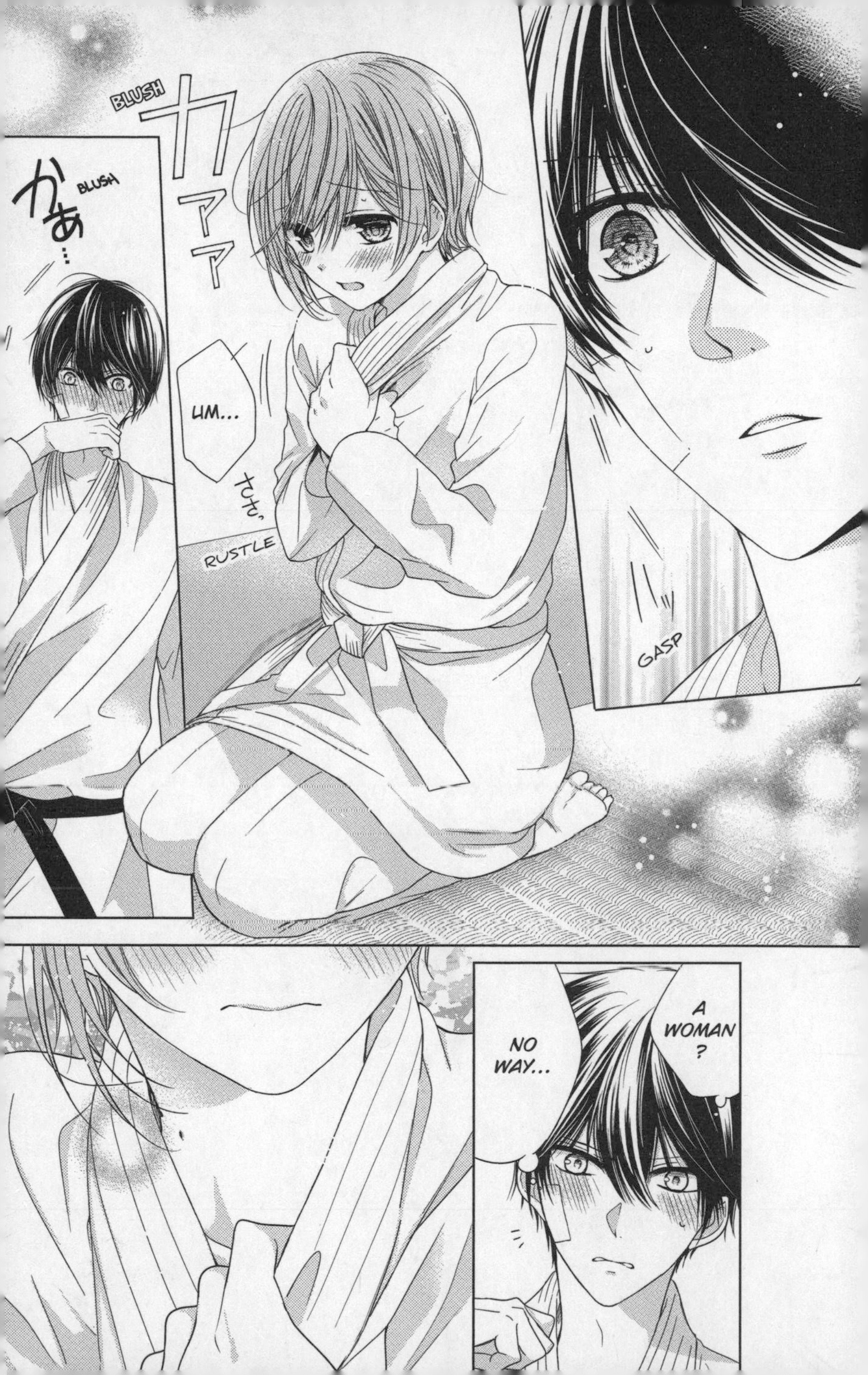

GASP
カァァ
BLUSH
UM...
ささ
RUSTLE
かあ…
BLUSH
A WOMAN?
NO WAY...

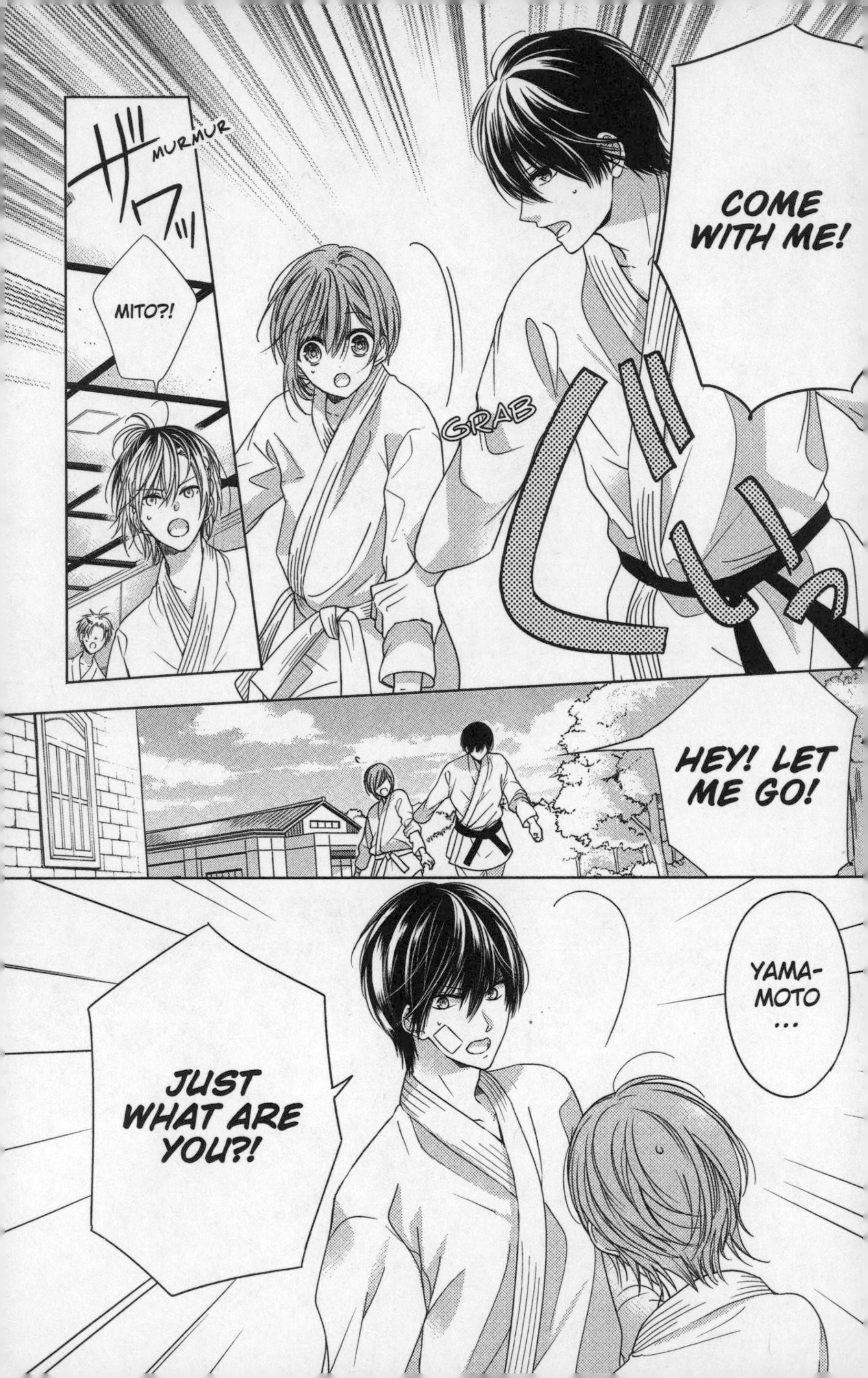
COME WITH ME!
GRAB
ザワッ
MURMUR
MITO?!
HEY! LET ME GO!
YAMA-MOTO...
JUST WHAT ARE YOU?!

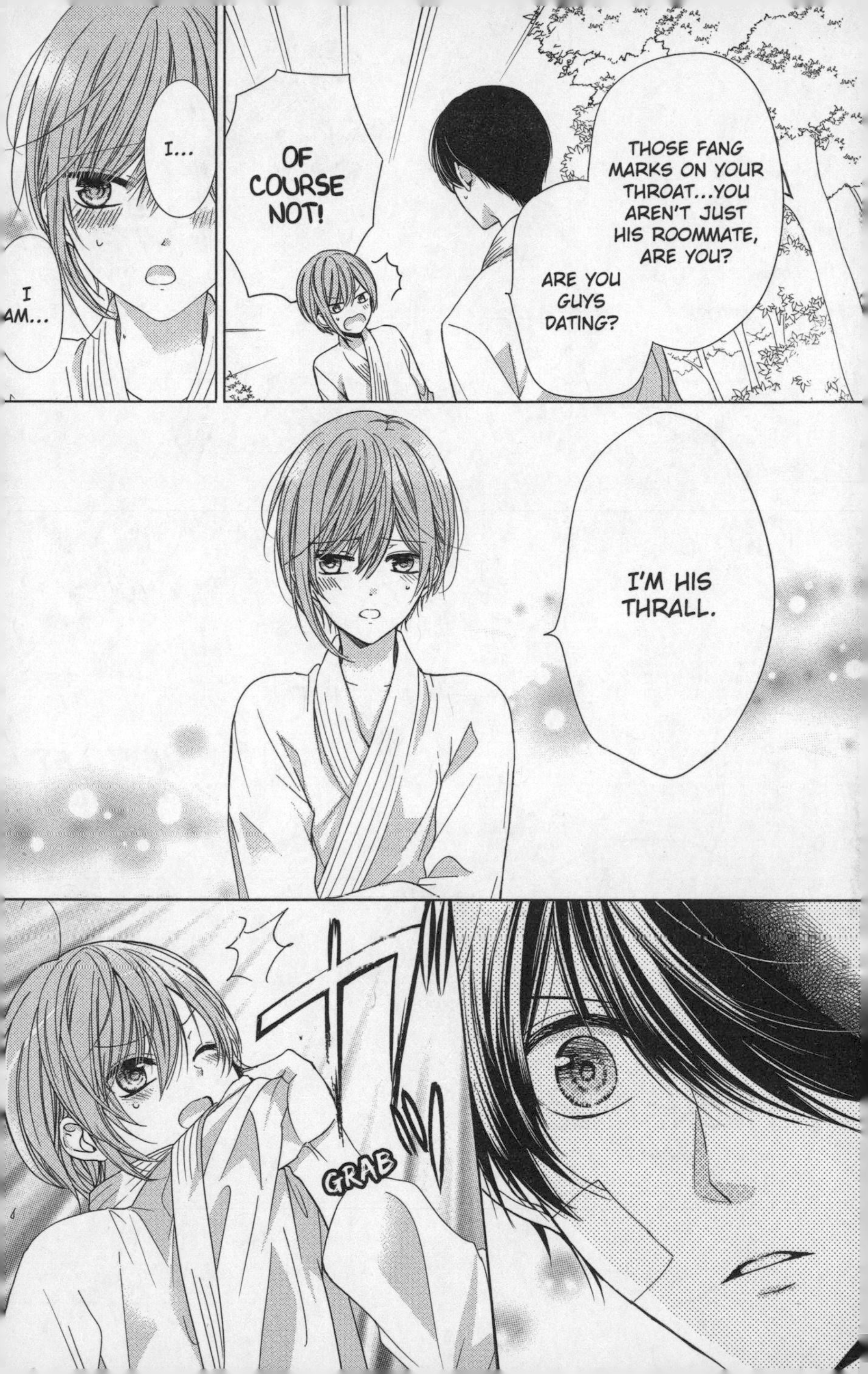
THOSE FANG MARKS ON YOUR THROAT...YOU AREN'T JUST HIS ROOMMATE, ARE YOU?
ARE YOU GUYS DATING?
OF COURSE NOT!
I...
I AM...
I'M HIS THRALL.
GRAB

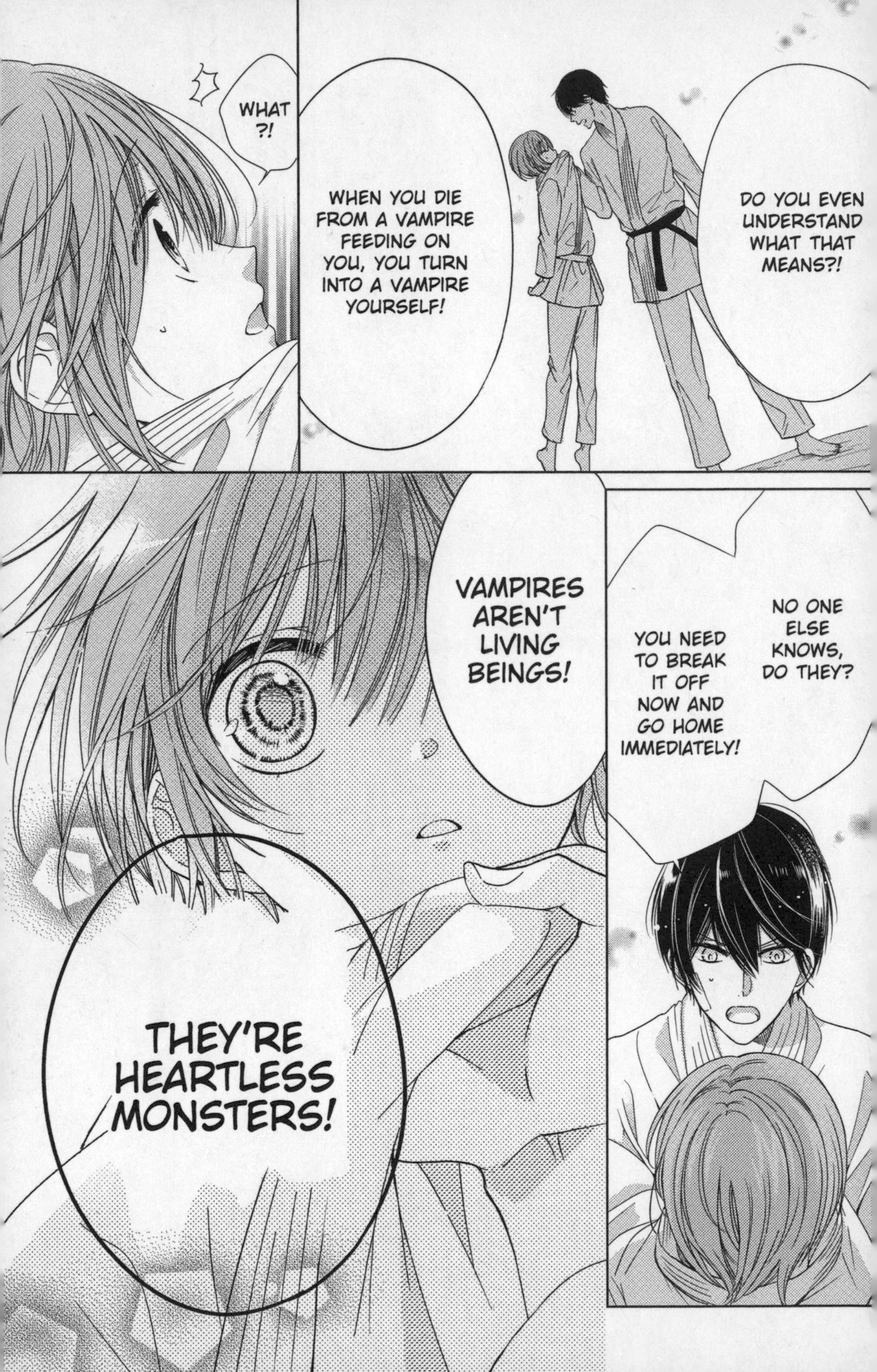
DO YOU EVEN UNDERSTAND WHAT THAT MEANS?!
WHEN YOU DIE FROM A VAMPIRE FEEDING ON YOU, YOU TURN INTO A VAMPIRE YOURSELF!
WHAT ?!
NO ONE ELSE KNOWS, DO THEY?
YOU NEED TO BREAK IT OFF NOW AND GO HOME IMMEDIATELY!
VAMPIRES AREN'T LIVING BEINGS!
THEY'RE HEARTLESS MONSTERS!

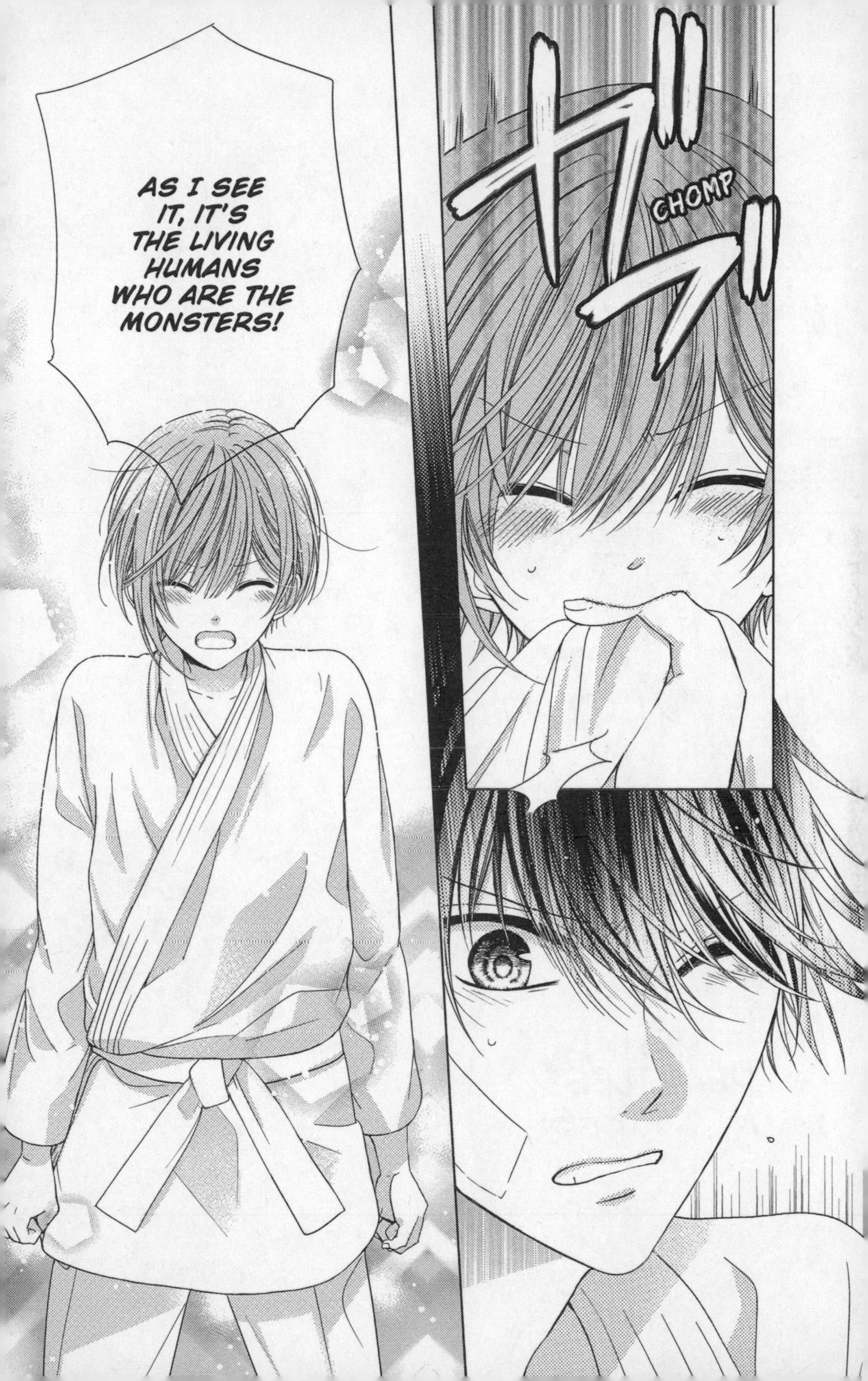
ガブ
CHOMP
AS I SEE IT, IT'S THE LIVING HUMANS WHO ARE THE MONSTERS!

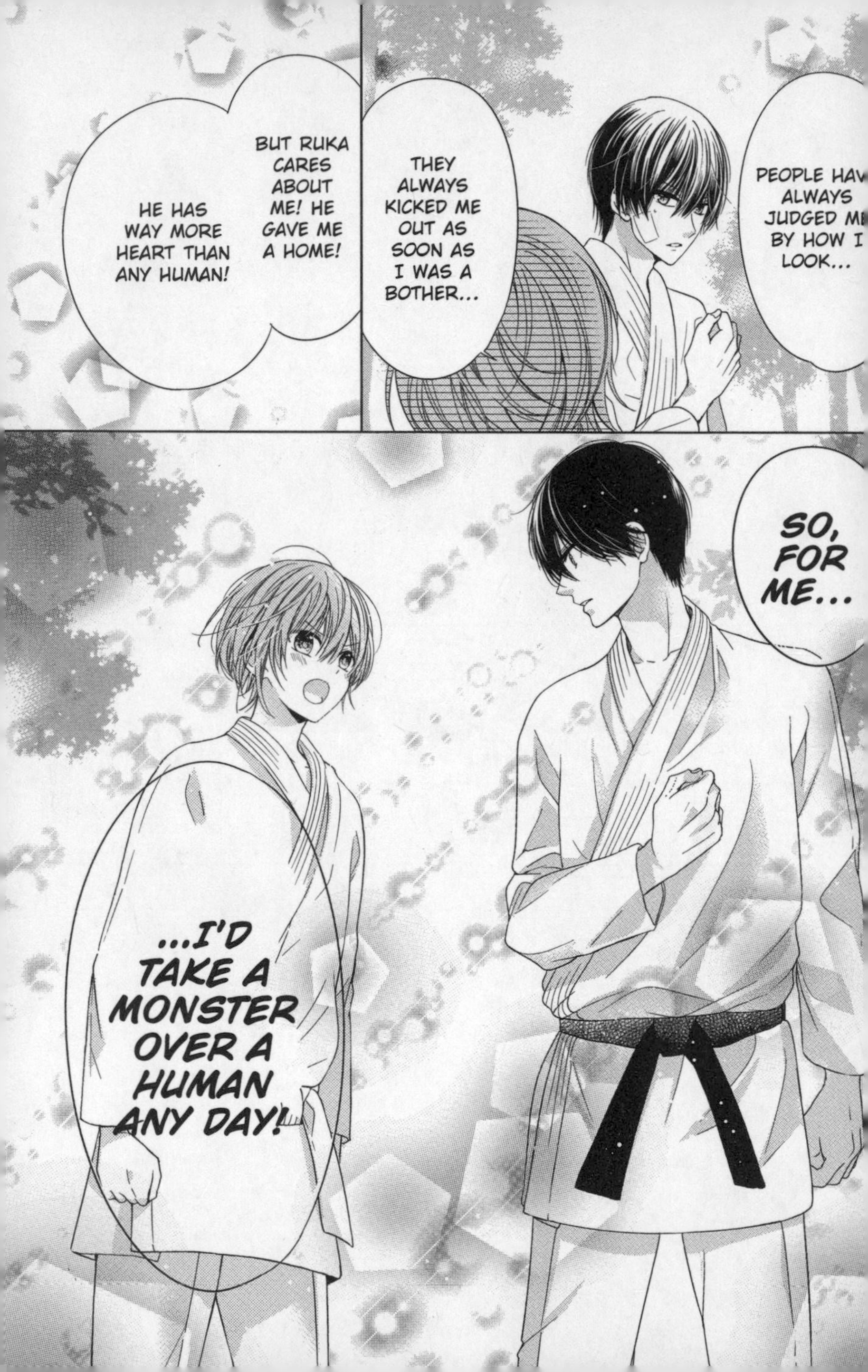
PEOPLE HAV ALWAYS JUDGED M BY HOW I LOOK...
THEY ALWAYS KICKED ME OUT AS SOON AS I WAS A BOTHER...
BUT RUKA CARES ABOUT ME! HE GAVE ME A HOME!
HE HAS WAY MORE HEART THAN ANY HUMAN!
SO, FOR ME...
...I'D TAKE A MONSTER OVER A HUMAN ANY DAY!

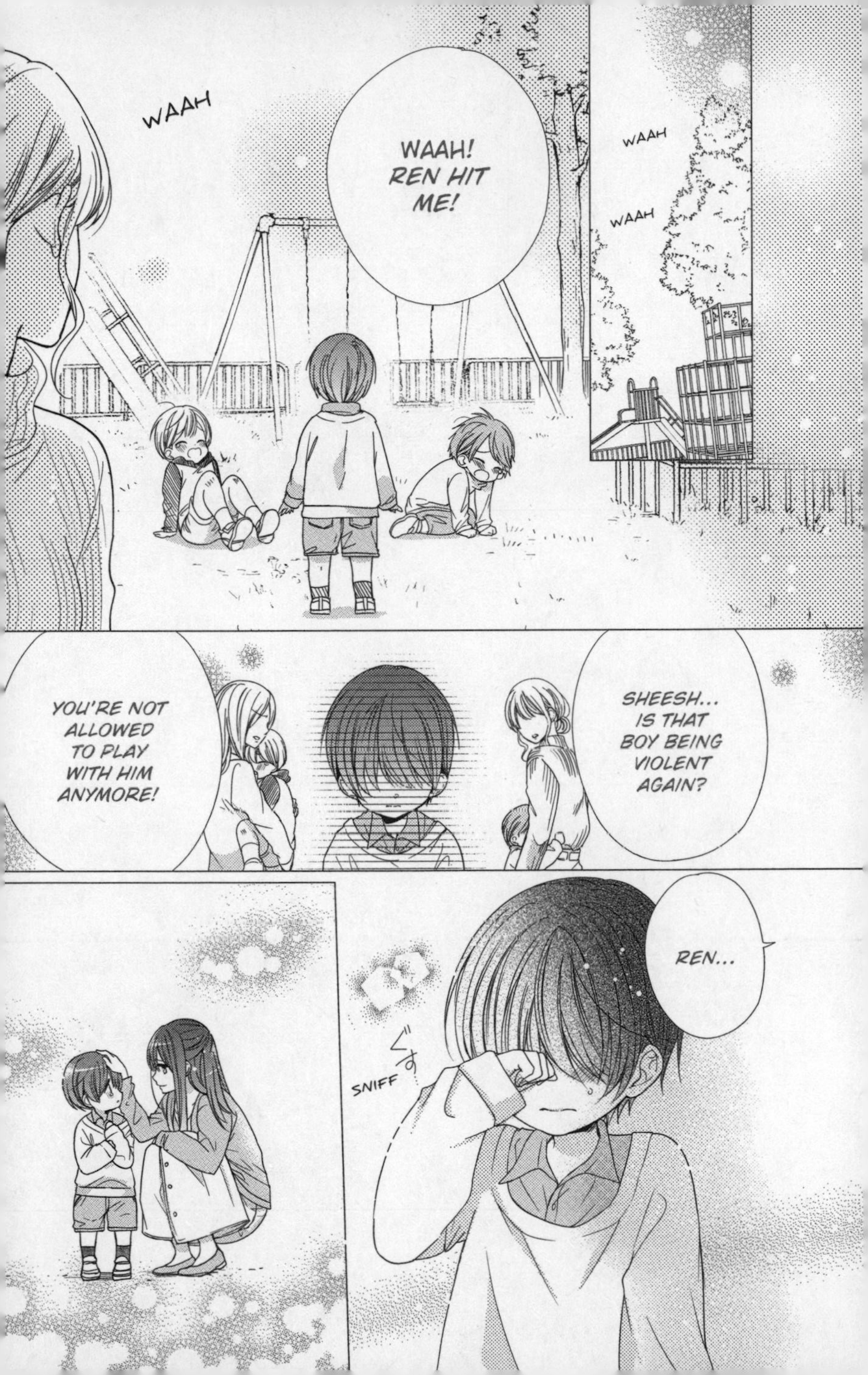
WAAH
WAAH
WAAH! REN HIT ME!
WAAH
SHEESH... IS THAT BOY BEING VIOLENT AGAIN?
YOU'RE NOT ALLOWED TO PLAY WITH HIM ANYMORE!
REN...
ぐす
SNIFF

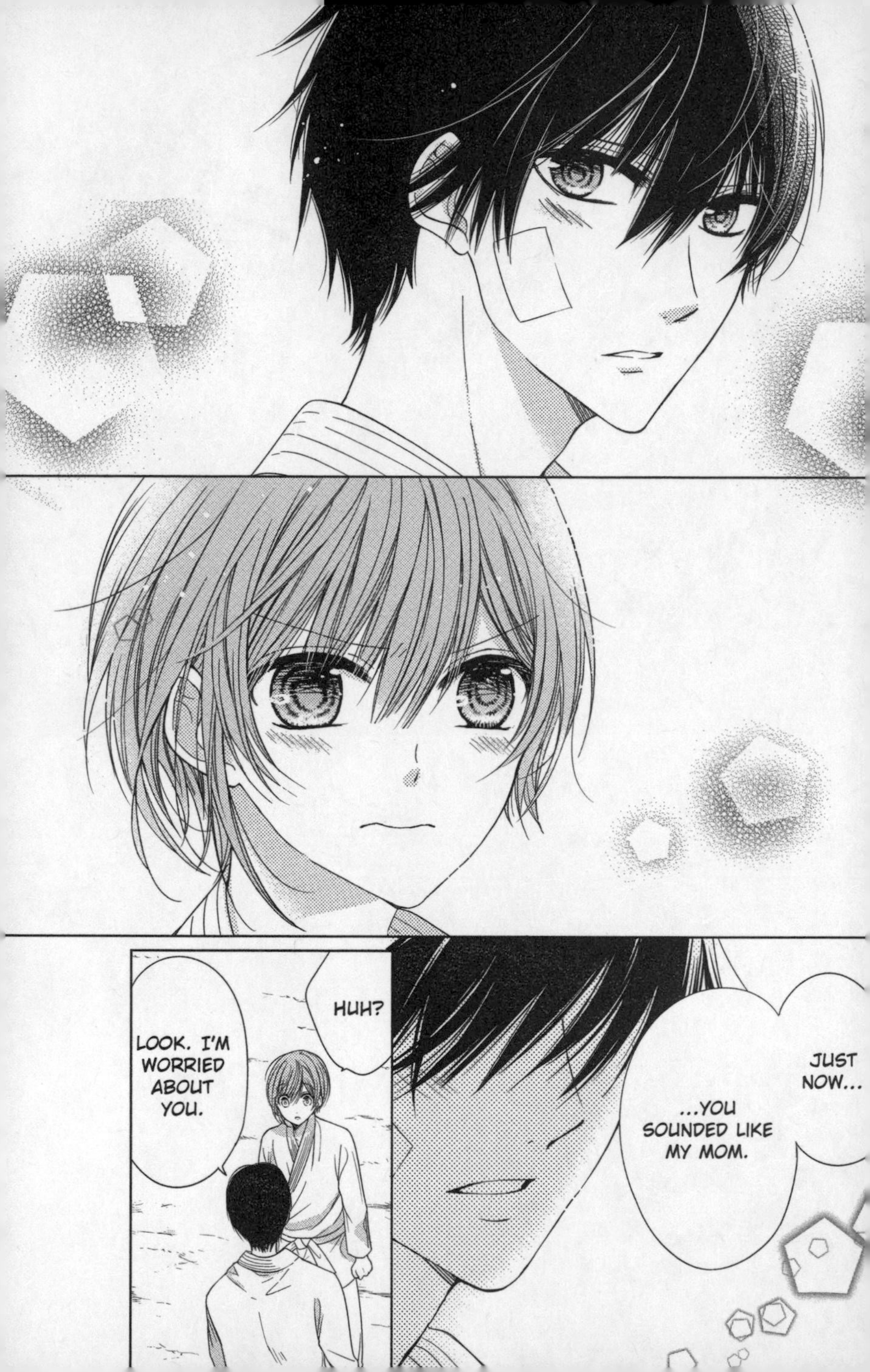
JUST NOW...
...YOU SOUNDED LIKE MY MOM.
HUH?
LOOK. I'M WORRIED ABOUT YOU.

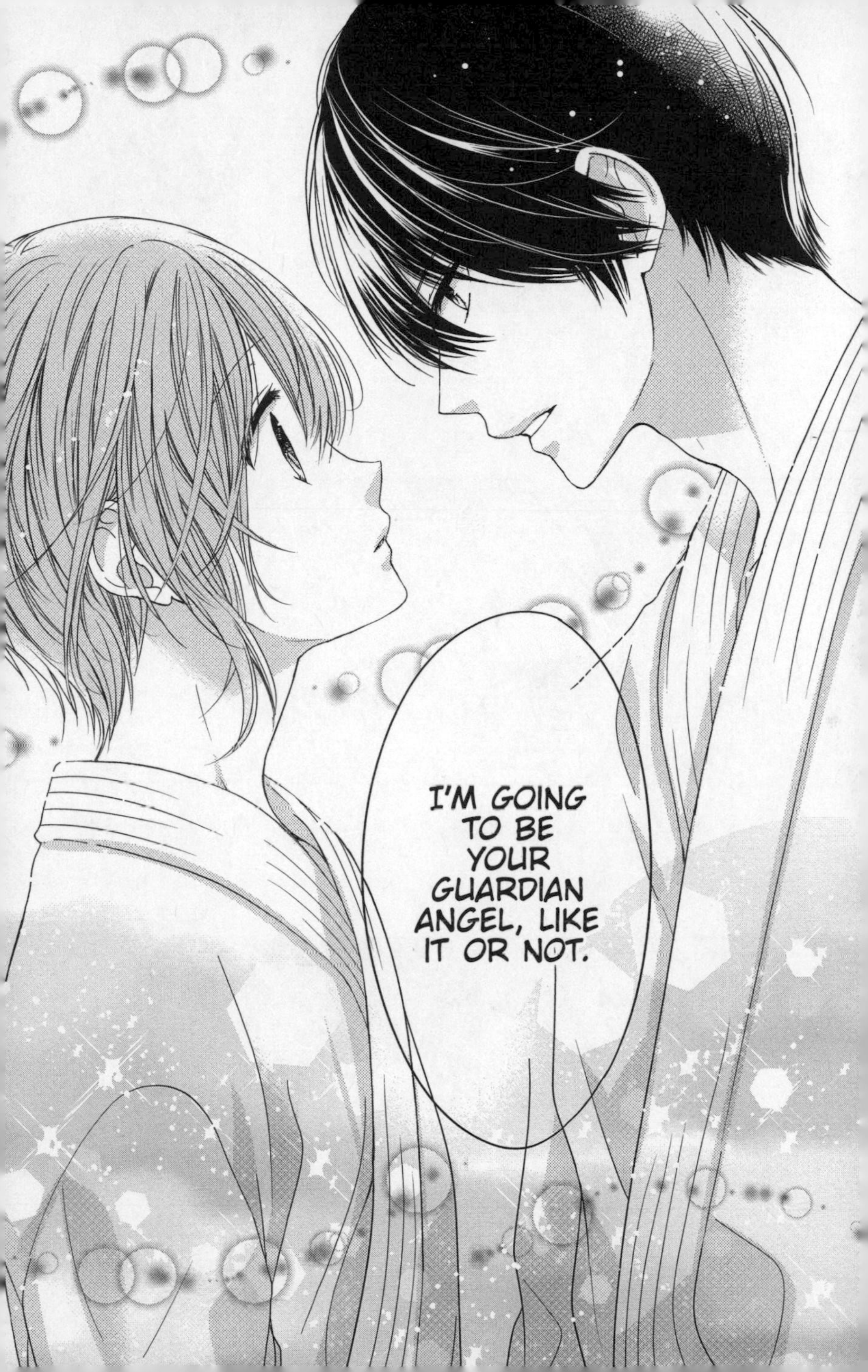
I'M GOING TO BE YOUR GUARDIAN ANGEL, LIKE IT OR NOT.

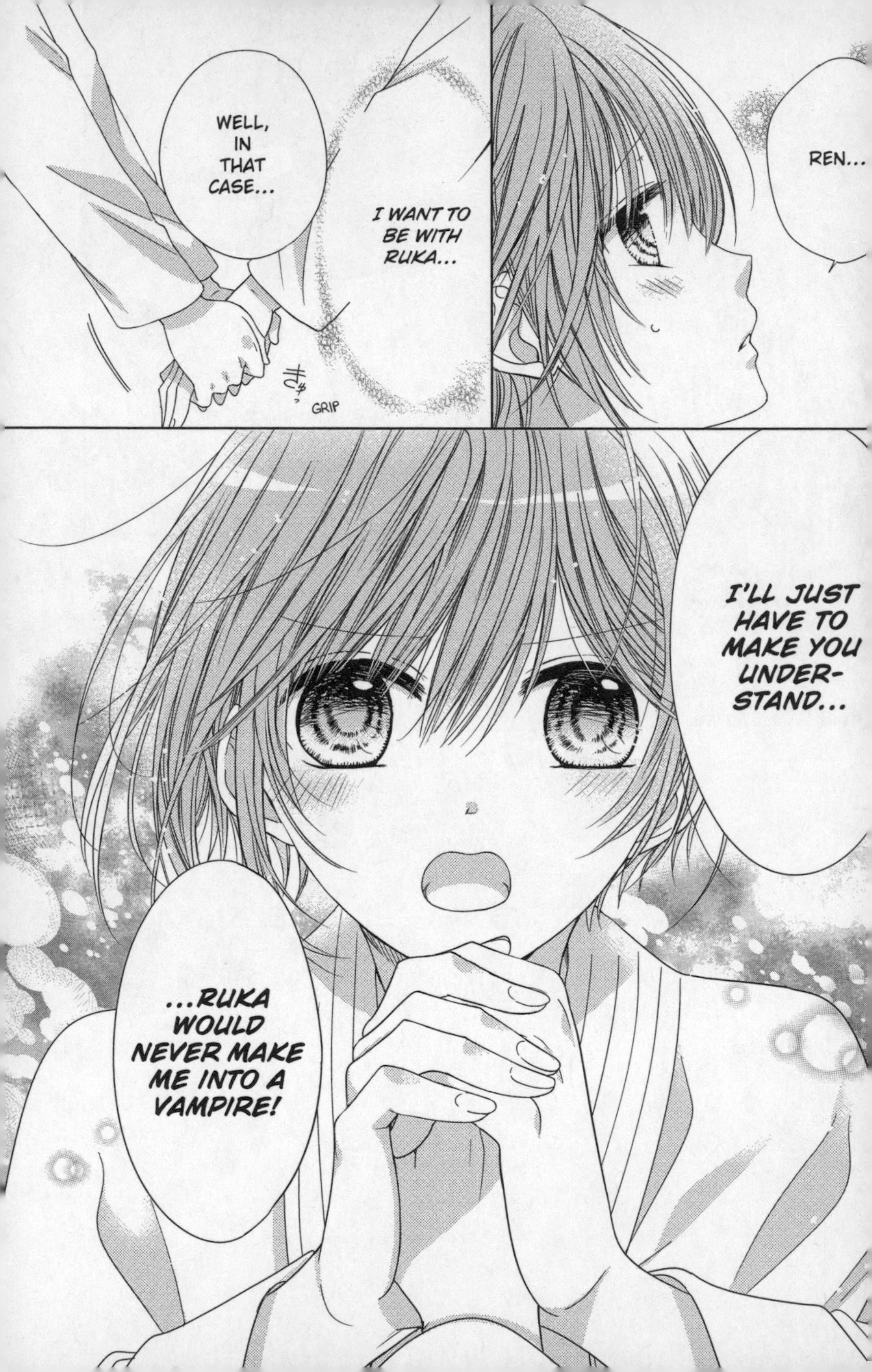
REN...
I WANT TO BE WITH RUKA...
WELL, IN THAT CASE...
GRIP
I'LL JUST HAVE TO MAKE YOU UNDER-STAND...
...RUKA WOULD NEVER MAKE ME INTO A VAMPIRE!

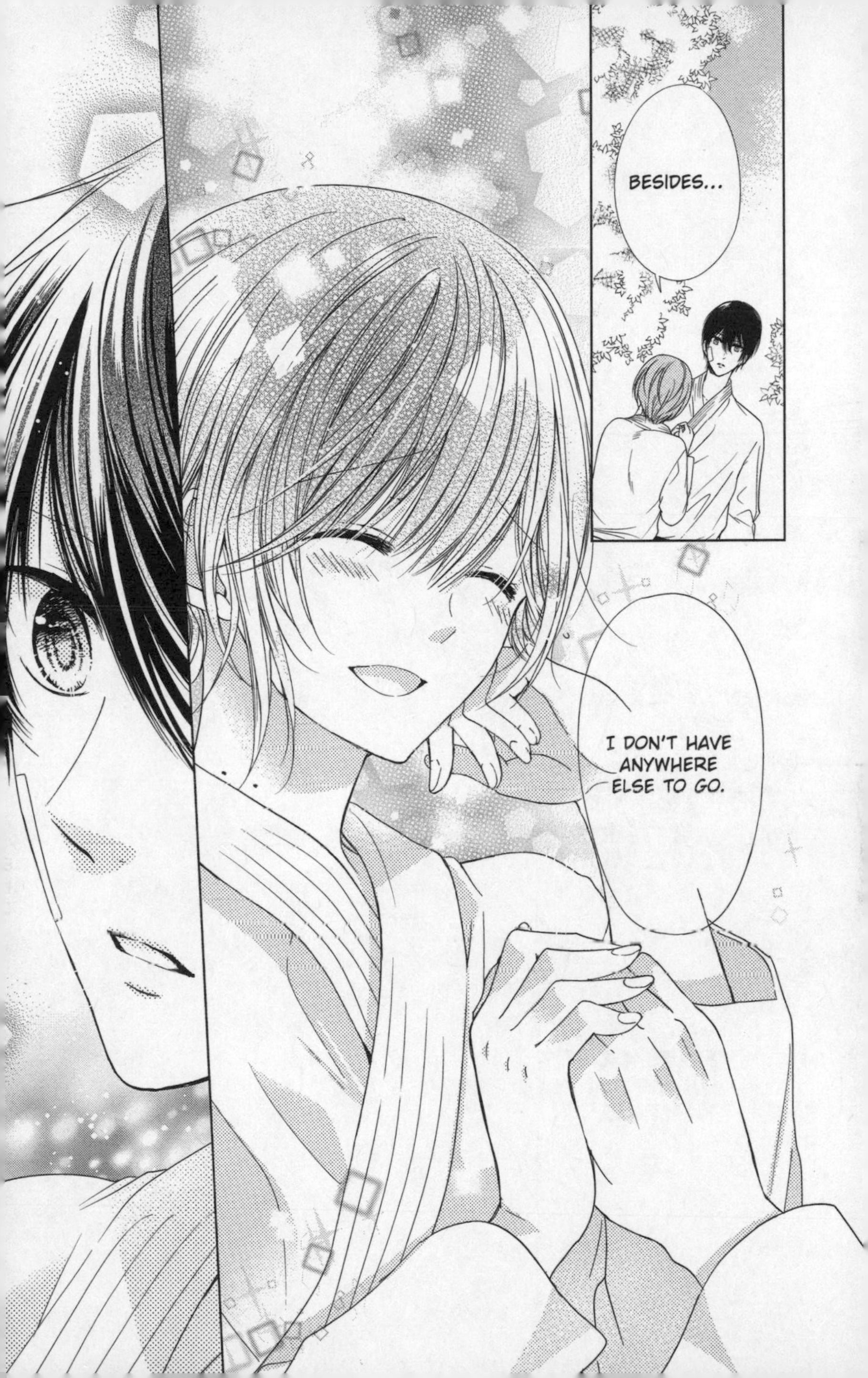
BESIDES...
I DON'T HAVE ANYWHERE ELSE TO GO.

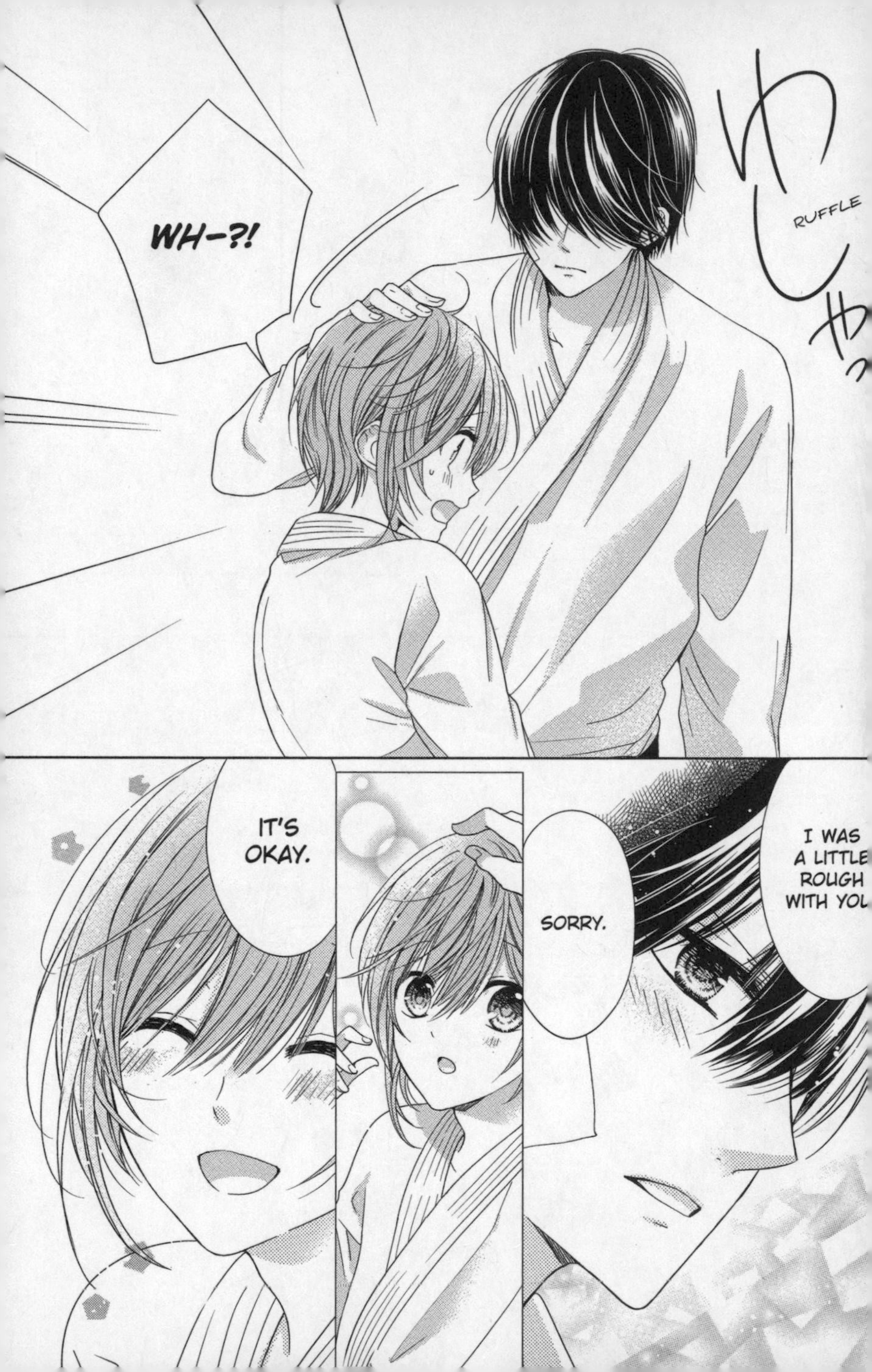
わしゃっ
RUFFLE
WH-?!
I WAS A LITTLE ROUGH WITH YOU
SORRY.
IT'S OKAY.

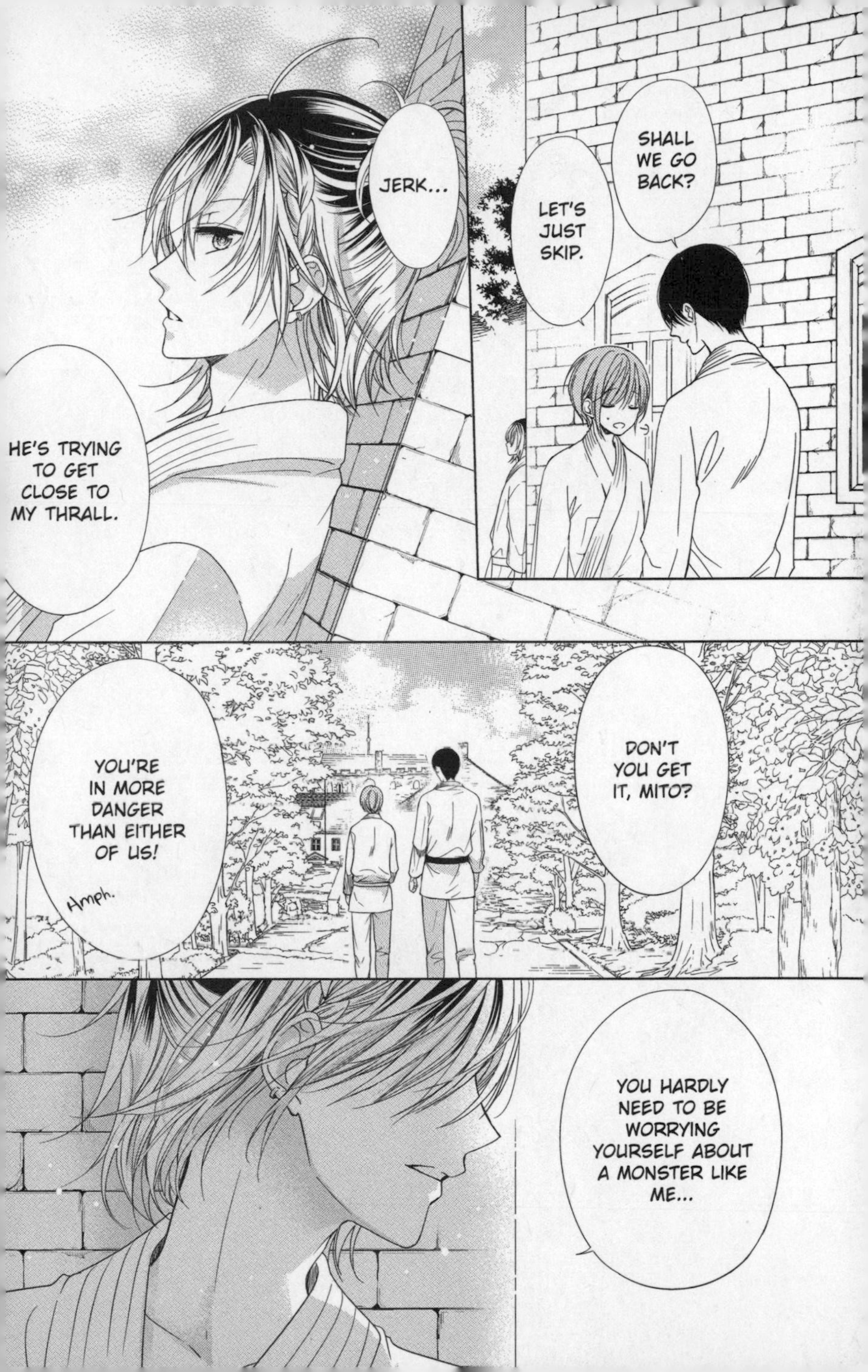
SHALL WE GO BACK?
LET'S JUST SKIP.
JERK...
HE'S TRYING TO GET CLOSE TO MY THRALL.
DON'T YOU GET IT, MITO?
YOU'RE IN MORE DANGER THAN EITHER OF US!
Hmph.
YOU HARDLY NEED TO BE WORRYING YOURSELF ABOUT A MONSTER LIKE ME...

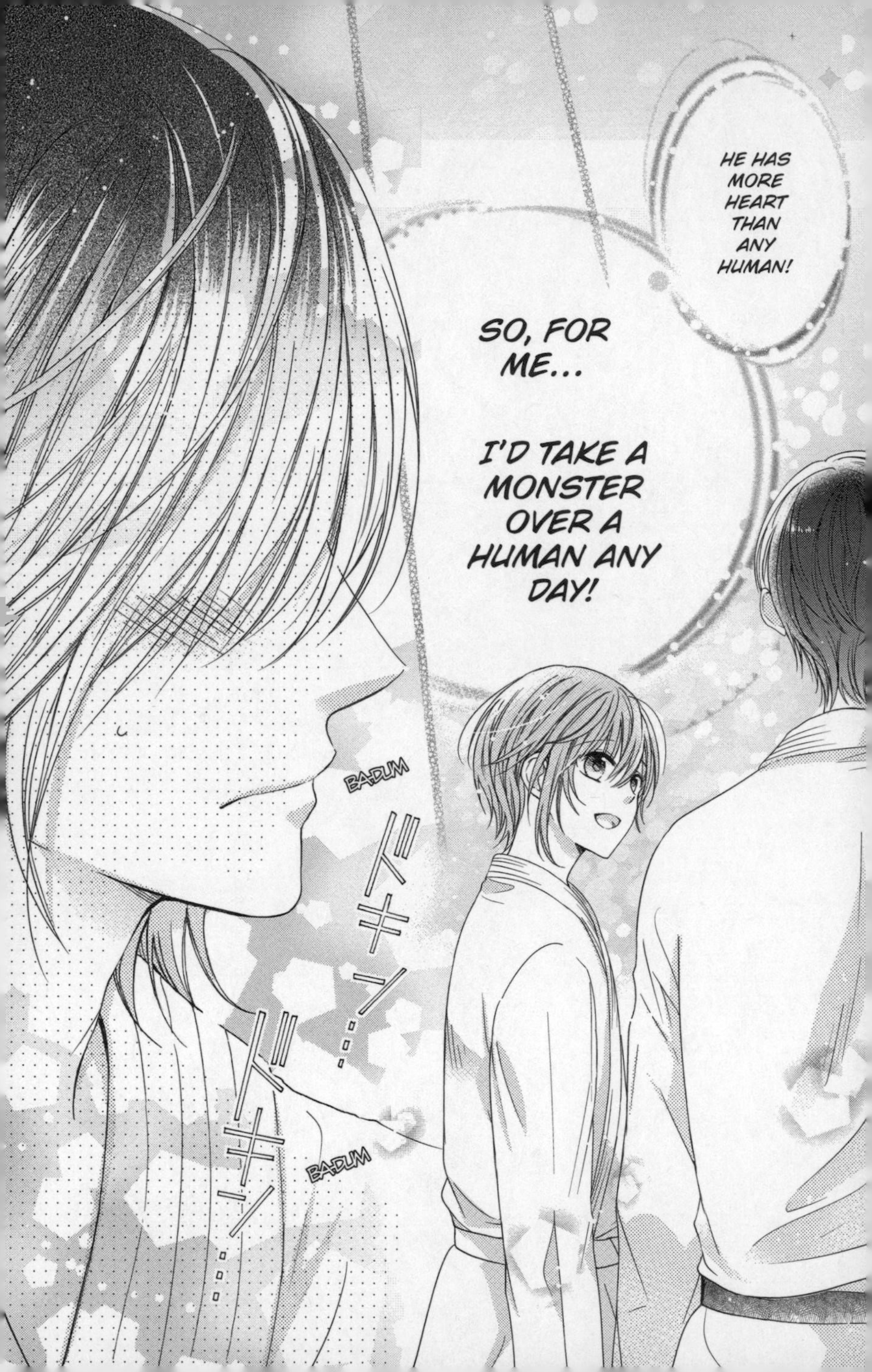
HE HAS MORE HEART THAN ANY HUMAN!
SO, FOR ME...
I'D TAKE A MONSTER OVER A HUMAN ANY DAY!
BA-DUM
BA-DUM

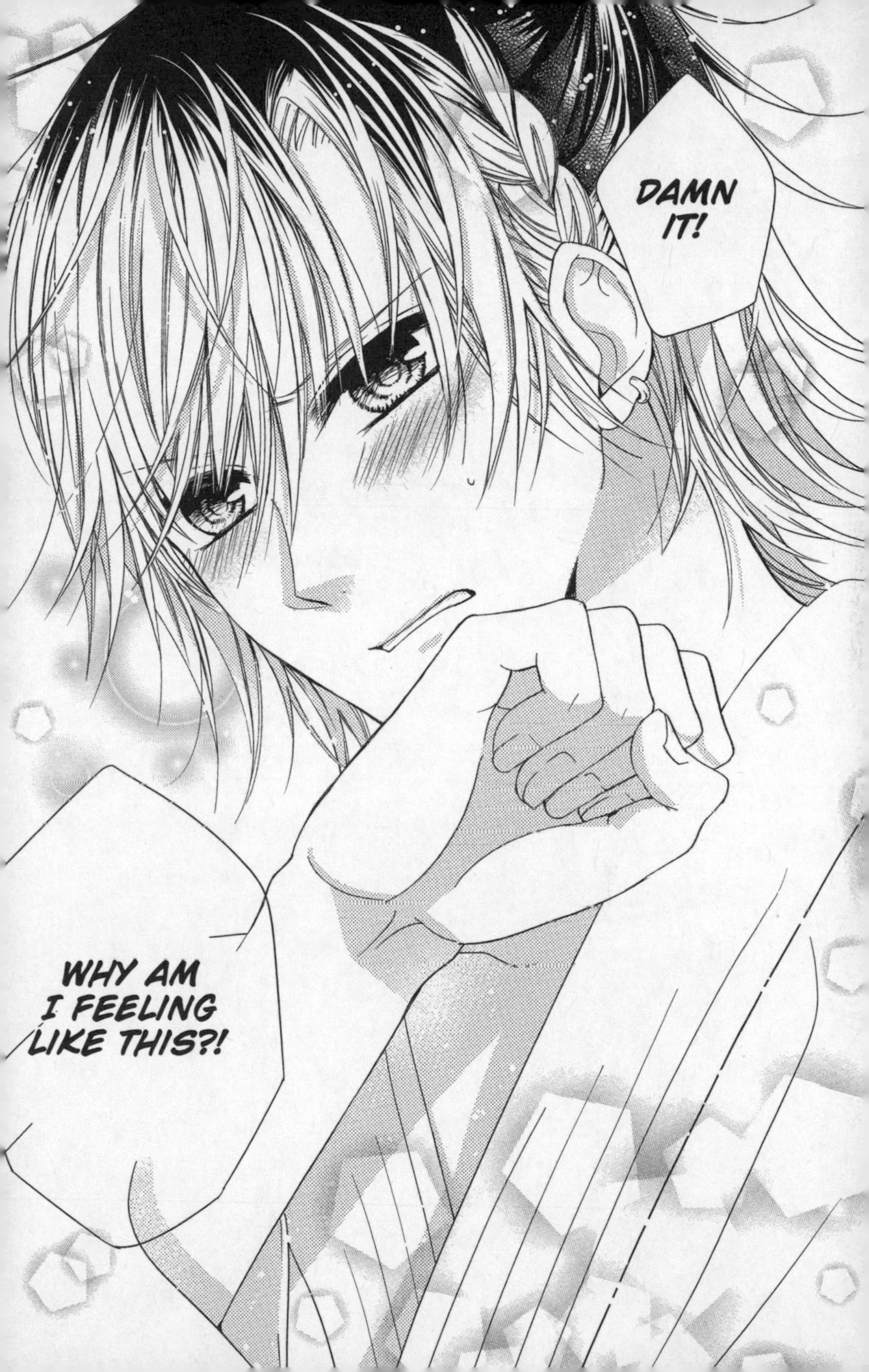
DAMN IT!
WHY AM I FEELING LIKE THIS?!

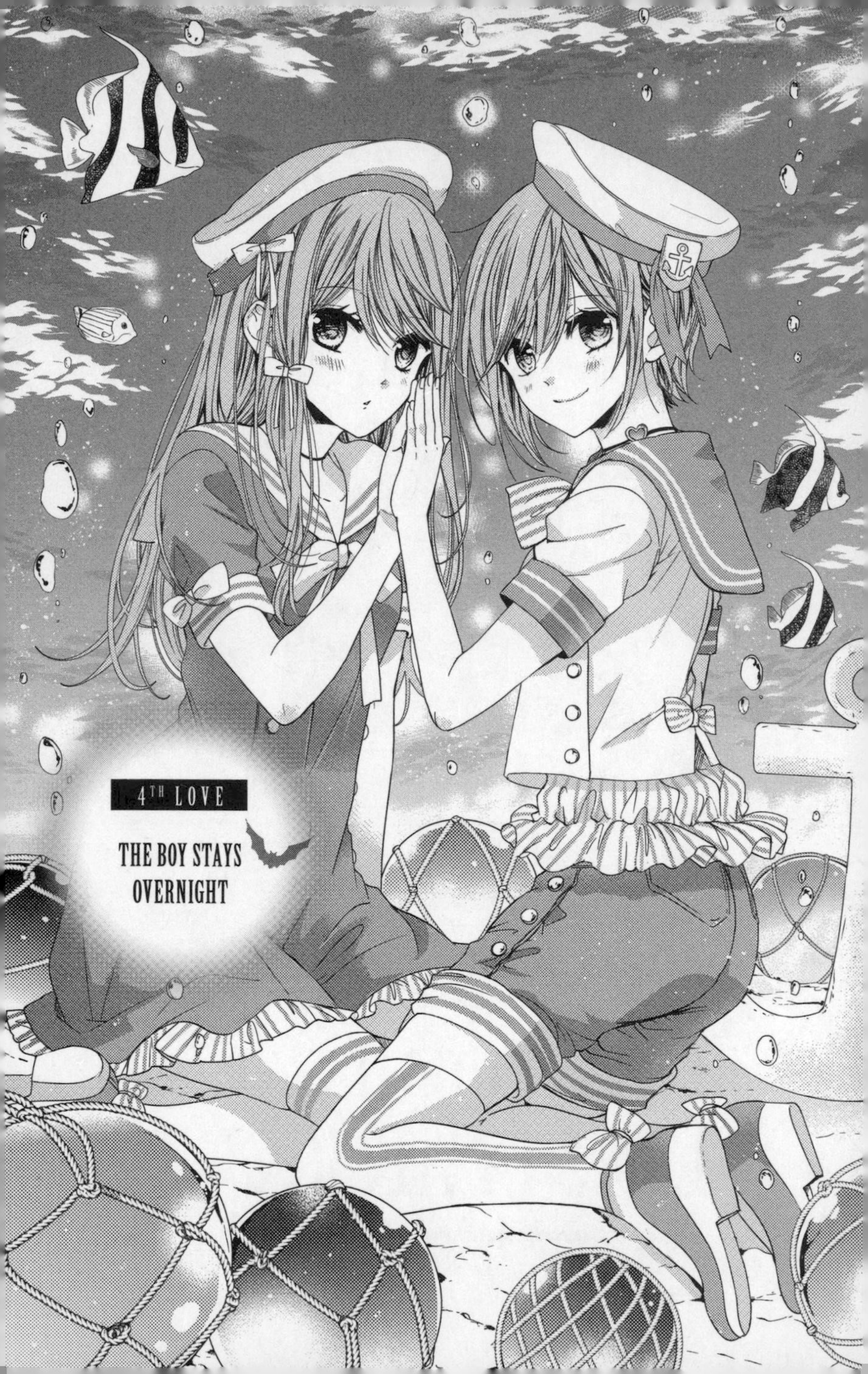
4TH LOVE
THE BOY STAYS OVERNIGHT

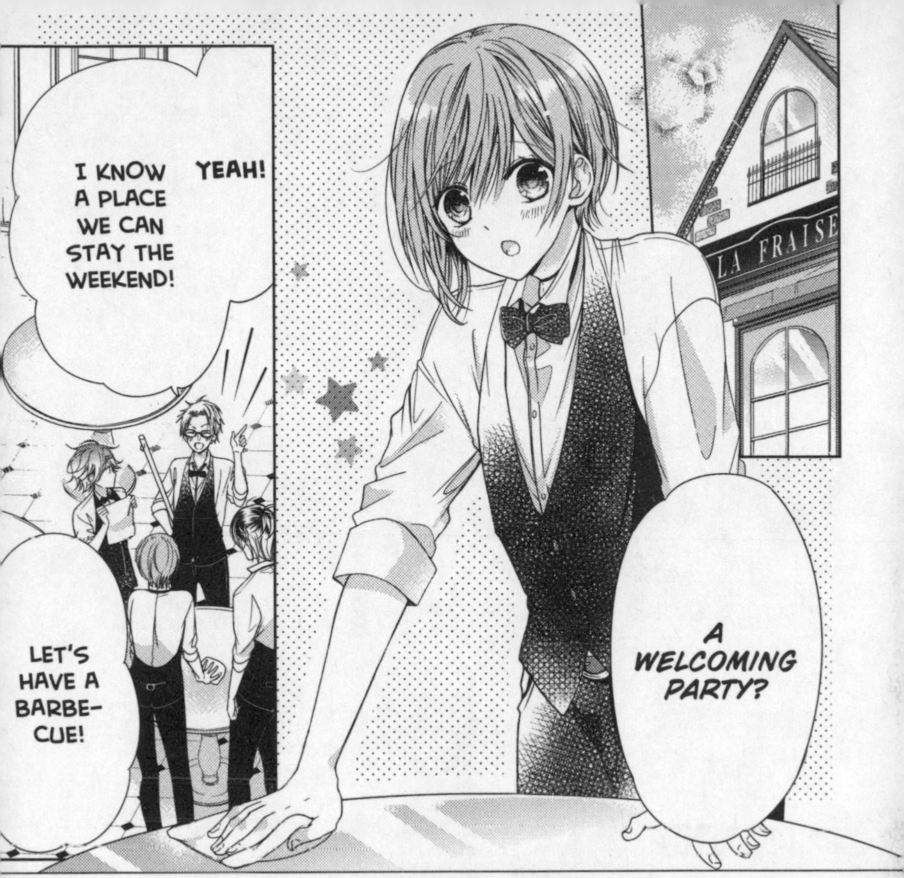
A WELCOMING PARTY?
LA FRAISE
YEAH!
I KNOW A PLACE WE CAN STAY THE WEEKEND!
LET'S HAVE A BARBE-CUE!

Vampire Dormitory

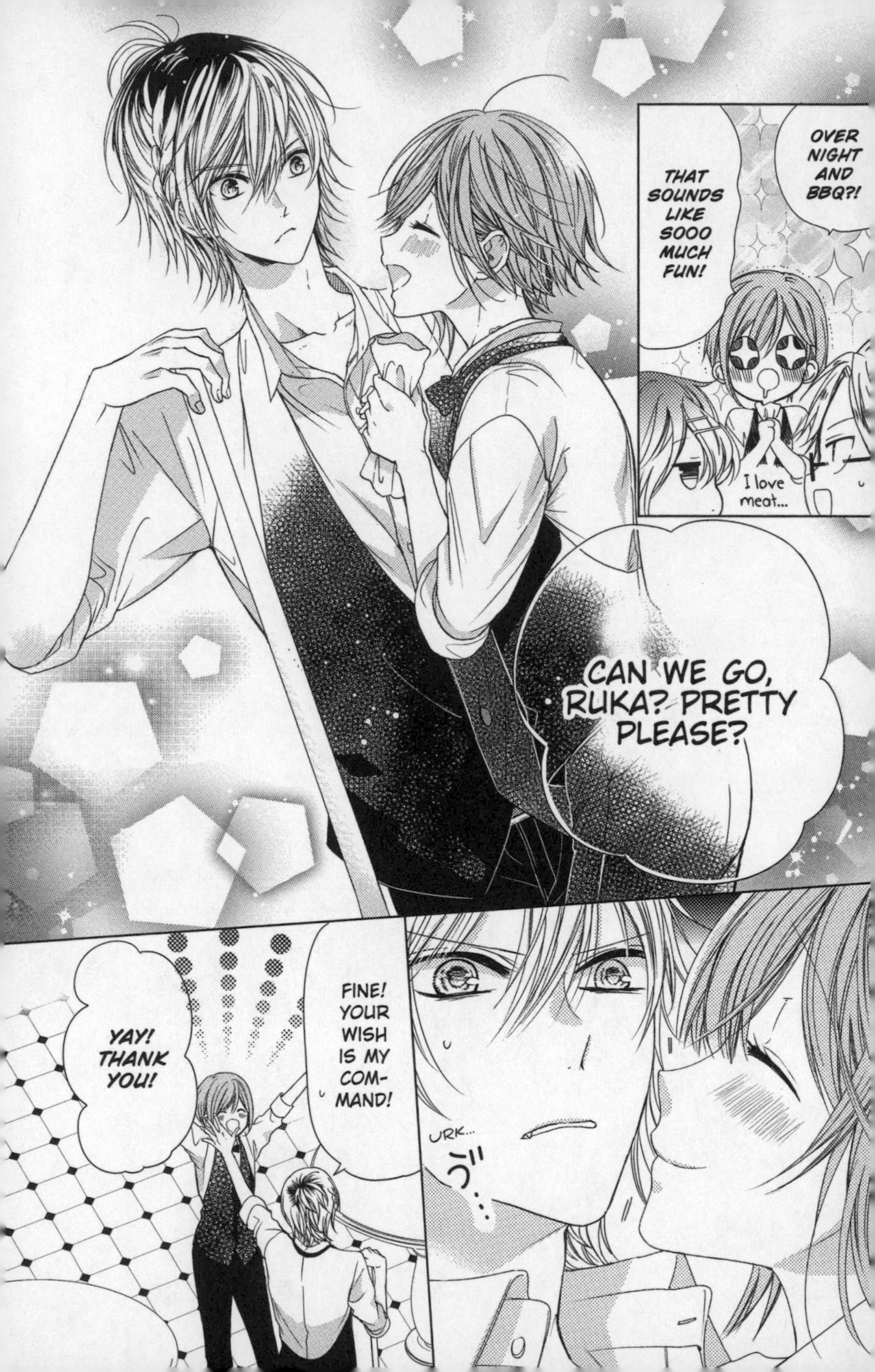
OVER NIGHT AND BBQ?!
THAT SOUNDS LIKE SOOO MUCH FUN!
I love meat...
CAN WE GO, RUKA? PRETTY PLEASE?
URK...
FINE! YOUR WISH IS MY COM- MAND!
YAY! THANK YOU!

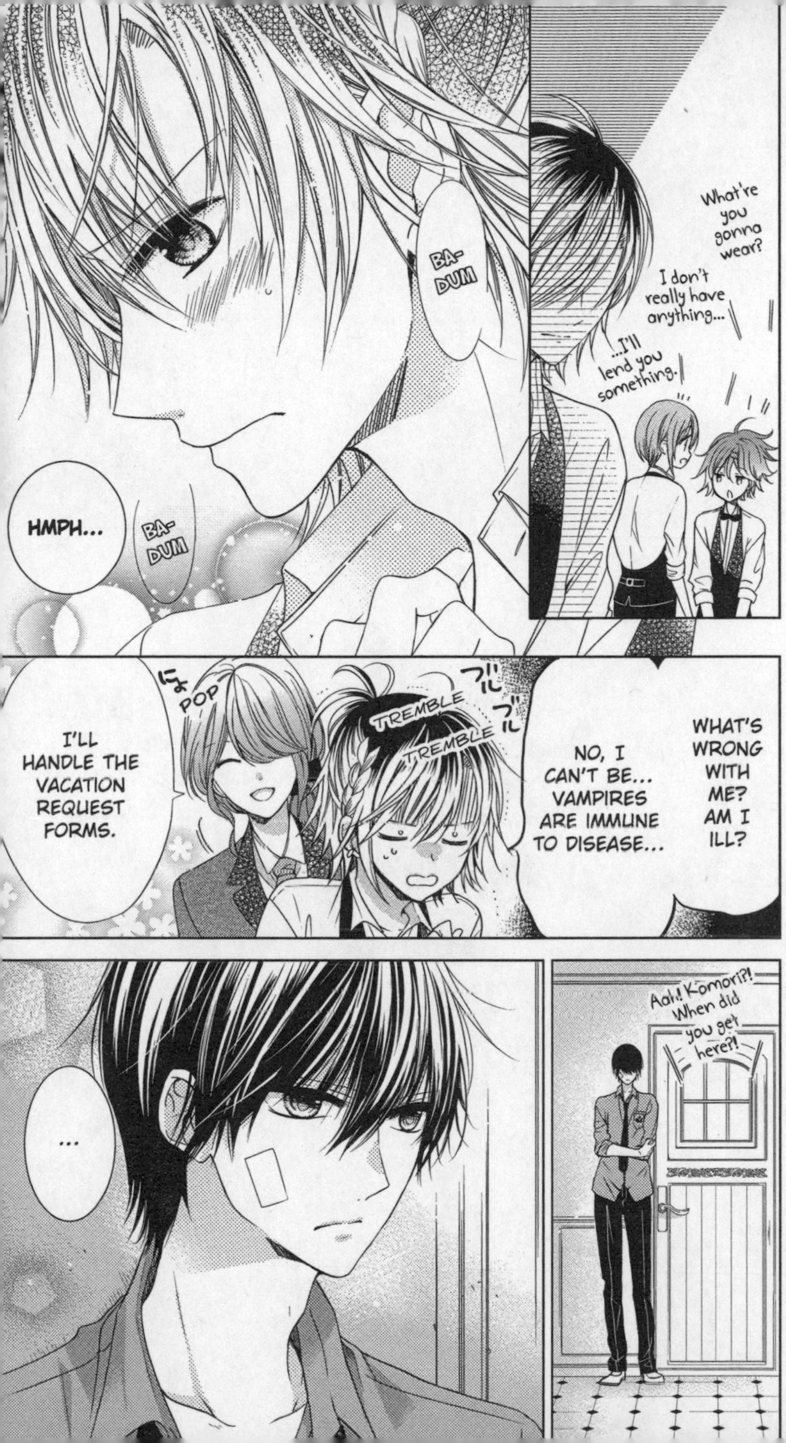
What're you gonna wear?
I don't really have anything...
...I'll lend you something.
BA-DUM
BA-DUM
HMPH...
WHAT'S WRONG WITH ME? AM I ILL?
NO, I CAN'T BE... VAMPIRES ARE IMMUNE TO DISEASE...
ブル TREMBLE
ブル TREMBLE
にょ POP
I'LL HANDLE THE VACATION REQUEST FORMS.
Aah! Komori?! When did you get here?!
...

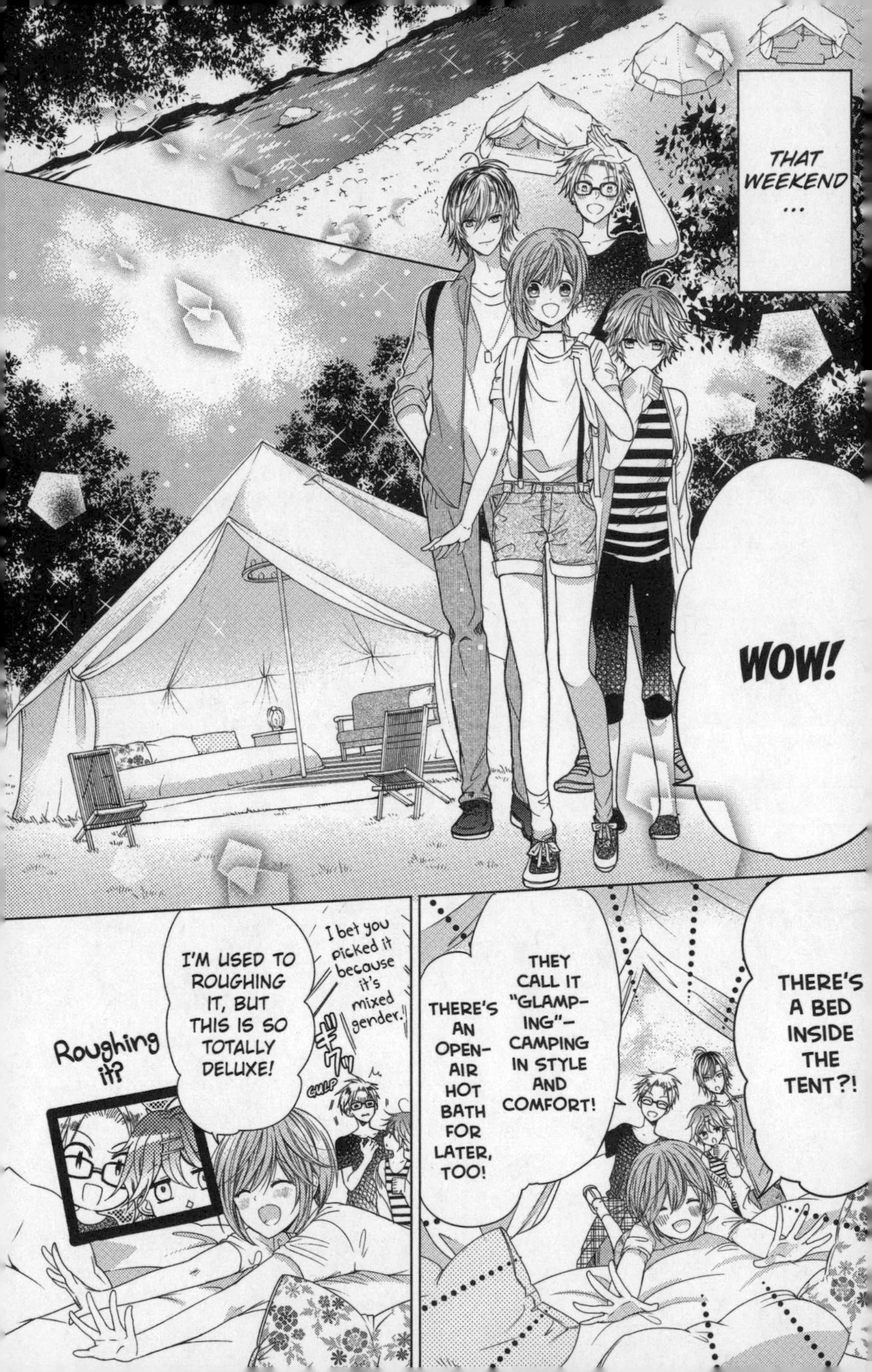
THAT WEEKEND...
WOW!
THERE'S A BED INSIDE THE TENT?!
THEY CALL IT "GLAMP-ING"—CAMPING IN STYLE AND COMFORT!
THERE'S AN OPEN-AIR HOT BATH FOR LATER, TOO!
I'M USED TO ROUGHING IT, BUT THIS IS SO TOTALLY DELUXE!
I bet you picked it because it's mixed gender.
GULP
Roughing it?

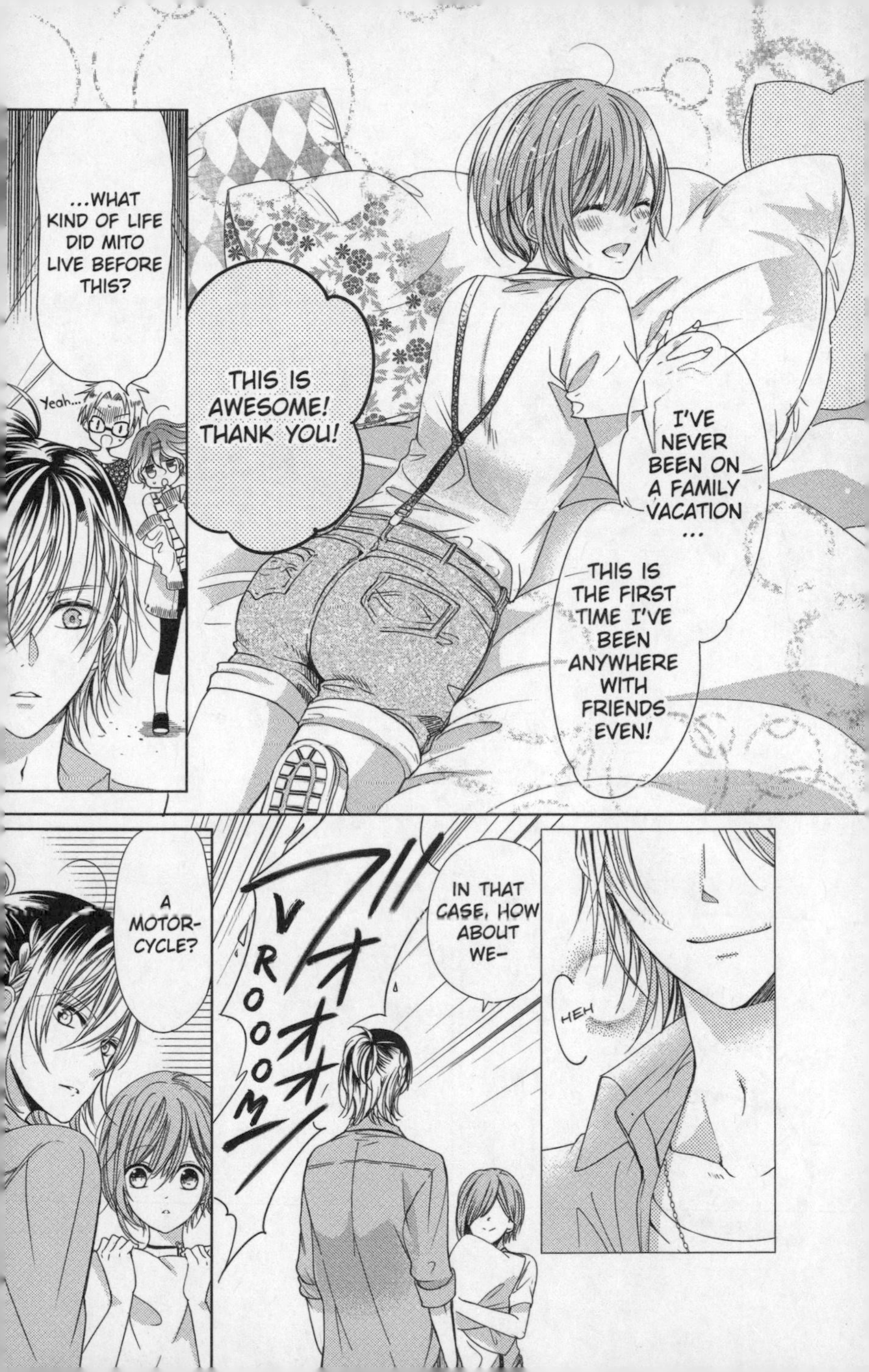
I'VE NEVER BEEN ON A FAMILY VACATION...
THIS IS THE FIRST TIME I'VE BEEN ANYWHERE WITH FRIENDS EVEN!
THIS IS AWESOME! THANK YOU!
...WHAT KIND OF LIFE DID MITO LIVE BEFORE THIS?
Yeah...
HEH
IN THAT CASE, HOW ABOUT WE-
VROOOOM!
A MOTOR-CYCLE?

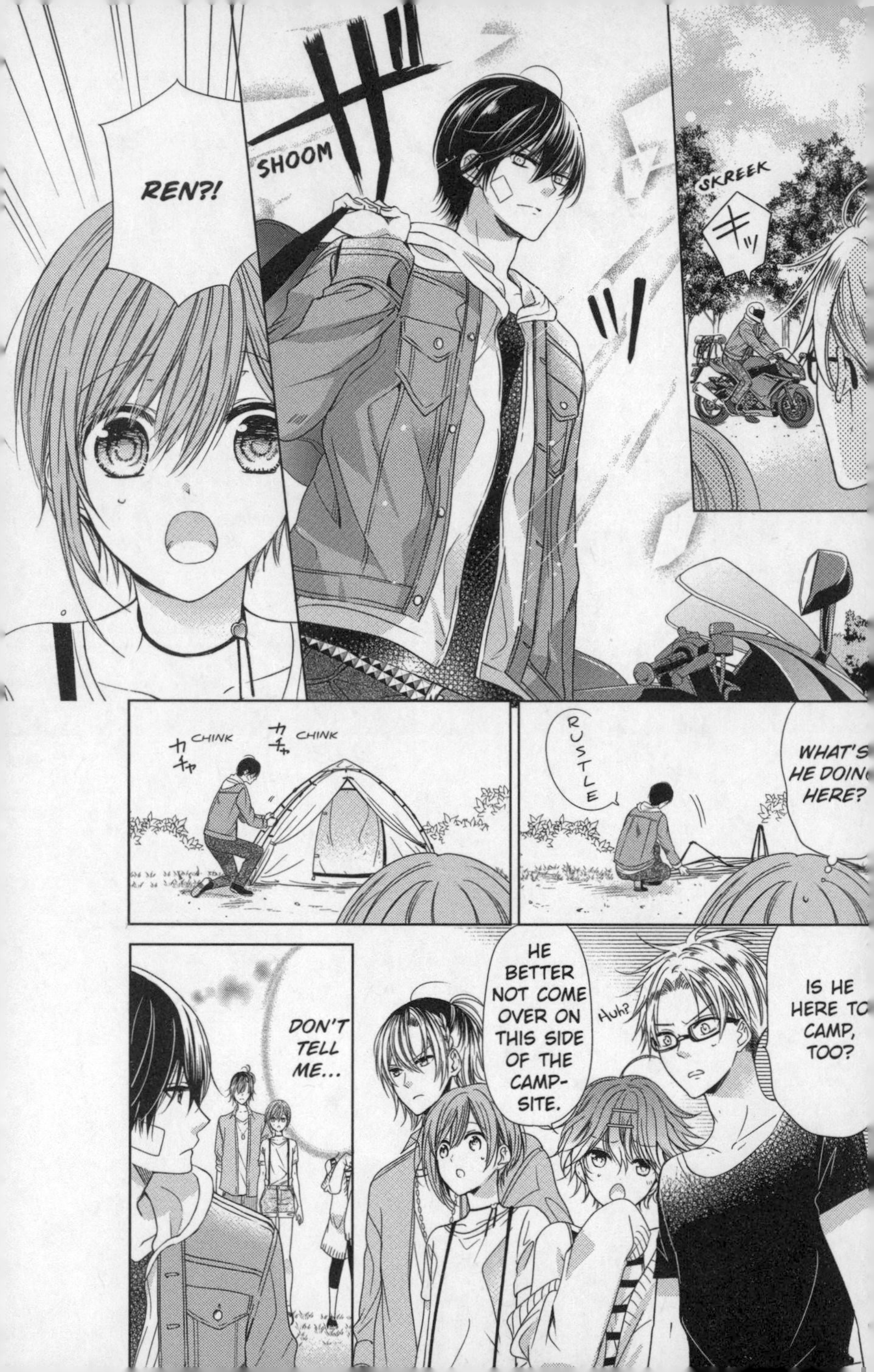
SKREEK
キッ
SHOOM
ザッ
REN?!
WHAT'S HE DOING HERE?
RUSTLE
カチャ
CHINK
カチャ
CHINK
IS HE HERE TO CAMP, TOO?
Huh?
HE BETTER NOT COME OVER ON THIS SIDE OF THE CAMP-SITE.
DON'T TELL ME...

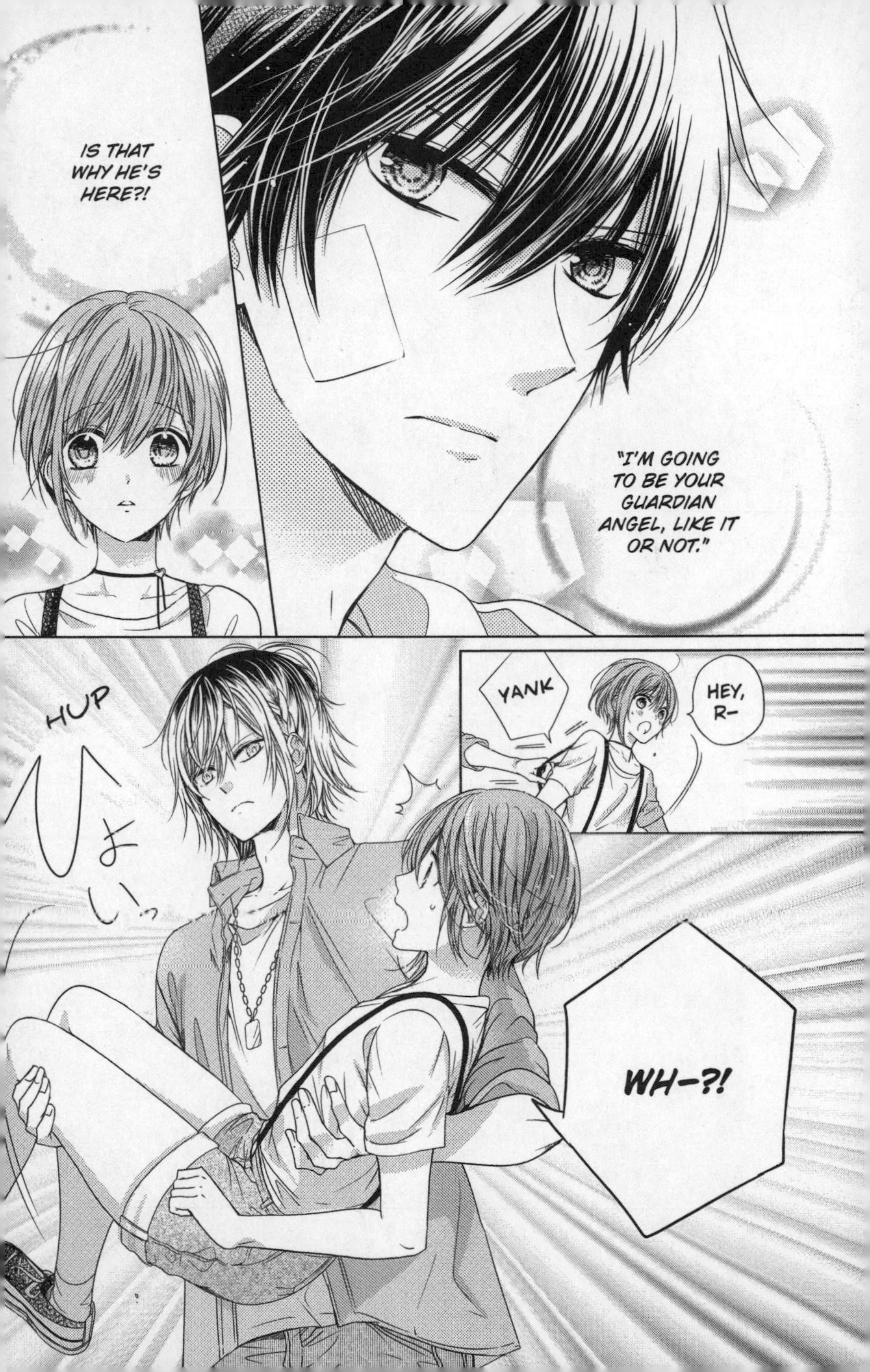
"I'M GOING TO BE YOUR GUARDIAN ANGEL, LIKE IT OR NOT."
IS THAT WHY HE'S HERE?!
HEY, R-
YANK
HUP
ひょいっ
WH-?!

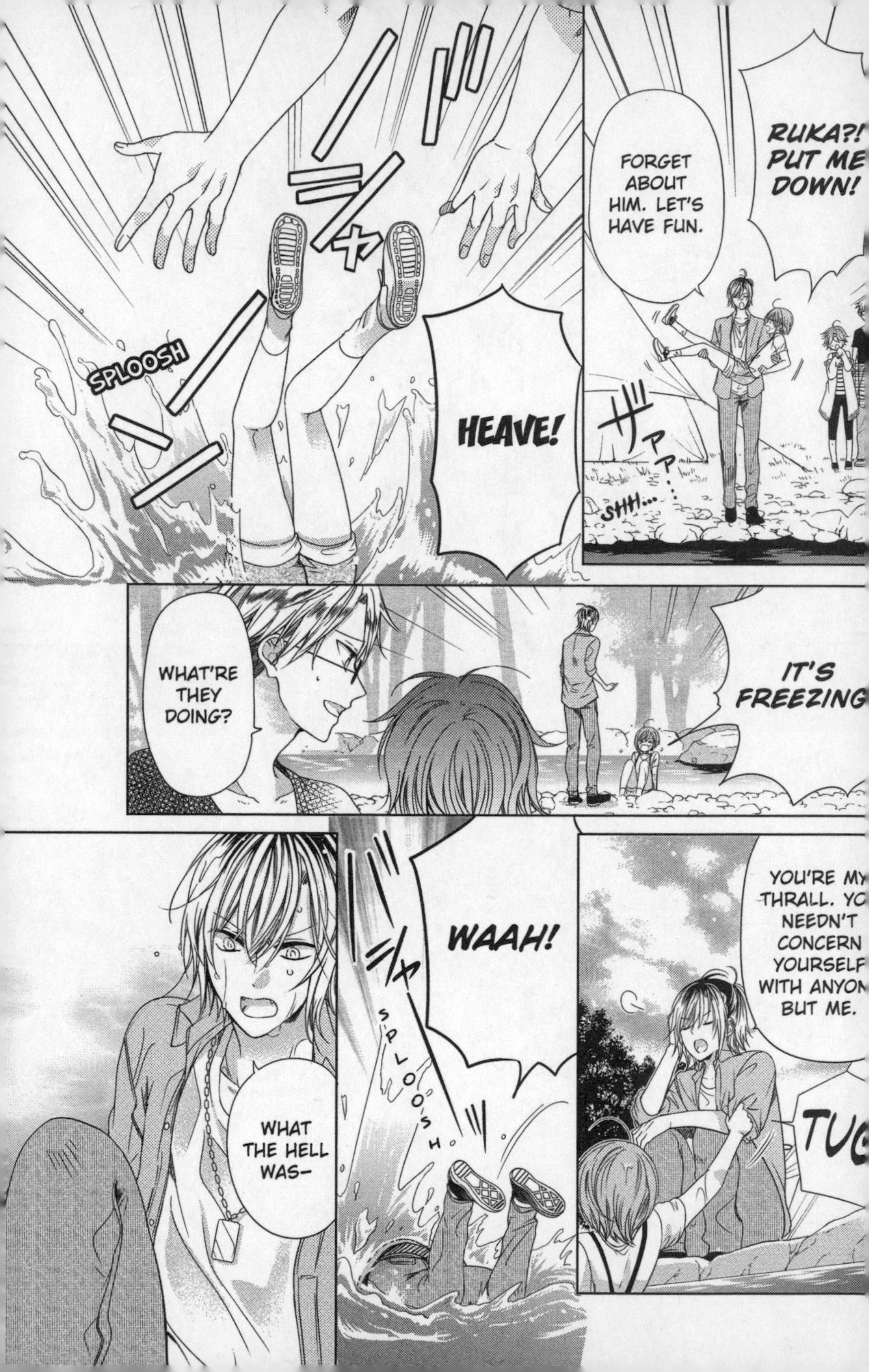
RUKA?! PUT ME DOWN!
FORGET ABOUT HIM. LET'S HAVE FUN.
ザァァ…
SHH...
HEAVE!
SPLOOSH
IT'S FREEZING
WHAT'RE THEY DOING?
YOU'RE MY THRALL. YO NEEDN'T CONCERN YOURSELF WITH ANYON BUT ME.
TUG
WAAH!
SPLOOSH
WHAT THE HELL WAS–

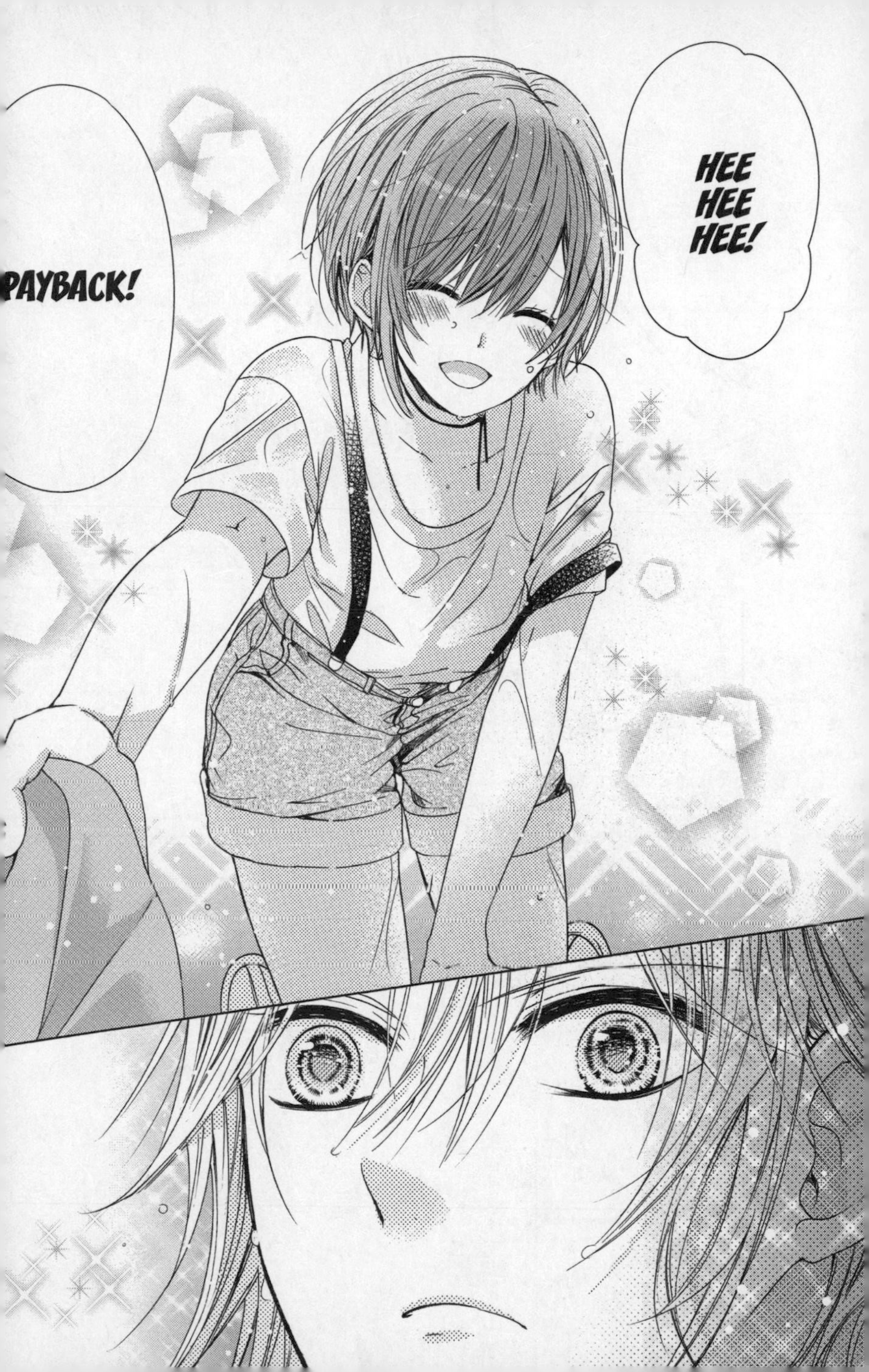
HEE HEE HEE!
PAYBACK!

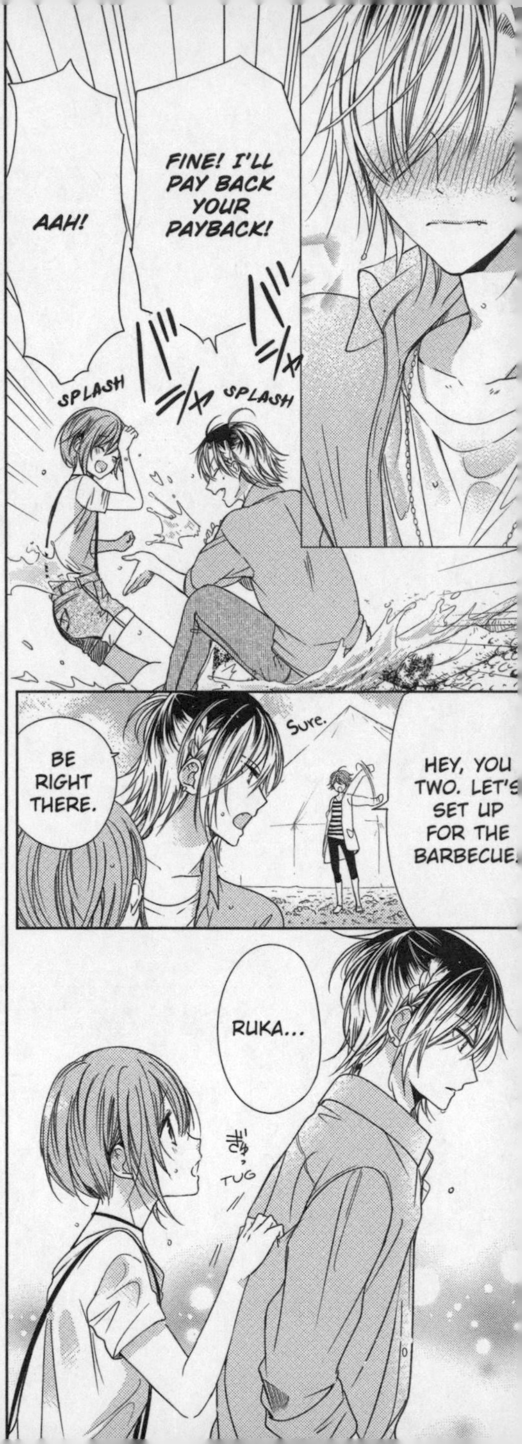
FINE! I'LL PAY BACK YOUR PAYBACK!
AAH!
SPLASH
SPLASH
HEY, YOU TWO. LET'S SET UP FOR THE BARBECUE.
Sure.
BE RIGHT THERE.
RUKA...
TUG

③

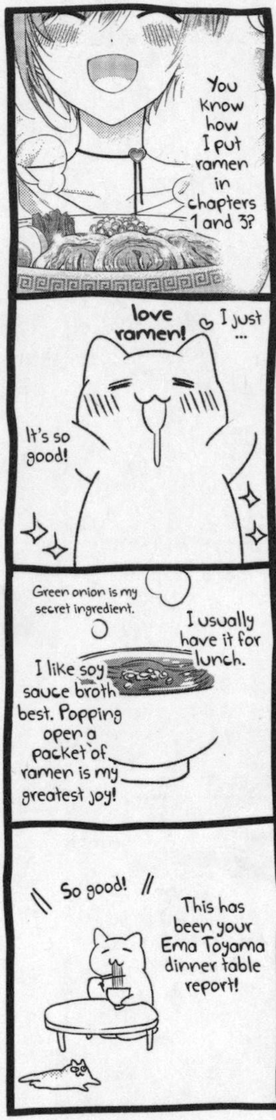
You know how I put ramen in chapters 1 and 3?
I just ... love ramen!
It's so good!
Green onion is my secret ingredient.
I usually have it for lunch.
I like soy sauce broth best. Popping open a packet of ramen is my greatest joy!
So good!
This has been your Ema Toyama dinner table report!

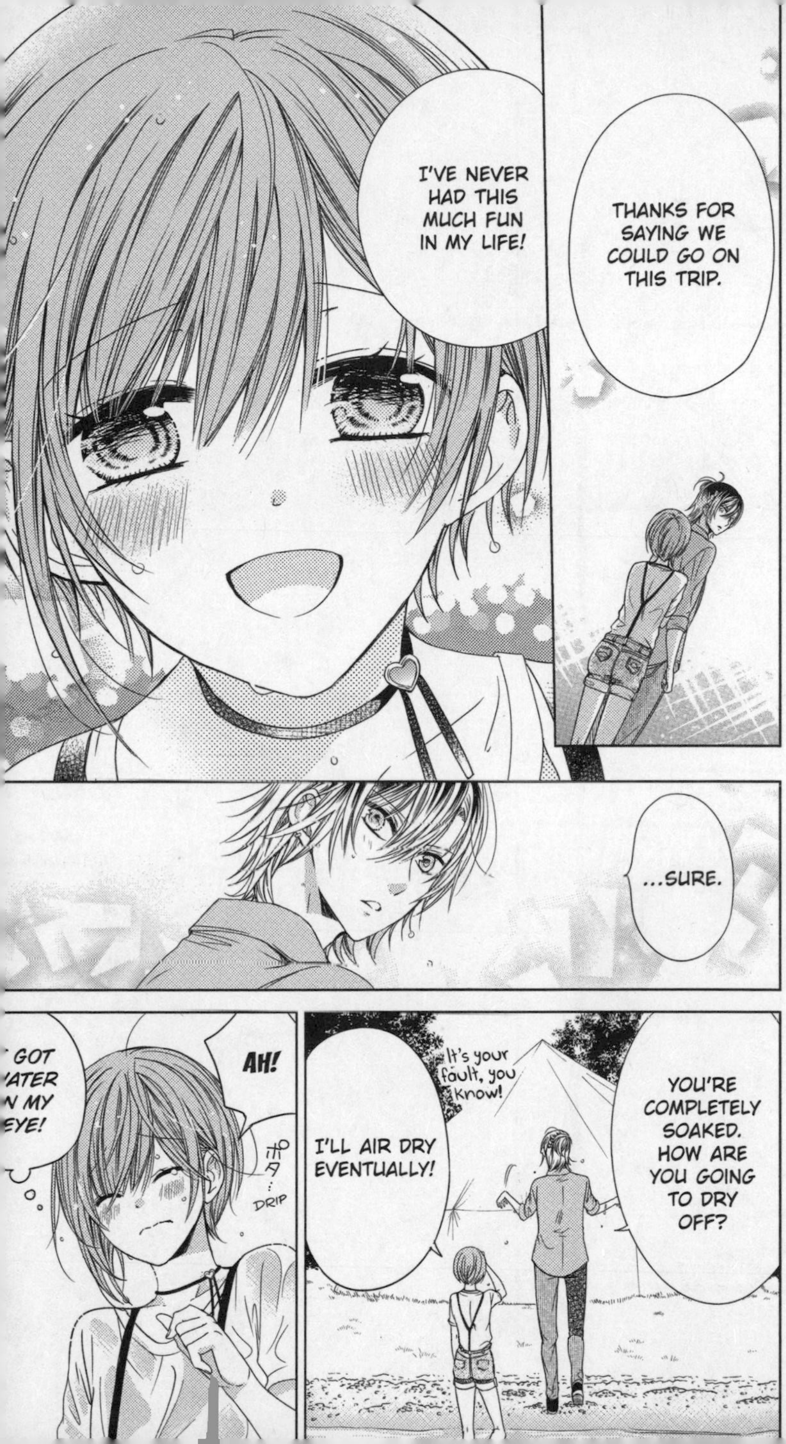

THANKS FOR SAYING WE COULD GO ON THIS TRIP.
I'VE NEVER HAD THIS MUCH FUN IN MY LIFE!
...SURE.
YOU'RE COMPLETELY SOAKED. HOW ARE YOU GOING TO DRY OFF?
It's your fault, you know!
I'LL AIR DRY EVENTUALLY!
AH!
ポタ… DRIP
GOT VATER N MY EYE!

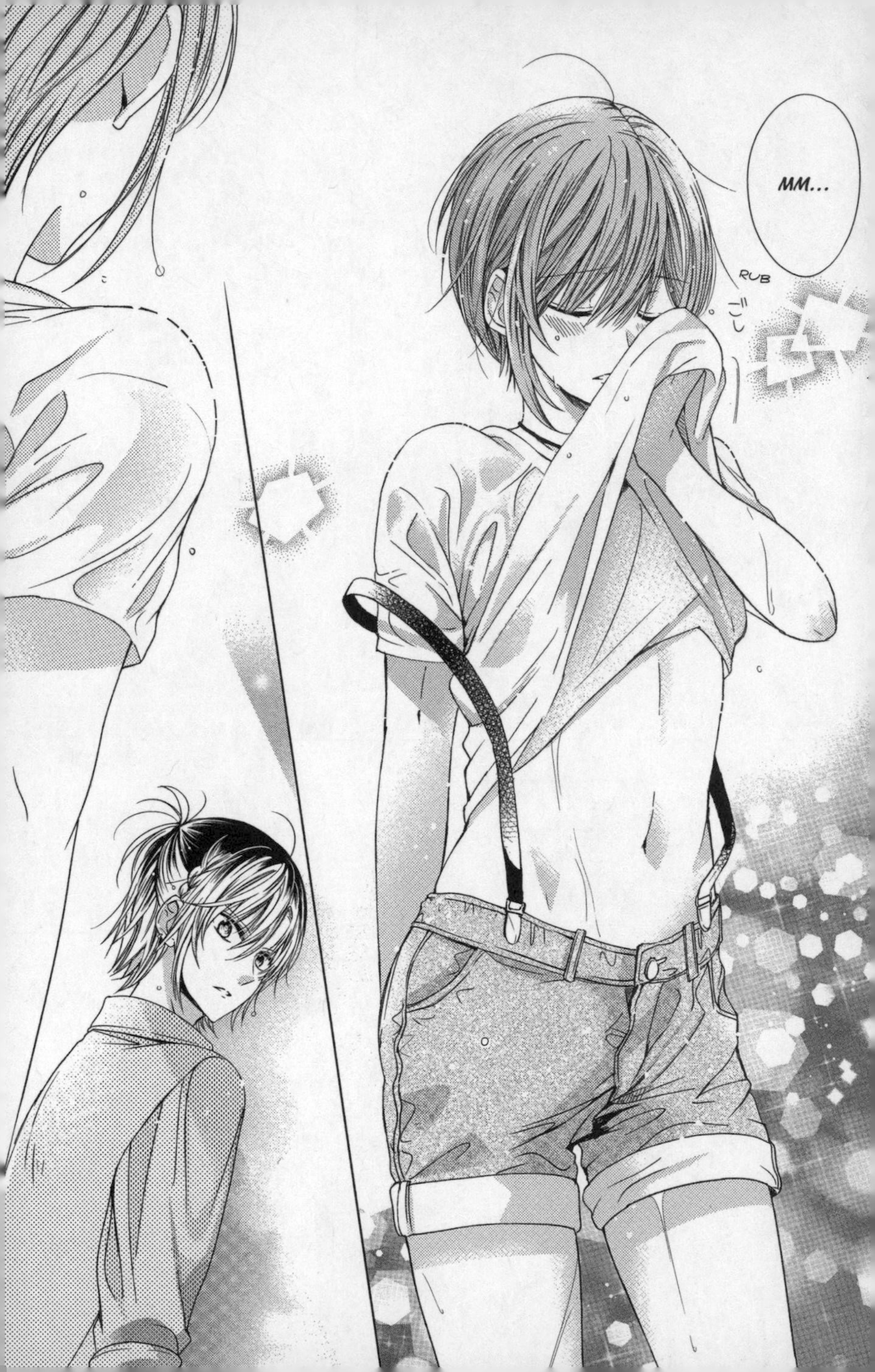
MM...
RUB
ごし

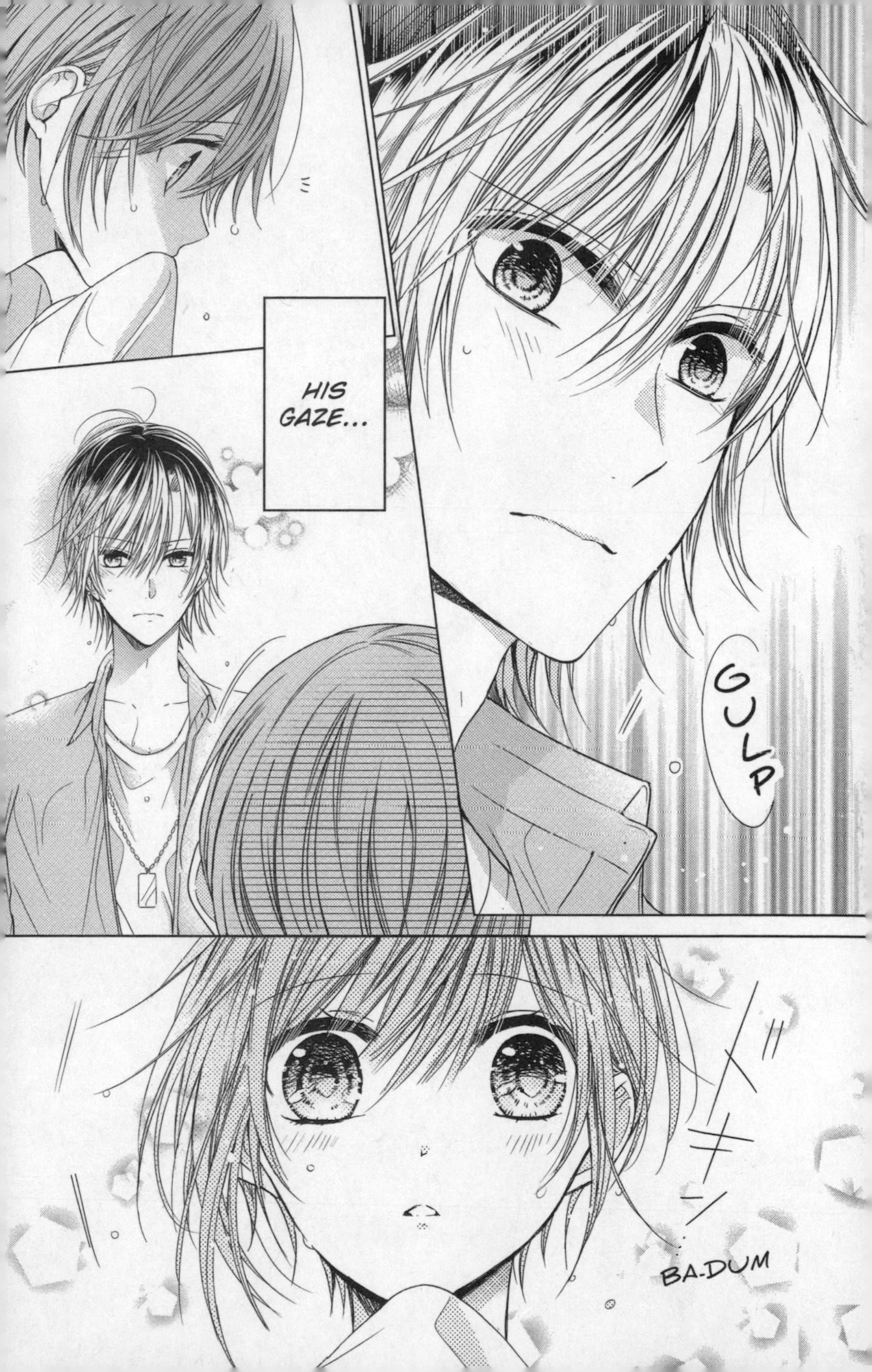
GULP
HIS GAZE...
BA-DUM

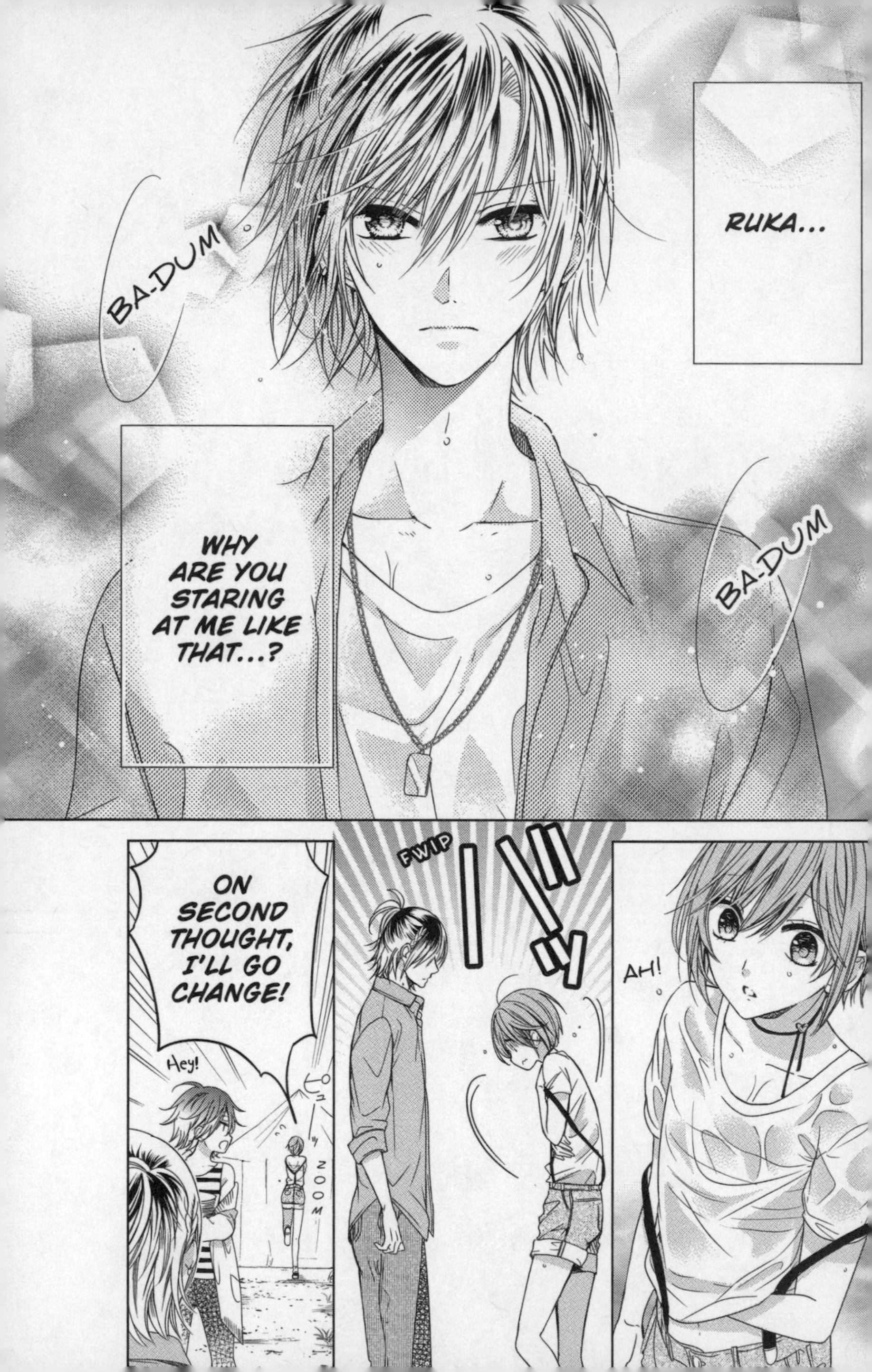
RUKA...
BA-DUM
WHY ARE YOU STARING AT ME LIKE THAT...?
BA-DUM
AH!
FWIP
ON SECOND THOUGHT, I'LL GO CHANGE!
Hey!
ZOOM

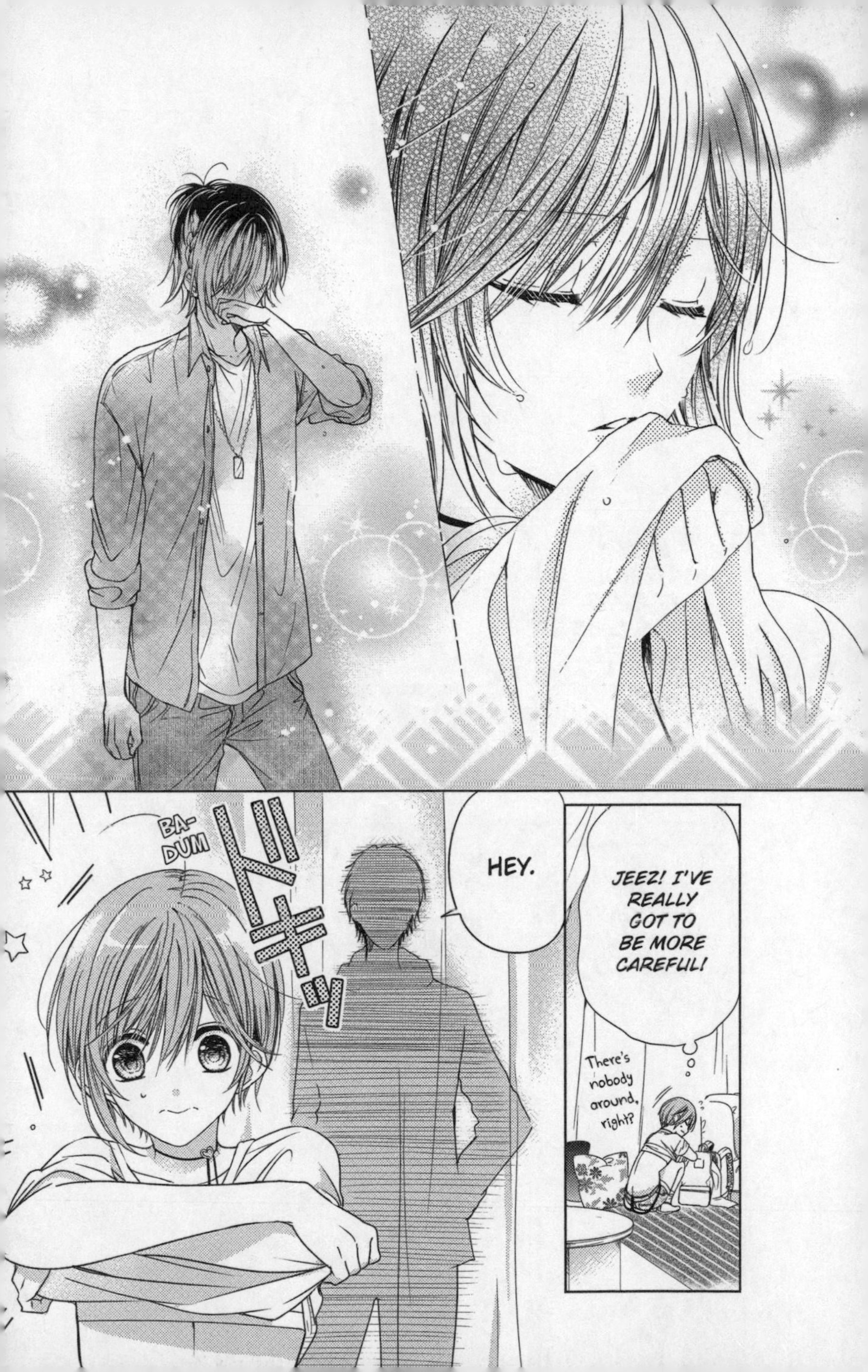
JEEZ! I'VE REALLY GOT TO BE MORE CAREFUL!
There's nobody around, right?
HEY.
BA-DUM
ドキッ

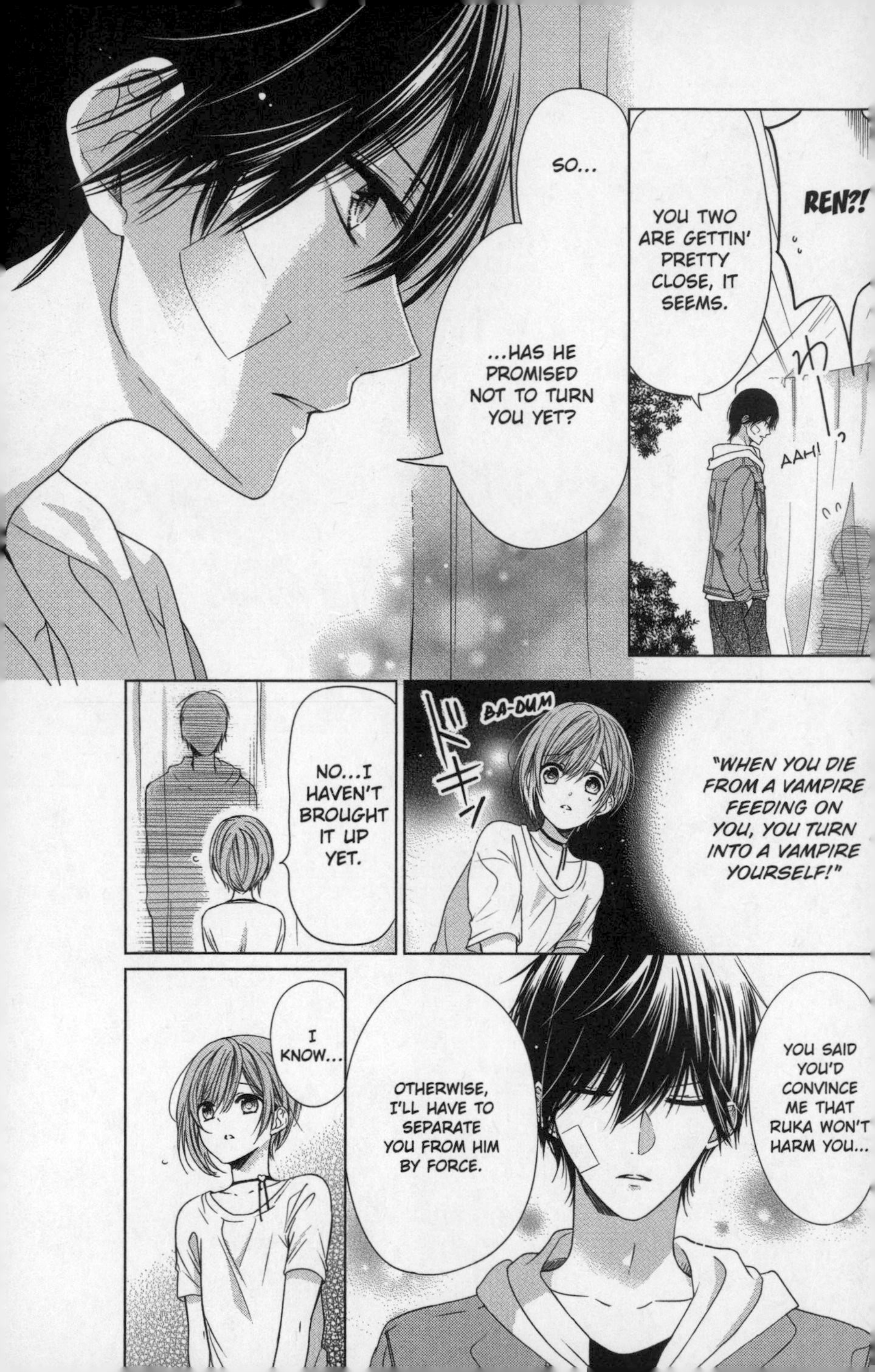
YOU TWO ARE GETTIN' PRETTY CLOSE, IT SEEMS.
REN?!
AAH!
SO...
...HAS HE PROMISED NOT TO TURN YOU YET?
"WHEN YOU DIE FROM A VAMPIRE FEEDING ON YOU, YOU TURN INTO A VAMPIRE YOURSELF!"
BA-DUM
NO...I HAVEN'T BROUGHT IT UP YET.
YOU SAID YOU'D CONVINCE ME THAT RUKA WON'T HARM YOU...
OTHERWISE, I'LL HAVE TO SEPARATE YOU FROM HIM BY FORCE.
I KNOW...

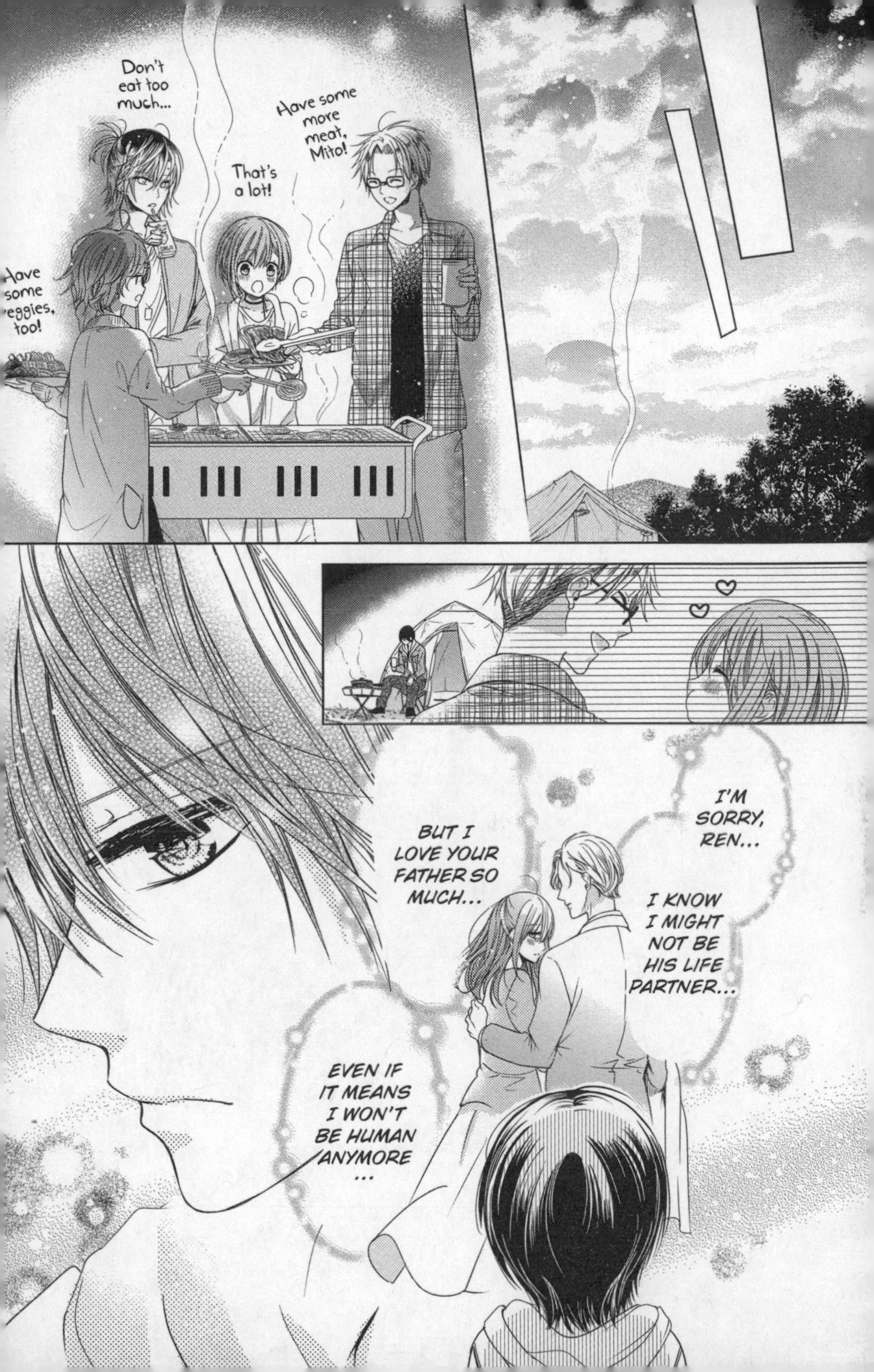
Have some more meat, Mito!
That's a lot!
Don't eat too much...
Have some veggies, too!
I'M SORRY, REN...
I KNOW I MIGHT NOT BE HIS LIFE PARTNER...
BUT I LOVE YOUR FATHER SO MUCH...
EVEN IF IT MEANS I WON'T BE HUMAN ANYMORE...

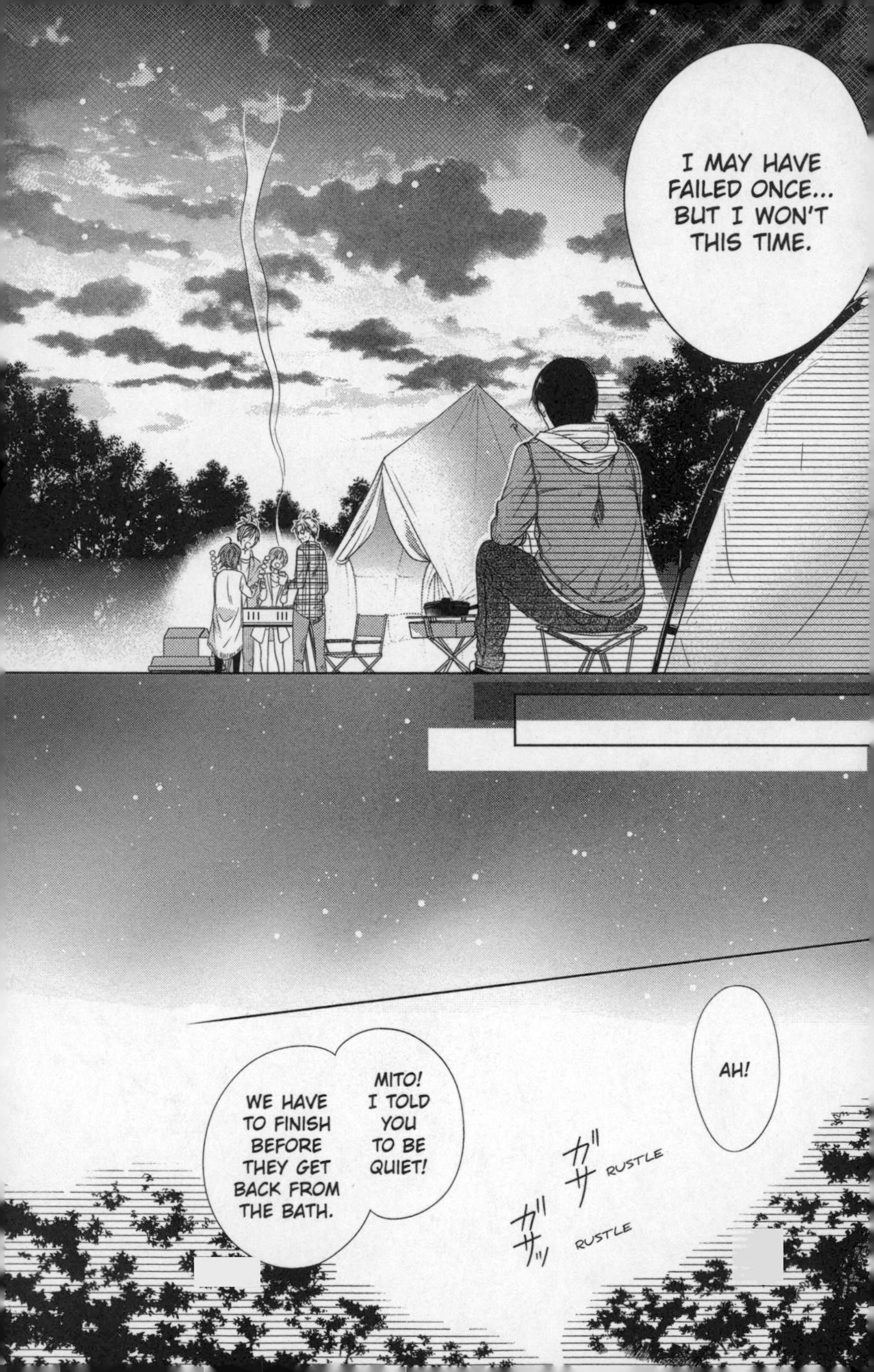
I MAY HAVE FAILED ONCE... BUT I WON'T THIS TIME.
AH!
ガサ RUSTLE
ガサッ RUSTLE
MITO! I TOLD YOU TO BE QUIET!
WE HAVE TO FINISH BEFORE THEY GET BACK FROM THE BATH.

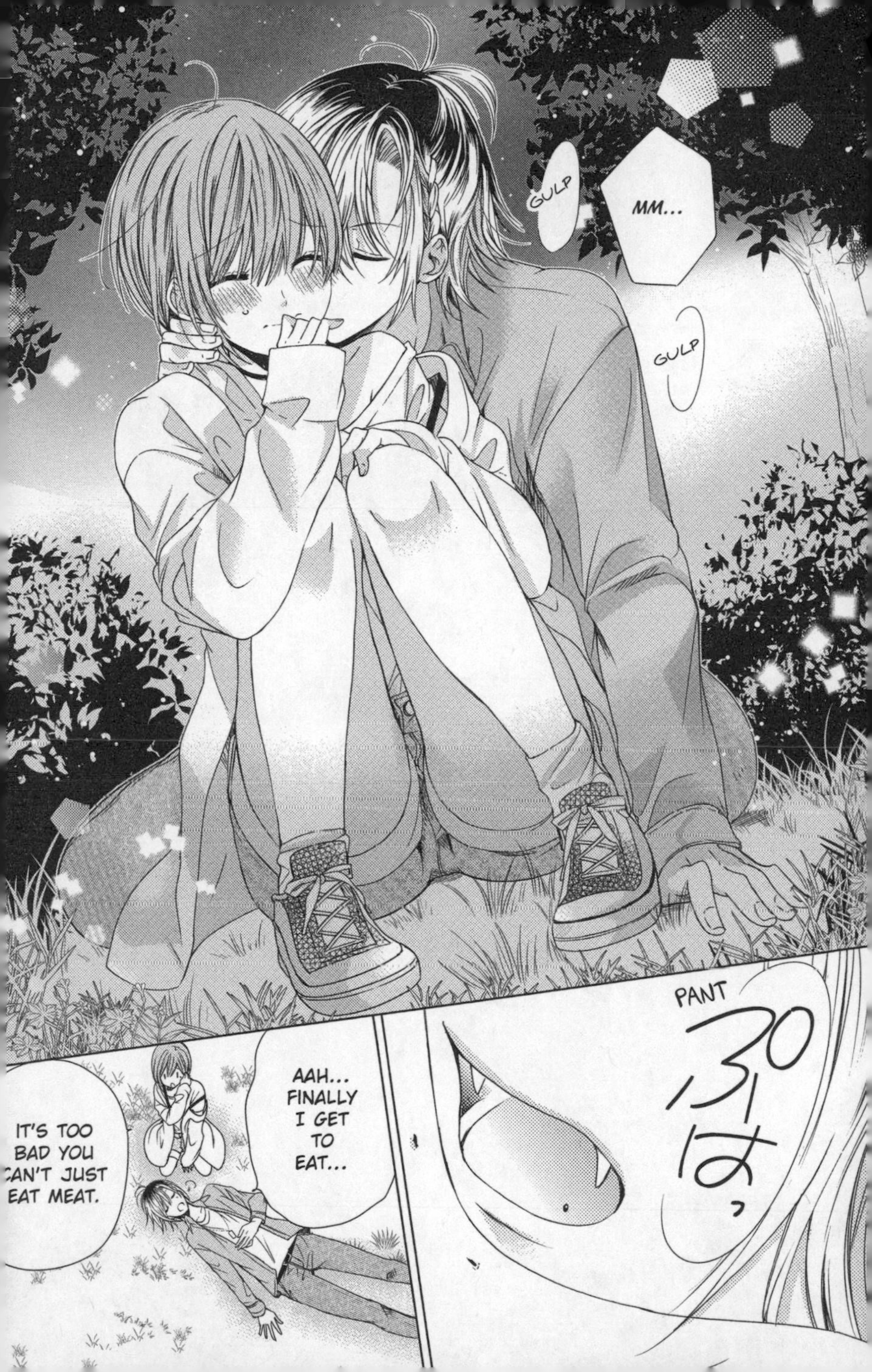
MM...
GULP
GULP
PANT
ふはっ
AAH... FINALLY I GET TO EAT...
IT'S TOO BAD YOU CAN'T JUST EAT MEAT.

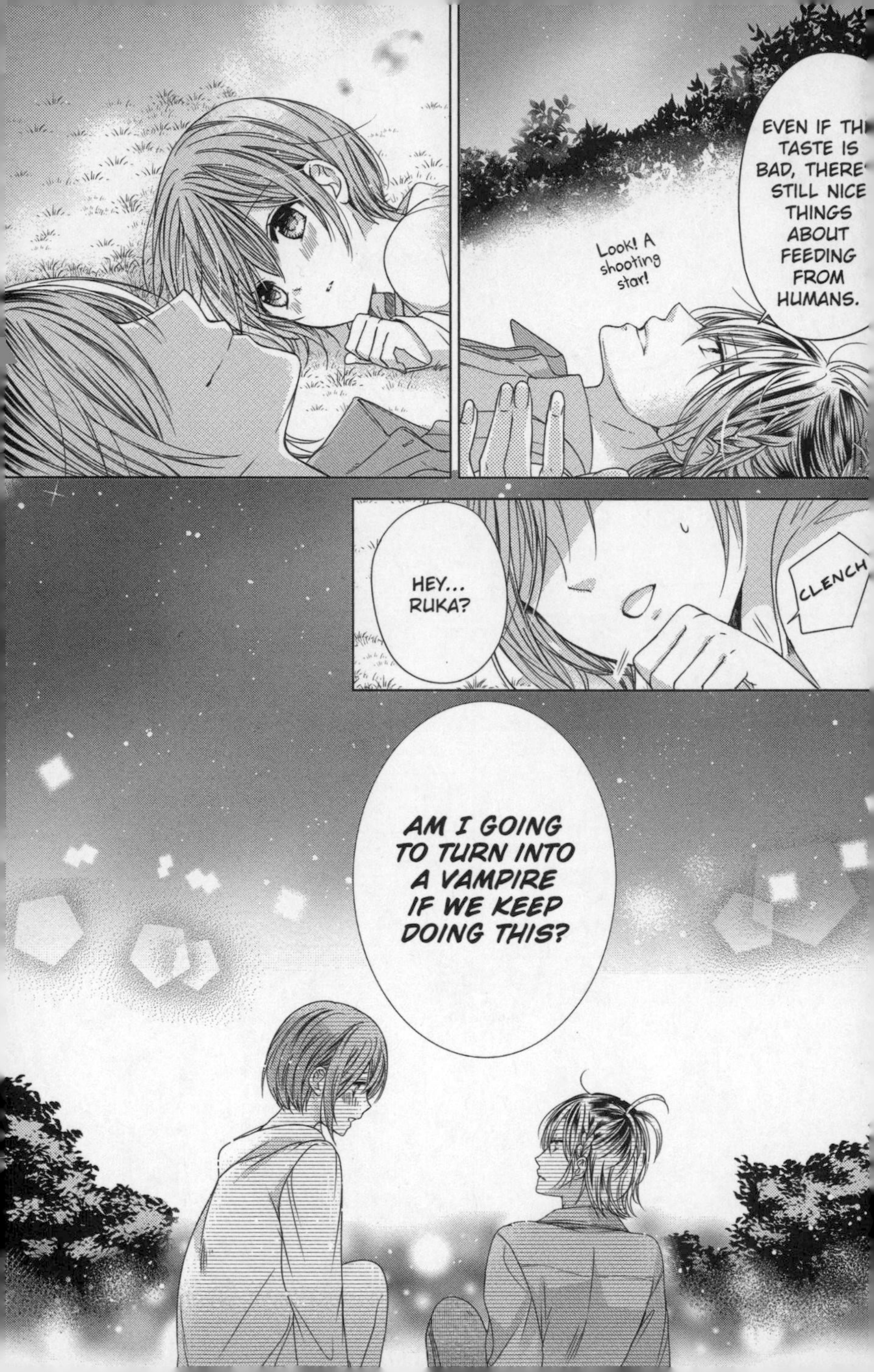
EVEN IF TH TASTE IS BAD, THERE STILL NICE THINGS ABOUT FEEDING FROM HUMANS.
Look! A shooting star!
CLENCH
HEY... RUKA?
AM I GOING TO TURN INTO A VAMPIRE IF WE KEEP DOING THIS?

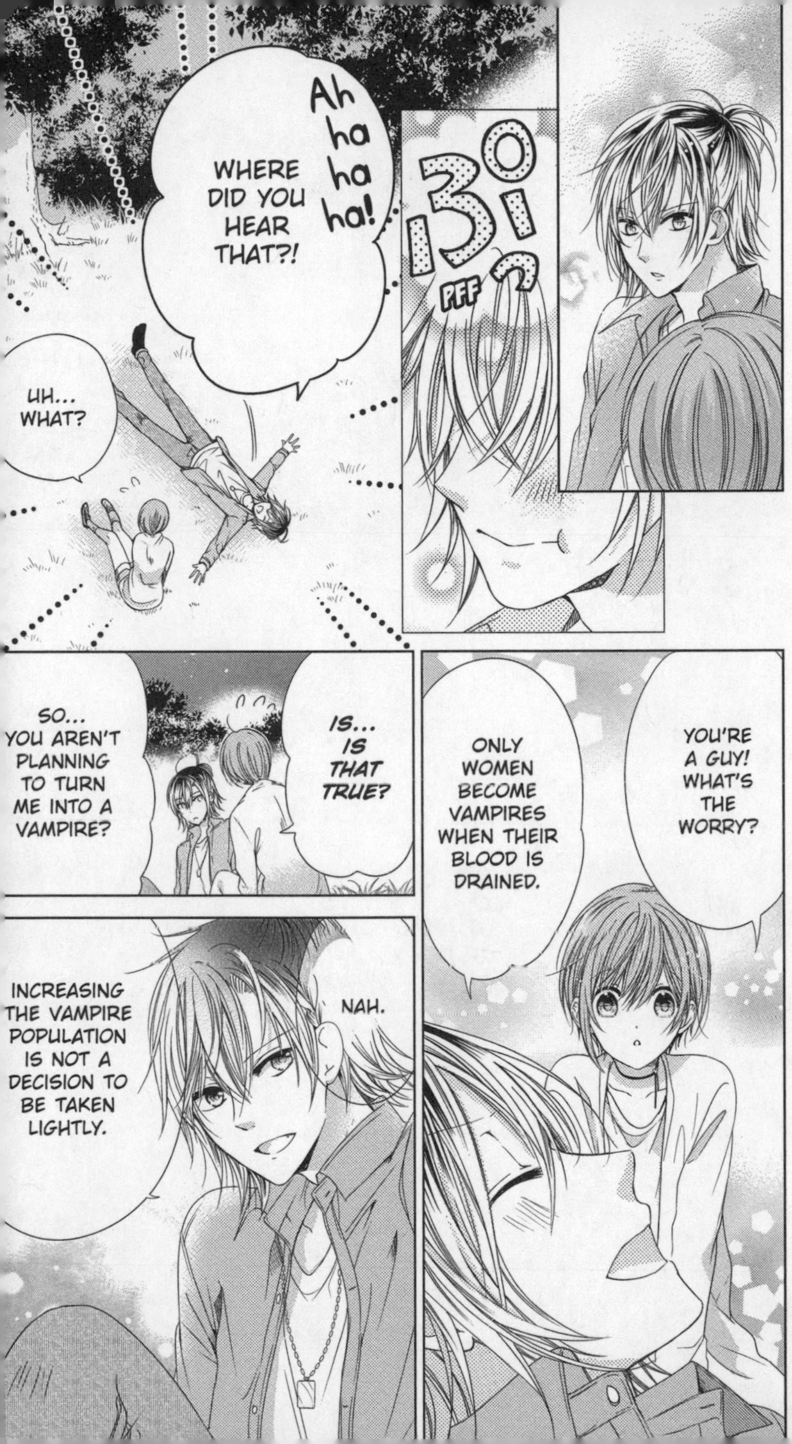
PFF
Ah ha ha ha!
WHERE DID YOU HEAR THAT?!
UH... WHAT?
YOU'RE A GUY! WHAT'S THE WORRY?
ONLY WOMEN BECOME VAMPIRES WHEN THEIR BLOOD IS DRAINED.
IS... IS THAT TRUE?
SO... YOU AREN'T PLANNING TO TURN ME INTO A VAMPIRE?
NAH.
INCREASING THE VAMPIRE POPULATION IS NOT A DECISION TO BE TAKEN LIGHTLY.

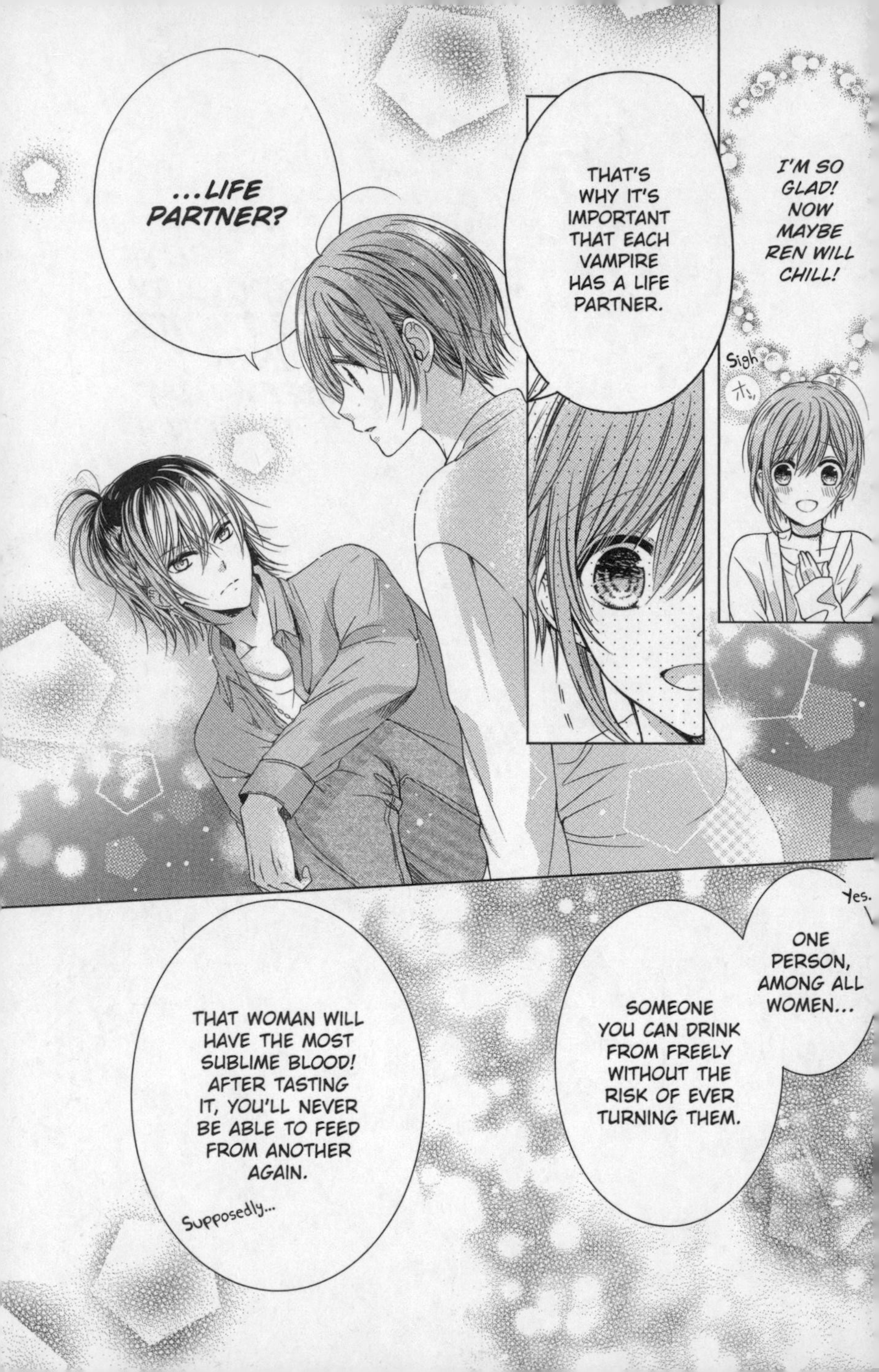
I'M SO GLAD! NOW MAYBE REN WILL CHILL!
Sigh
ホッ
THAT'S WHY IT'S IMPORTANT THAT EACH VAMPIRE HAS A LIFE PARTNER.
...LIFE PARTNER?
Yes.
ONE PERSON, AMONG ALL WOMEN...
SOMEONE YOU CAN DRINK FROM FREELY WITHOUT THE RISK OF EVER TURNING THEM.
THAT WOMAN WILL HAVE THE MOST SUBLIME BLOOD! AFTER TASTING IT, YOU'LL NEVER BE ABLE TO FEED FROM ANOTHER AGAIN.
Supposedly...

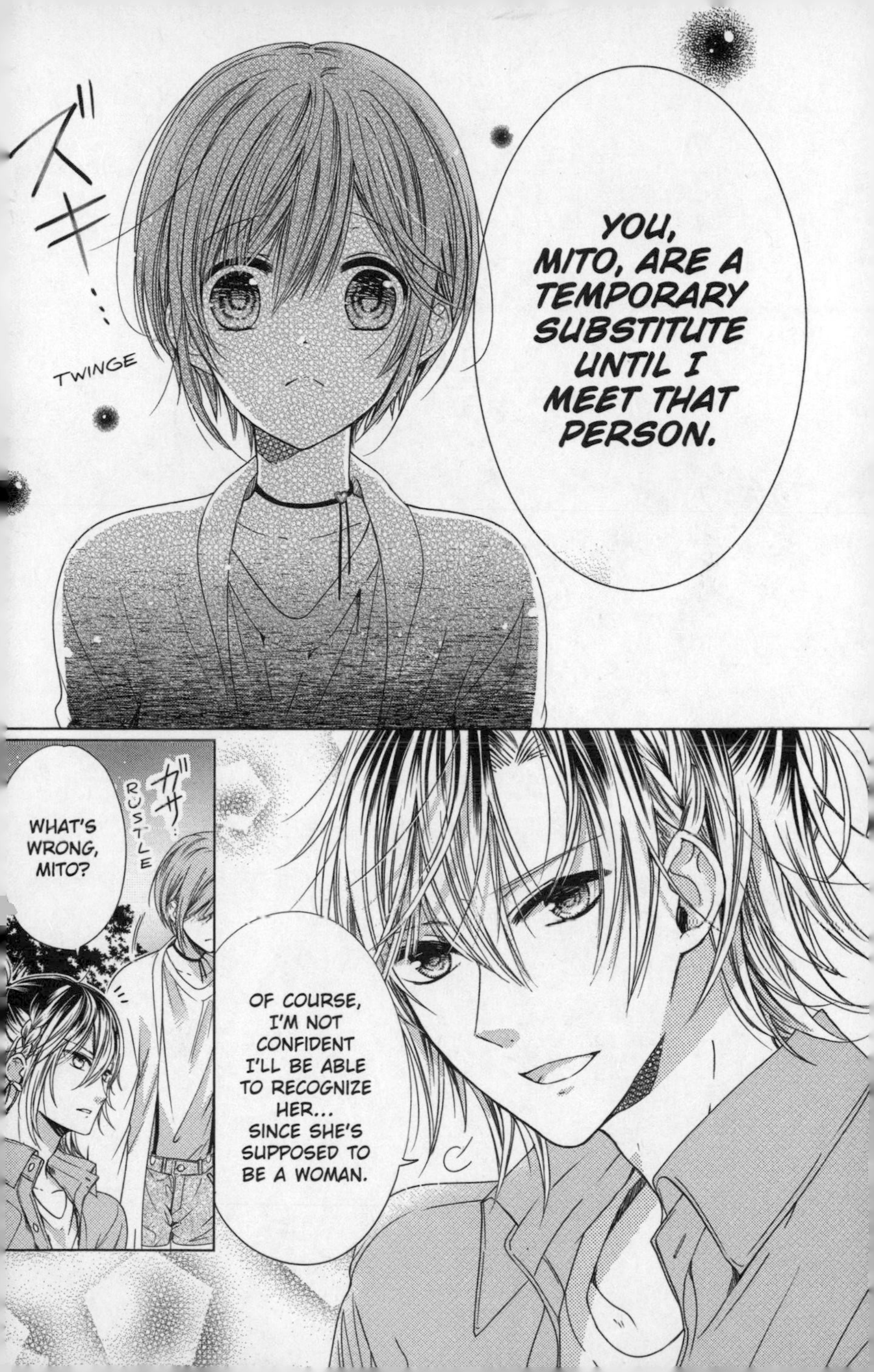
YOU, MITO, ARE A TEMPORARY SUBSTITUTE UNTIL I MEET THAT PERSON.
ズキ…
TWINGE
OF COURSE, I'M NOT CONFIDENT I'LL BE ABLE TO RECOGNIZE HER… SINCE SHE'S SUPPOSED TO BE A WOMAN.
ガサ…
RUSTLE
WHAT'S WRONG, MITO?

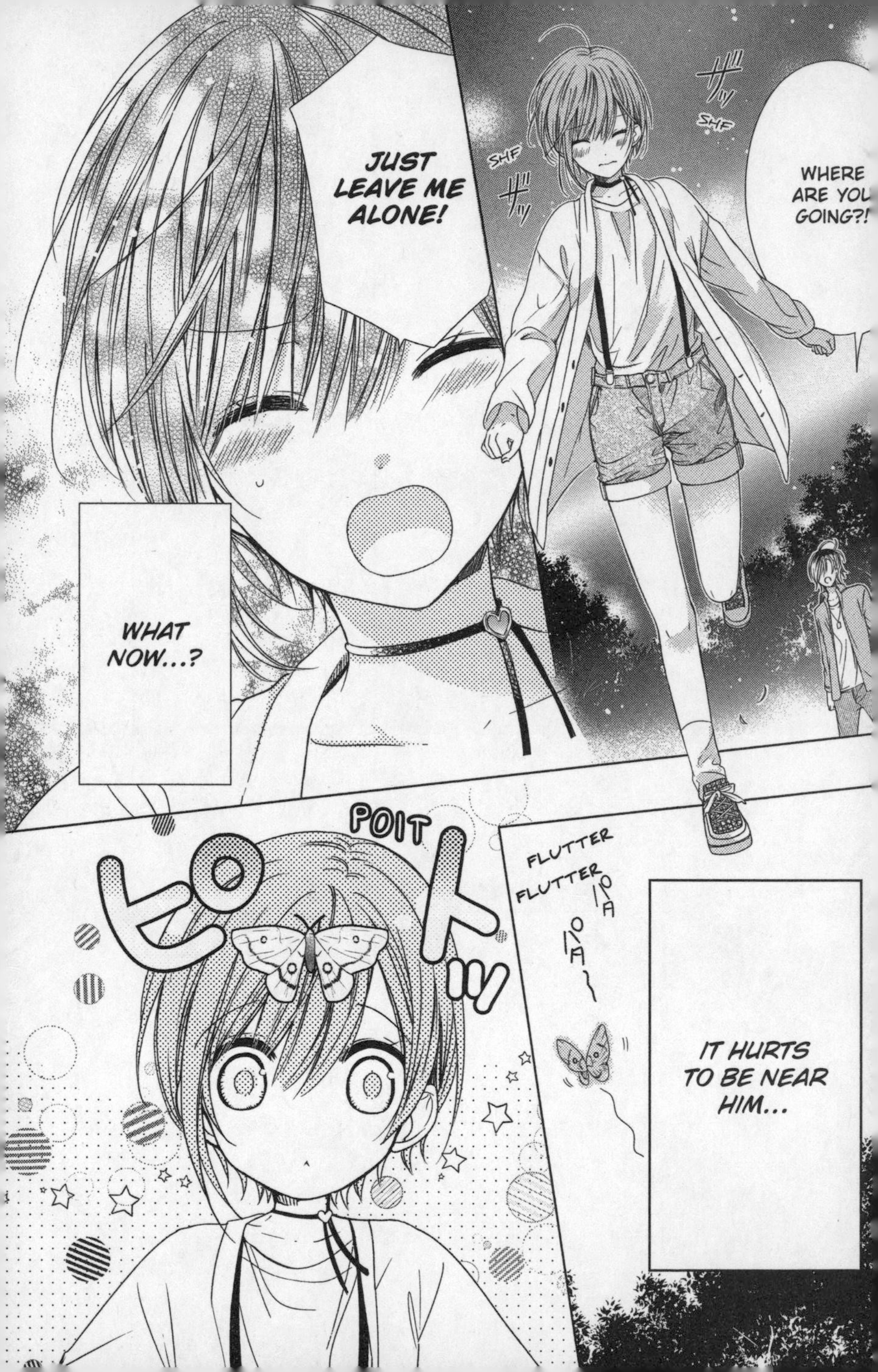

WHERE ARE YOU GOING?!
SHF
SHF
JUST LEAVE ME ALONE!
WHAT NOW...?
IT HURTS TO BE NEAR HIM...
FLUTTER FLUTTER
POIT

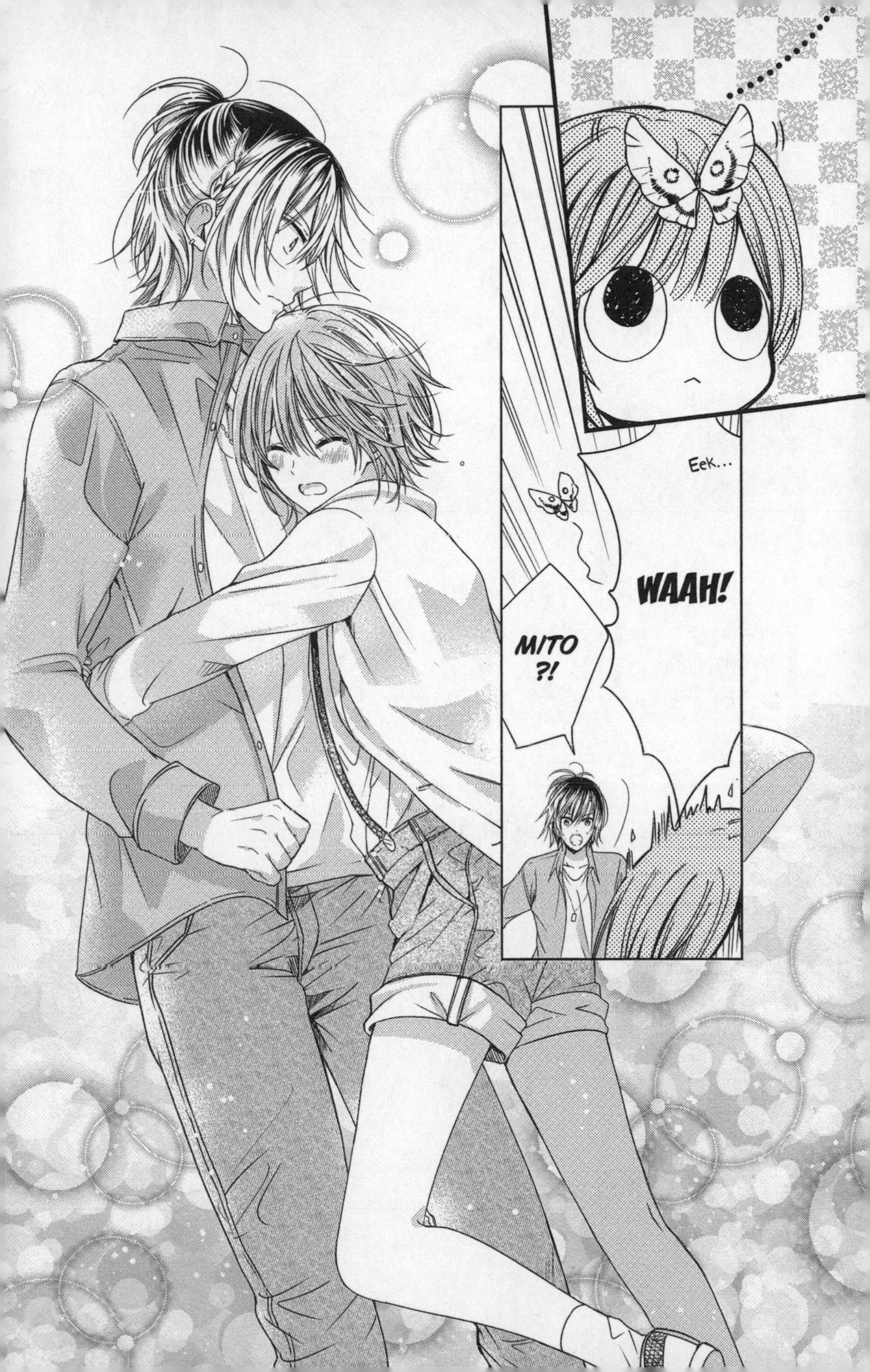
Eek...
WAAH!
MITO ?!

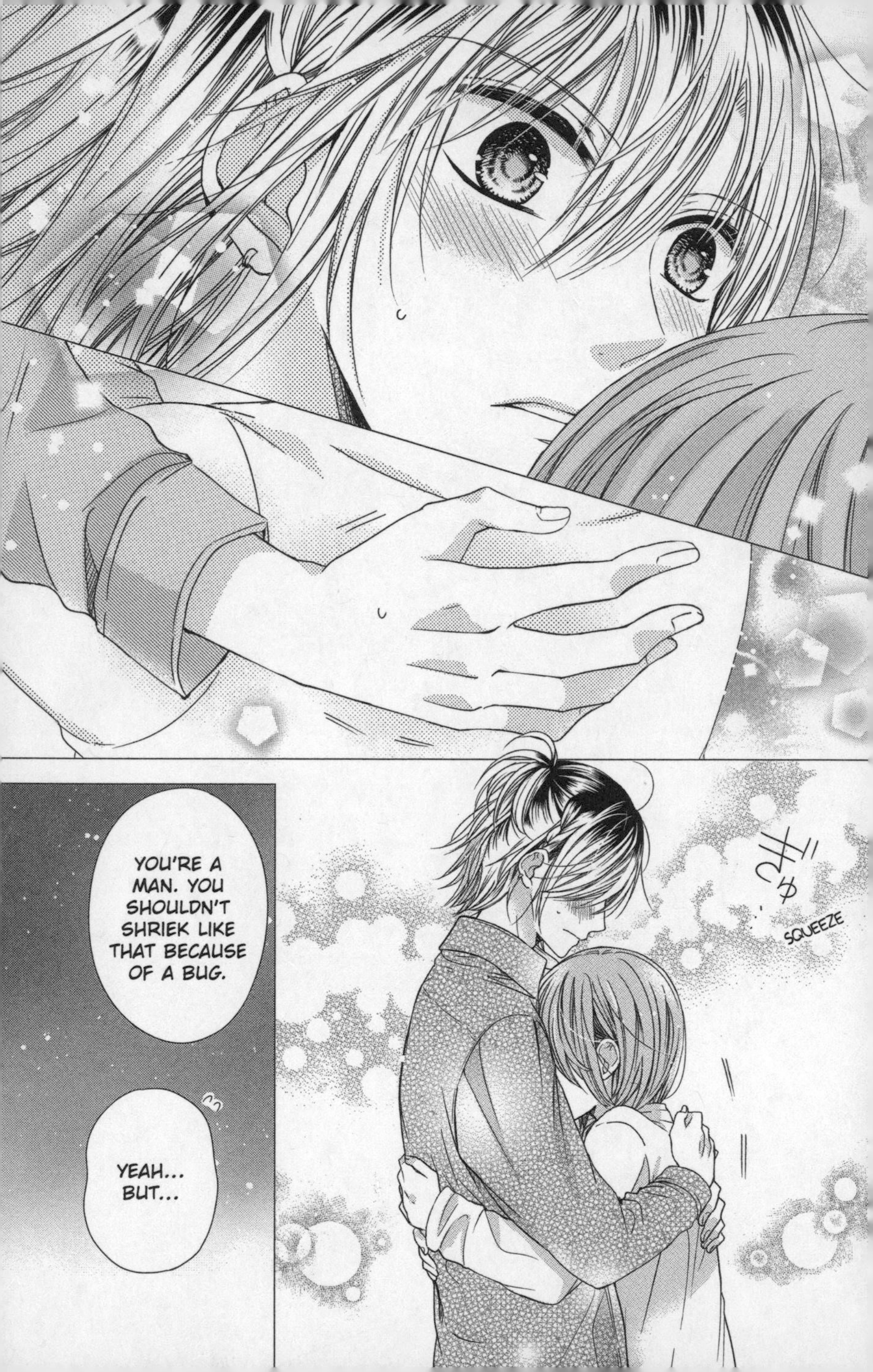
ぎゅ
SQUEEZE
YOU'RE A MAN. YOU SHOULDN'T SHRIEK LIKE THAT BECAUSE OF A BUG.
YEAH... BUT...

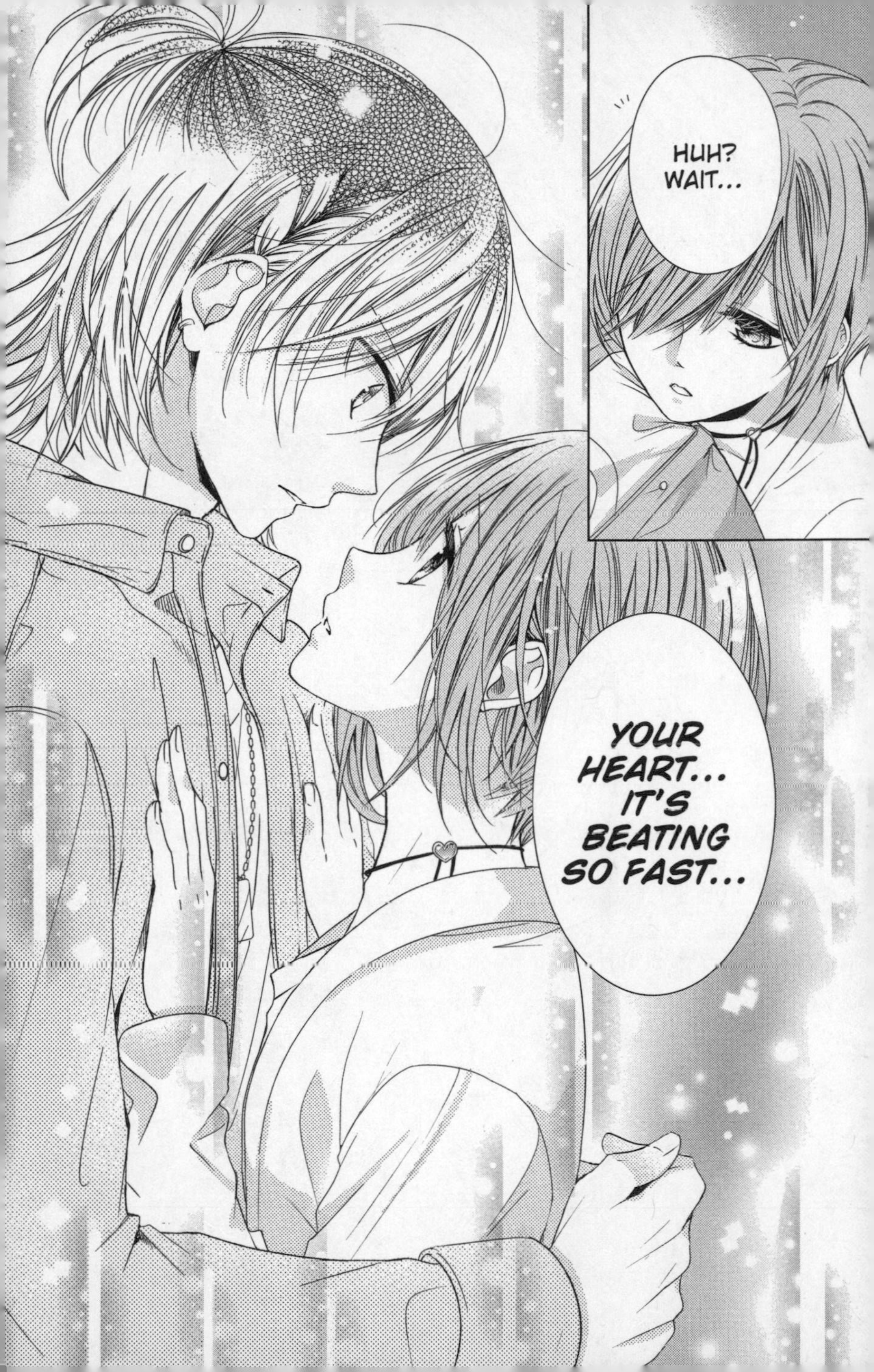
HUH? WAIT...
YOUR HEART... IT'S BEATING SO FAST...

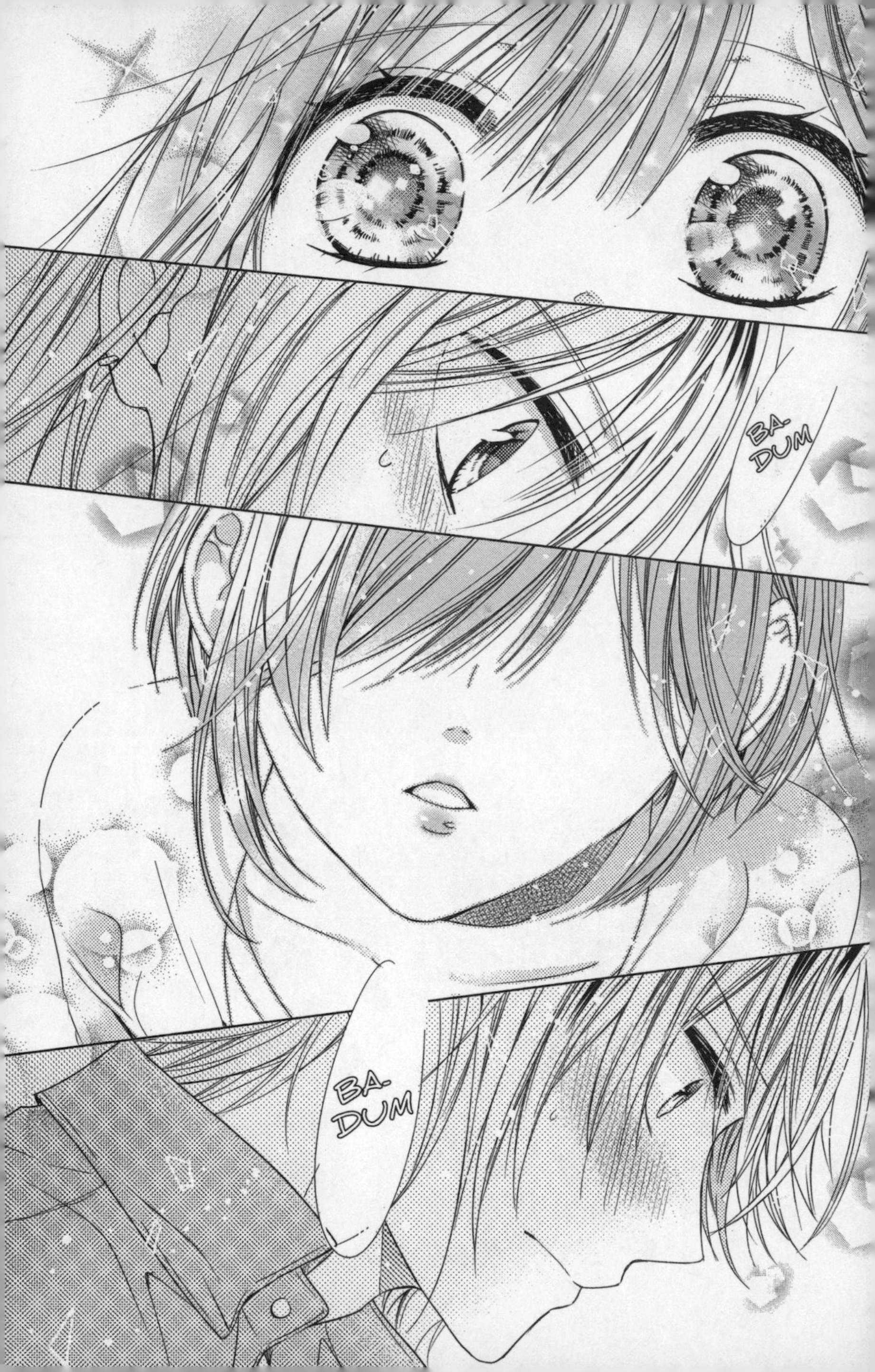
BA-
DUM
BA-
DUM

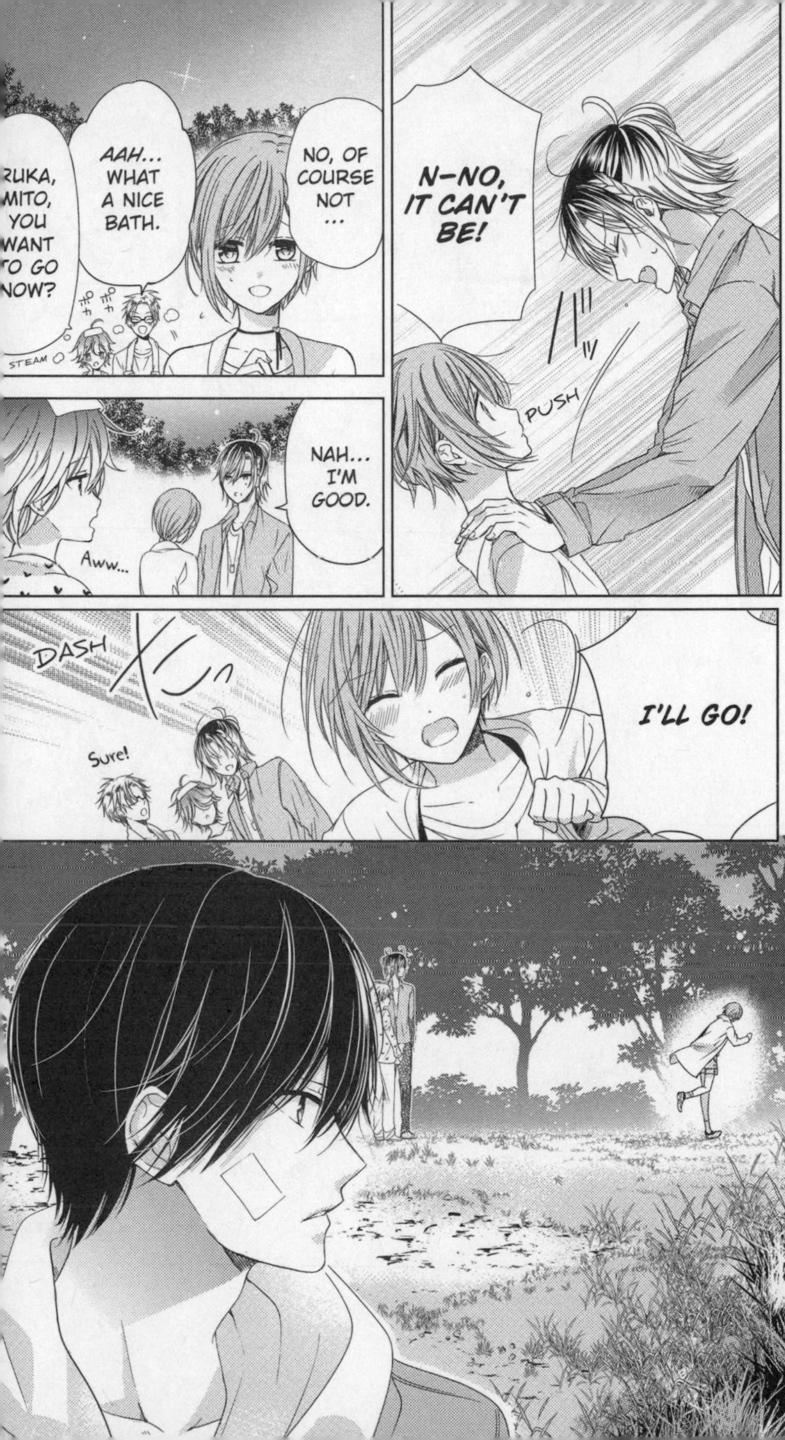
N-NO, IT CAN'T BE!
PUSH
NO, OF COURSE NOT ...
AAH... WHAT A NICE BATH.
RUKA, MITO, YOU WANT TO GO NOW?
STEAM
NAH... I'M GOOD.
Aww...
I'LL GO!
DASH
Sure!

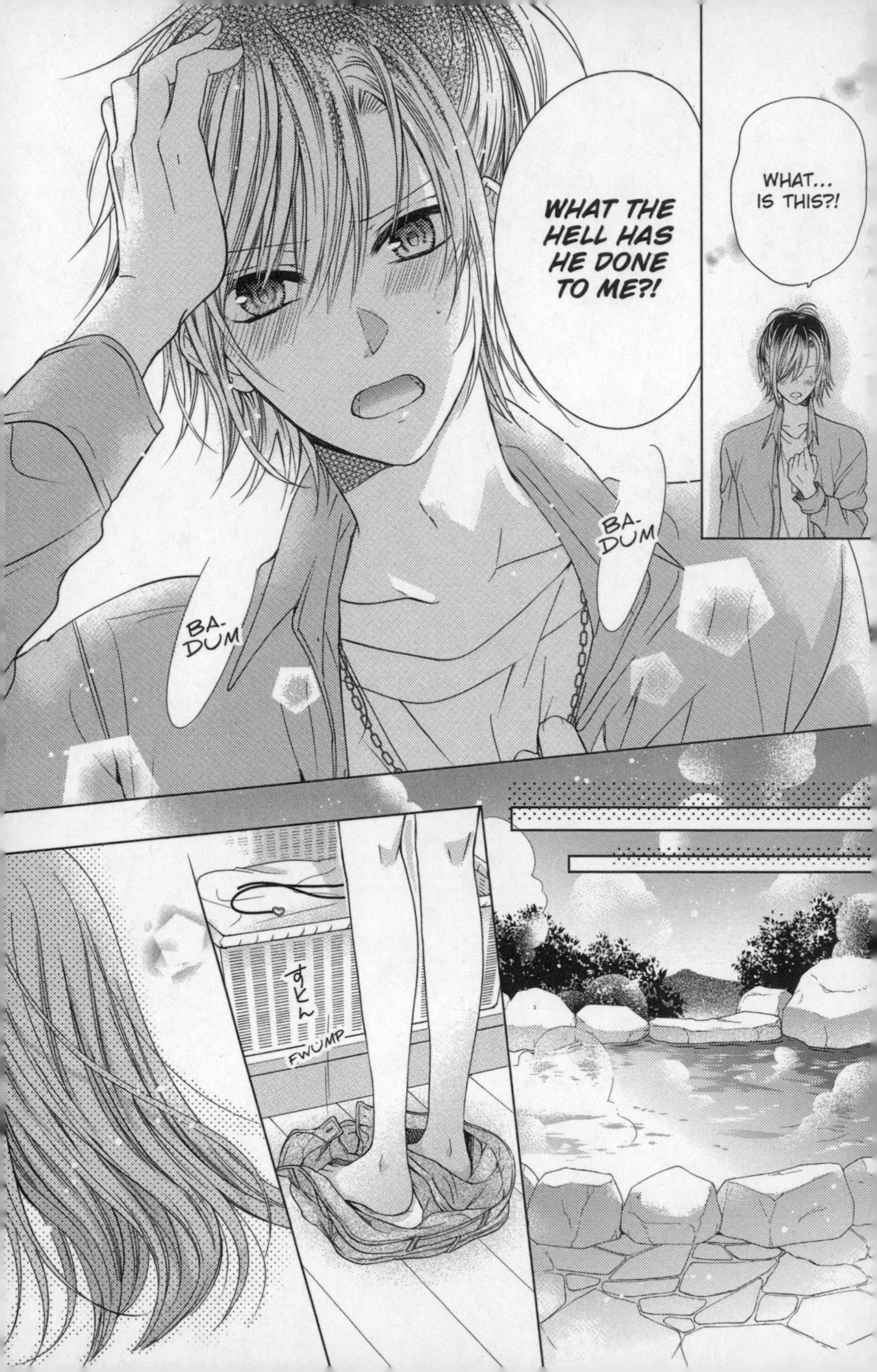
WHAT... IS THIS?!
WHAT THE HELL HAS HE DONE TO ME?!
BA-DUM
BA-DUM
すとん
FWUMP

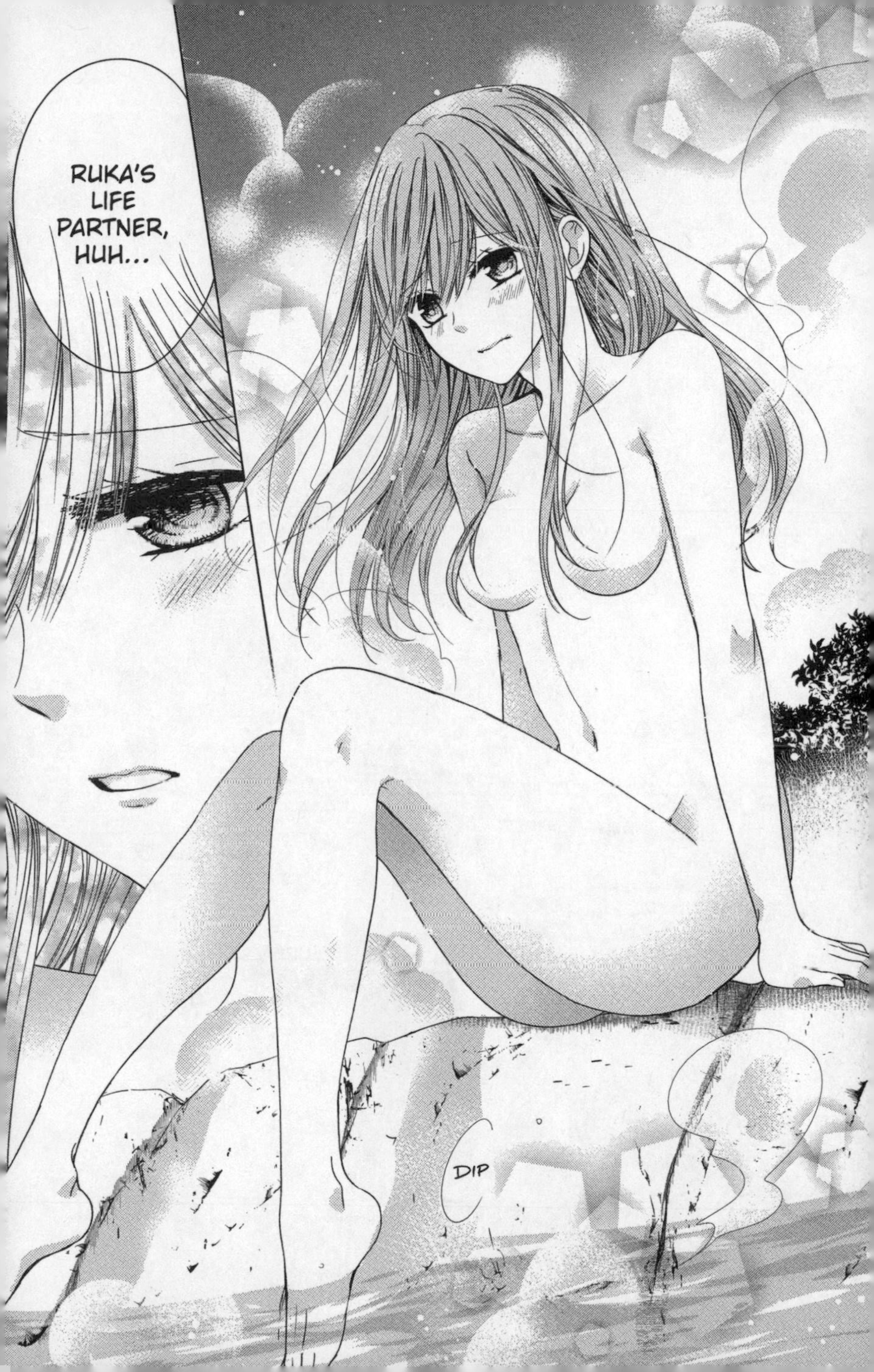
RUKA'S LIFE PARTNER, HUH...
DIP

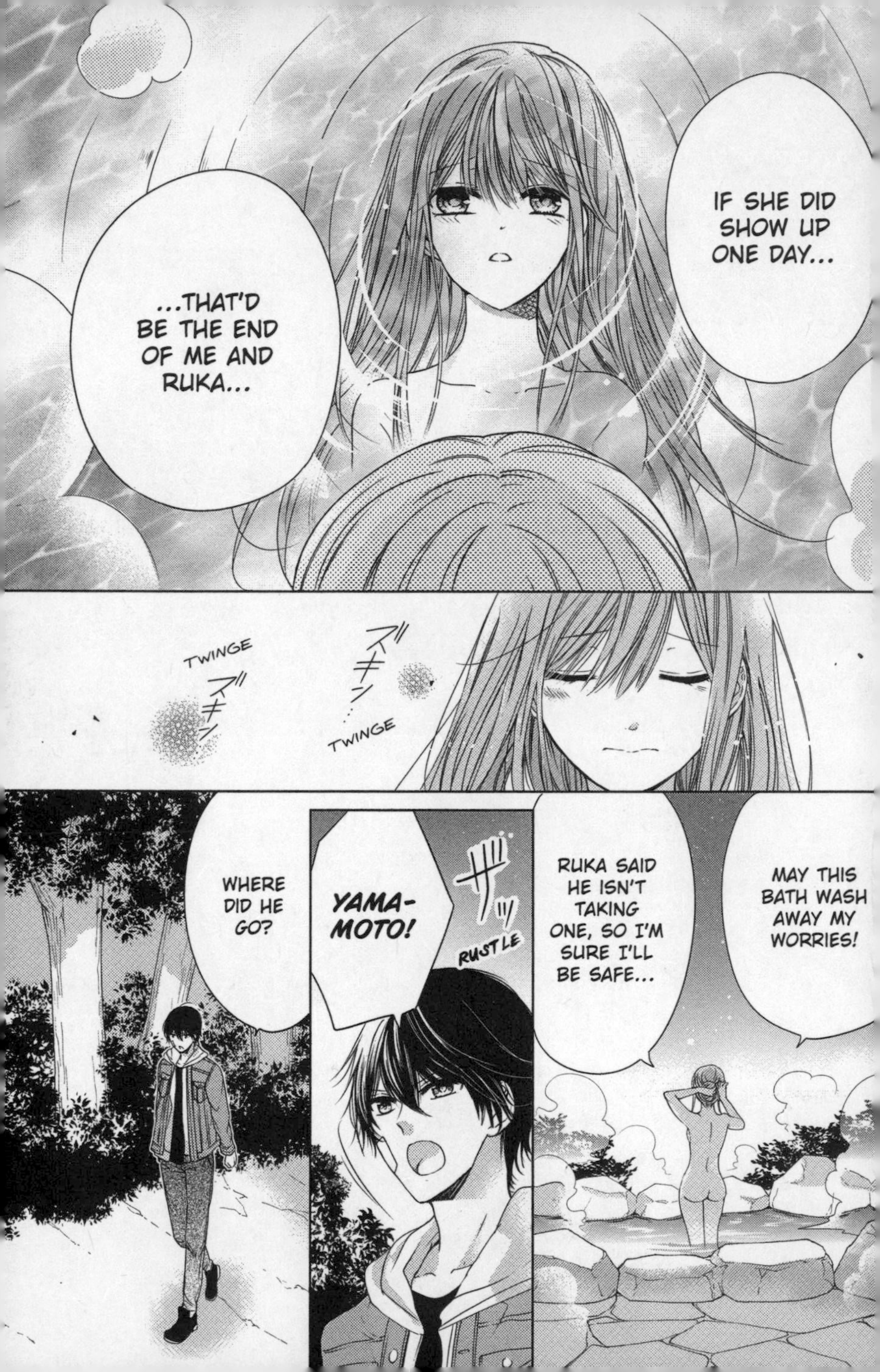
IF SHE DID SHOW UP ONE DAY...
...THAT'D BE THE END OF ME AND RUKA...
ズキン
TWINGE
ズキン
TWINGE
MAY THIS BATH WASH AWAY MY WORRIES!
RUKA SAID HE ISN'T TAKING ONE, SO I'M SURE I'LL BE SAFE...
ザッ
RUSTLE
YAMA-MOTO!
WHERE DID HE GO?

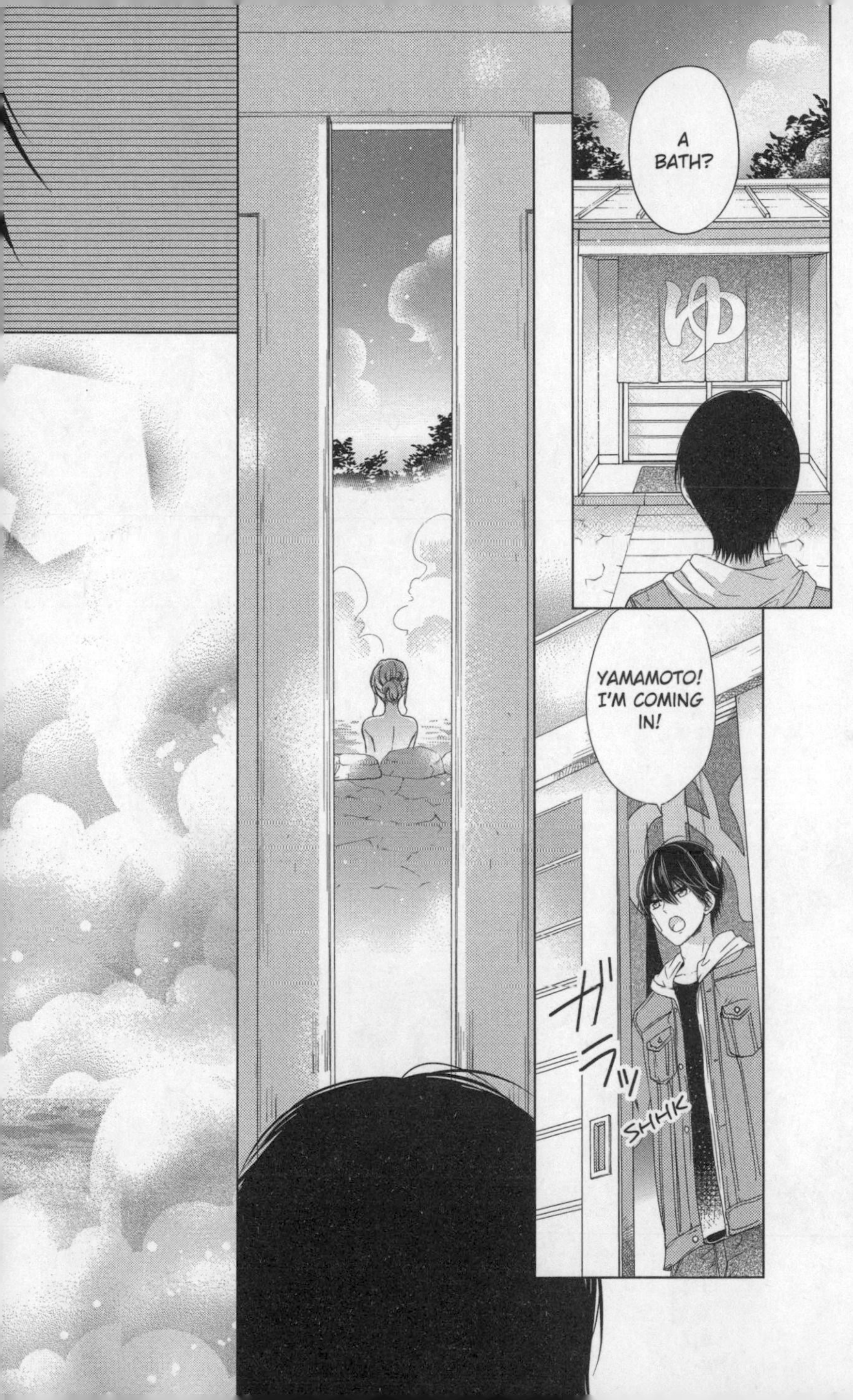
A BATH?
YAMAMOTO! I'M COMING IN!
ガラッ
SHHK

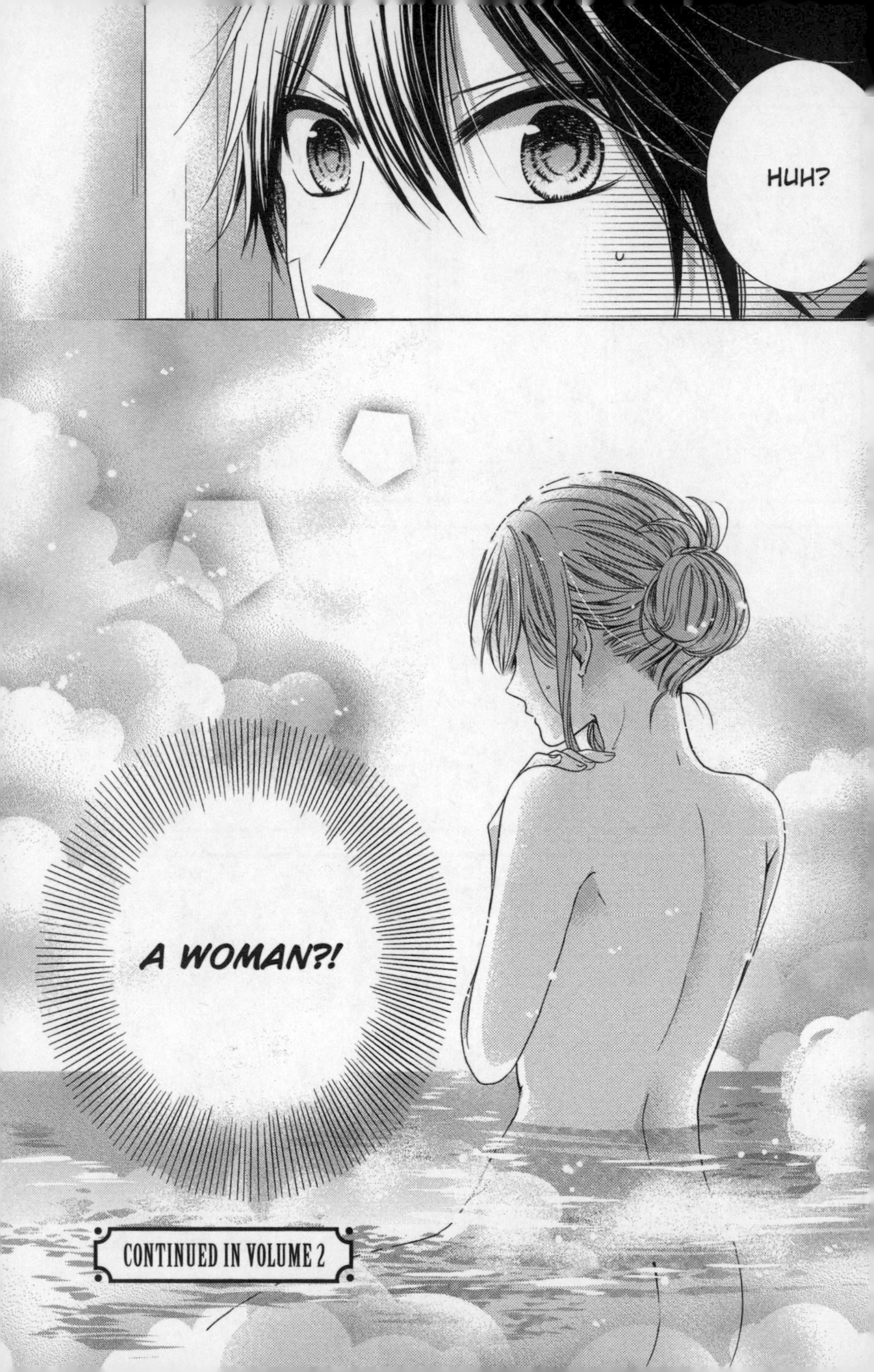
HUH?
A WOMAN?!
CONTINUED IN VOLUME 2

AFTERWORD

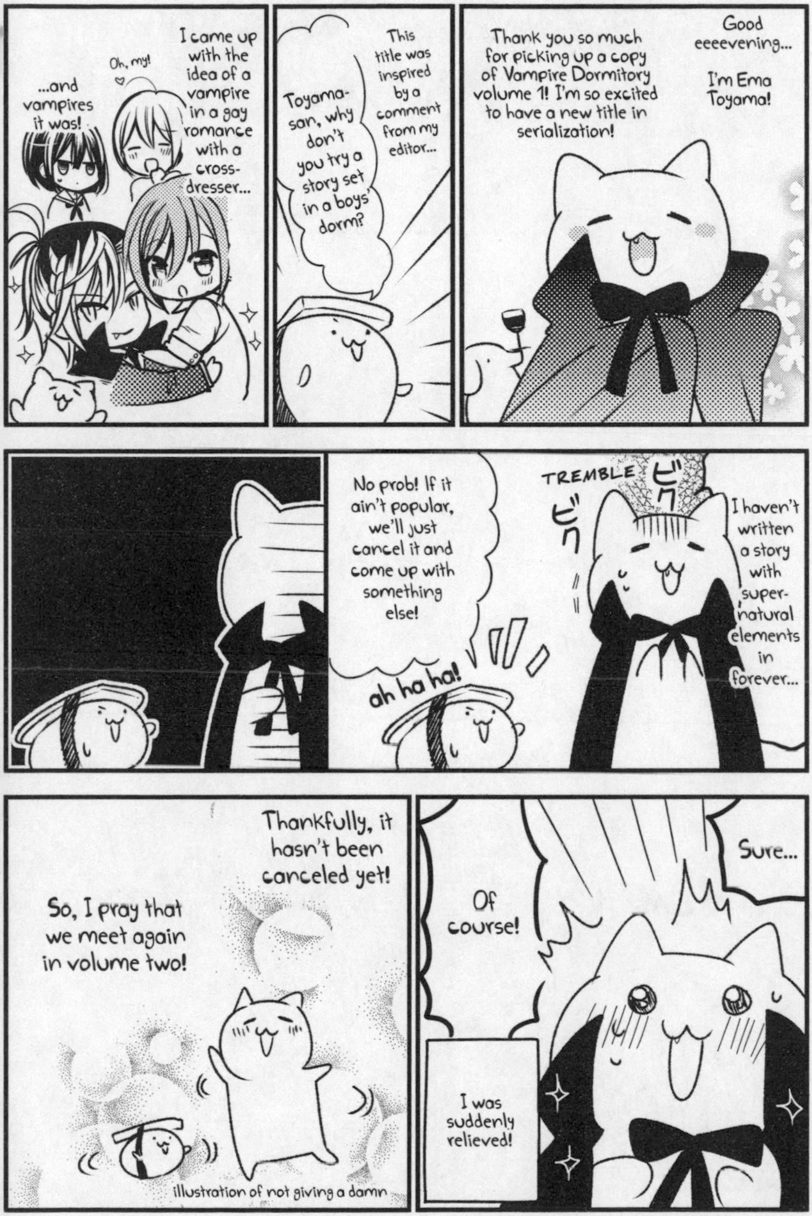
Good eeeevening... I'm Ema Toyama!
Thank you so much for picking up a copy of Vampire Dormitory volume 1! I'm so excited to have a new title in serialization!
This title was inspired by a comment from my editor...
Toyama-san, why don't you try a story set in a boys' dorm?
I came up with the idea of a vampire in a gay romance with a cross-dresser...
Oh, my!
...and vampires it was!
I haven't written a story with super-natural elements in forever...
TREMBLE
ビク
ビク
No prob! If it ain't popular, we'll just cancel it and come up with something else!
ah ha ha!
Sure...
Of course!
I was suddenly relieved!
Thankfully, it hasn't been canceled yet!
So, I pray that we meet again in volume two!
illustration of not giving a damn